Alfonso Gálvez

Ecclesiastical Winter

New Jersey
U.S.A. - 2024

CATALOGING DATA

Author: Gálvez, Alfonso, 1932–2022
Title: Ecclesiastical Winter

First Printing   New Jersey, 2012
Second Printing   New Jersey, 2024

Library of Congress Control Number: 2024902763

ISBN: 978-1-953170-39-2 (Hardcover)
      978-1-953170-40-8 (E-book)

**Published by
Shoreless Lake Press
P.O. Box 157
Stewartsville, New Jersey 08886**

INTRODUCTION

First, let me proclaim at the outset my strong love for the Church, whose son I consider myself to be through divine goodness. I have devoted my entire life to Her, and in Her I have exercised my priestly office in Spain and in South America; even, not infrequently, at the risk of my life. I always put my trust in the mercy of God, from Whom I hope to receive the grace to die in the Catholic Church, where I was born to the supernatural life and which I acknowledge as the Only True One founded by Christ.

It is important for me to make this initial statement, given the nature of this book. In it I have tried to warn about the causes and effects of the crisis that the Church is suffering since the death of Pius XII;[1] to this end, I found myself with the need to describe, with some harshness at times, some of the evils that are so acrimoniously afflicting the Institution founded by Jesus Christ. Of course, some will argue the existence of this crisis and will disagree with all or most of what is said in this book.

Since the idea of trying to impose my own views is far from my mind, any attempt to argue about what is said in this book is totally

---

[1] In recent years, there is a tendency, everyday more common among Catholic intellectuals, to advance the start of the crisis to the times of Pius XII —and even before him, according to some. Without denying categorically whatever truth such a statement may contain —it is very difficult to pinpoint the roots and the complete historical background of a social event—, I certainly puzzle at the efforts to exonerate the Second Vatican Council as the beginning of the causes that have led to the current problems.

ruled out, for my part. Therefore, this does not claim to be a work of denunciation —although, generally speaking, the reader may be led to think otherwise— but rather a kind of painful exposition, deeply felt, of the evils that, in my opinion, are afflicting the Church. Evils which I have tried to place, in regard to time, during an era which started approximately in the second half of the last century (Pius XII died in 1958) and expands to the present.

Hence the title of this book: *Ecclesiastical Winter*. Indeed it has been a cold and hard *Winter* which has been lashing the Church during the aftermath of the Second Vatican Council; something quite different from the *Ecclesiastical Springtime* which was so solemnly proclaimed from the first moments that followed this event. The reality of the facts, however, imposed itself once again, which has reduced the frequency of these allusions to the best season of the year, which was considered, with not a little optimism, like the aura that enlivened the *New Church*. The Council was called by Pope John XXIII —inspired, so he said, by the Holy Spirit— in 1959, although it did not see its beginnings until 1962. Even today this triumphal spirit that inspired it is maintained in the Church; although well enough diminished, I must say, because anyone can perceive nowadays that the old clamorous euphoric shouts have been muted.[2] In fact, regarding the beginning of the new millennium, far from witnessing the arrival of the *New Pentecost*, so insistently proclaimed by Pope John Paul II, it seems that such a happy event has been postponed, put on a perpetual hold; which has given way, in contrast, to an indefinite prolongation of the darkness of Good Friday.

---

[2]The current situation —the second decade of the first century of the third millennium— is more complicated than that. Not a few serious and well–founded analyses are being done, motivated no doubt by the disastrous consequences that emerged in the post–Conciliar times.

Shortly after the Council ended, the first protests arose, directed against clear abuses which tried, at all costs, to hide themselves behind its shadow. Those protests were weak reactions at first, but they became stronger as time passed.[3] In general, they were directed almost exclusively against the anarchy in the Liturgy, which relegated the most important danger of doctrinal error to the background; errors which were barely perceived, rarely reported, and never, or almost never, impeded. Isolated cases, like that of Cardinal Ottaviani and Archbishop Lefebvre, went unnoticed and were not heard. However, the Hierarchy defended its positions by claiming a *faulty interpretation* of the conciliar texts, and rightly so; although it had been more honest to add that those interpretations, rather than being wrong, were not infrequently clearly malicious.

But there came a time when the theory of a *faulty interpretation* of the texts of the Council became unsustainable. The most radical attacks proceeded from the group of Lefebvrists, but there were other more serene studies that denounced the ambiguities and the dangers of many passages present in the conciliar documents.[4] Consequently, an idea began to emerge: there was a possibility of a break with Tradition and the pre–Conciliar Magisterium.

Perhaps this was the reason why Pope Benedict XVI chanted his strategy regarding his defense of the Council. A new theory, namely, *the hermeneutic of continuity,* conceived by this Pontiff, replaced that of the *faulty interpretation.* The Pope introduced it as the only possible orthodox position in the face of the *hermeneutic of rupture* which he openly rejected. According to the Pontiff, there was no

---

[3]Although we are talking in the past tense, the problem, in fact, currently remains the same, and even worse.

[4]The latter, however, remained faithful to the Council and to the Hierarchy of the Church, unlike the followers of Archbishop Lefebvre.

other approach but to acknowledge a perfect continuity between the pre–Conciliar and the post–Conciliar Magisterium.

Needless to say, Pope Benedict XVI had right on his side, at least according to the sense of his words. It is not possible to admit a breach between two periods of the Magisterium of the Church because it cannot be but only one. Unfortunately, however, the apparently simple problem became complicated due to a number of facts which, except the main one,[5] cannot be commented on sufficiently here.

In effect, the main obstacle for the premise of the *hermeneutic of continuity* was the fact that the Pontiff himself, before and during his Pontificate, has spoken in open contradiction to his own theory. Among the many testimonies that one could bring forward here, one suffices which, precisely because of its forcefulness, had wide repercussions. According to Cardinal Ratzinger, the Conciliar Document *Gaudium et Spes* is a veritable *contra–Syllabus*; and there is no need to delay here for more details of this case.[6] Later, as Pontiff, he has never recanted his position —that we know at least. It is not worth it to resort here to the Encyclicals of John Paul II (especially those known as the *Trinitarian*) or to some Documents of the Council that have been subjected to documented studies which affirm that serious problems have been detected with them.

---

[5]Another problem, which is not easy to solve to the satisfaction of everybody, is the fact that the Council itself repeatedly and persistently claimed that it was *merely pastoral and not dogmatic* in nature (unlike all the Ecumenical Councils celebrated by the Church throughout Her History). In addition to this, the Hierarchy was always bent on *not imposing anything by authority, in order to welcome an attitude that has since become thoroughly accepted —none other than dialogue and paying attention to the "sensus fidei fidelium."*

[6]Joseph Cardinal Ratzinger, *Les Principes de la Théologie Catholique*, Paris, Téqui, 1982, pp. 426–427.

But the efforts of the Pope were not able to dispel the idea that, in effect, there is a breach between the pre–and the post–Conciliar Magisterium. With all due respect to the present Pontiff, the opinion is forcefully making its way through which maintains that either there is no such continuity or that it is difficult to recognize it; which is some doctrinal point of no little importance. The mere fact that this issue has become the object of studies and has given rise to polemics (not only within extremist circles) proves that the problem *is there*, according to the adage *where there is smoke, there is fire.*[7]

According to news agencies, *today*, in the *Center for the Study of Vatican II*, at the Pontifical University of Lateran, a presentation of three important books in connection with this issue took place: *The Legacy of the Magisterium of Pius XII*; *The Church of Croatia and the Second Vatican Council*; and *John Paul II and Vatican II. A Challenge and a Duty.* The event was presided over by the Rector of the Pontifical University of Lateran, Monsignor Enrico Dal Covolo, who said in his speech: *These three books foster a new interpretative synthesis of Vatican II, which can overcome the paralysis of partial interpretations: on the one hand, the interpretation of an unbalanced total discontinuity; on the other, the interpretation which unilaterally and solely insists on continuity.*[8]

As one can see, the question is still open to discussion —a fact that cannot be attributed solely to radical groups or to those opposed to the Hierarchy.

Moreover, a new book about this issue has been published in Italy. This book is considered to be among the most widely read in this country and has been acclaimed by both sides of the fence: *Il Concilio Vaticano II. Una storia mai scrita*, by Roberto de Mattei, a Professor of Church history and the vice–president of the National Research Council and a consultant at the Pontifical Committee of Historical Science. The author says in the Introduction: *Unlike other Councils, Vatican II poses a new problem for the historian. Councils, under the Pope and*

---

[7]Today, one cannot resort to the sophism, so fashionable during the first years after the Council, stating that *post hoc, et non propter hoc*, which refers to the plausible causality on the part of the Council regarding the post–Conciliar catastrophes, with the clear intention of exonerating the Council. After all, the sophism sounded good but was still clumsy; hence, it was useful only for a time.

[8]Taken from the Internet. *Religion in Freedom.* 03/31/11.

with the Pope, exercise a Solemn Magisterium in matters of Faith and morals and act like supreme judges and legislators in what concerns the law of the Church. Vatican Council II, however, did not pass any laws or deliberate in an infallible (definitive) manner on questions of Faith and morals. Without any dogmatic definition, inevitably the door was open to discussions on the nature of the Council documents and on their application in the so–called 'post–Conciliar' period.

And the author continues:

The formula of the Council in the light of Tradition, or if you prefer, the 'hermeneutic of continuity,' undoubtedly offers an authoritative statement to the faithful in order to clarify the issue of the proper reception of the conciliar texts but leaves open a basic problem: given that the correct interpretation is that of 'continuity,' it remains to be explained why after Vatican II something happened that had never happened in the aftermath of any council in history; namely that two (or more) contrary hermeneutics have faced off, and, as Pope Benedict XVI says, are 'quarreling' among themselves. The very existence of a variety of hermeneutics shows a certain ambiguity or ambivalence in the documents themselves.[9]

In short, the issue, as one can easily see, is far from definitively settled. In the meantime, doctrinal errors (which are condemned late, imperfectly, and almost never) are being spread; liturgical anarchy continues; the crisis of discipline goes on, along with the uncertainty and confusion of many Catholics —not counting those who opted for desertion or those who preferred indifference, abandoning in fact any religious practice.

As for the small group of faithful people who ask, as Saint Peter did, *To whom shall we go?* (Jn 6:68) or as he might as well have said: *Where shall we go?* they must be reminded that if it is true that *the just man lives on faith* (Heb 10:38), it is also true that he feeds on hope (Rom 5:5; 1 Thess 2:19; 1 Pet 1:21). They, therefore, should never forget Our Lord's promise referring to the perennial character of His Church and addressed to His followers of all ages: *And the gates of hell shall not prevail against Her* (Mt 16:18).

---

[9]Taken from *The Latin Mass, The Journal of Catholic Culture and Tradition*, Vol. 20, n. 1, Winter, 2011, p. 4.

But to those in open rebellion against the Hierarchy —whom they consider responsible for all the evils in the Church— and to those who are extremely worried but still faithful, although confused, I would advise them to consider that God takes care of His Church; that, consequently, He will allow things to go only as far as He permits them to go.

On the other hand, after a closer look, one easily discovers that the problem is more perceived than real. Is the existence of two contradictory Magisteria possible...? Or the existence of two different hermeneutics...? Should we admit the *hermeneutic of continuity,* does it sufficiently guarantee the continuity of the *new* doctrines with the perennial Magisterium of the Church...?

First of all, we have to firmly maintain that in the Catholic Church, since She is the Only True One founded by Jesus Christ, two contradictory, or even distinct, Magisteria cannot coexist. If it is true —as it is— that the Holy Spirit is the Soul and Life of the Church, it is impossible that two Magisteria meet together in Her. This is an undisputable point.

Nevertheless, some people will say that, *de facto,* one finds doctrinal points about which the post–Conciliar Magisterium is very different from, and even contrary to, the pre–Conciliar Magisterium. The discrepancies *are there*, and very noticeable. Are we facing then an insoluble problem...?

As we ponder this issue well, everything seems to indicate that we need not search for an answer... for there is no issue. The faithful need not be subjected to a situation that keeps them immersed in uncertainty. Nevertheless it is true that they are faced with an alternative: on the one hand, *there are indeed doctrinal teachings that claim for themselves a magisterial nature, demanding also from the faithful their complete acquiescence.* This is the pre–Conciliar Magisterium.[10] On the other, the faithful are offered *other doctrines which not only expressly deny their infallible character but which also expect from the faithful only a mere acceptance —never a binding consent— which, in addition, is supposedly obtained through dialogue and the consent of the community.* This is precisely the post–Conciliar Doctrine.[11]

As can be seen, the mere posing of the dilemma offers the solution to the problem, in that the Christian people can easily know what to expect. Let us try to explain.

According to what has been said, there is indeed a corpus of doctrine —a number of teachings— that demands the assent of the faithful. We also found a number of conciliar propositions that claim for themselves a merely *practical and pastoral* nature; they also utterly reject having an infallible character because they merely claim to furnish the faithful with behavioral guidelines, mainly referring to matters of discipline and worship (for instance, the new liturgical laws).[12] It should be noted here, however, that even when the post–Conciliar popes offer to the faithful a certain body of doctrine, such as Encyclicals, Exhortations, Public Catechesis, there is always the assumption —explicitly or implicitly expressed— of the absence of intent to compromise the Magisterial Authority of the Church.[13]

In addition to all this, it should be taken into account that when it comes to disciplinary rules, such as the introduction of specific changes in liturgical laws, then a situation arises in which the be-

---

[10]It does not necessarily demand the character of infallibility for all its teachings.

[11]For the progressive theology of the *New Church*, infallibility rests rather with the *sensus fidei* of the People of God than with the Hierarchy.

[12]There is a noticeable influence of the philosophy of praxis (Marxism) in the Church, especially since the days of John XXIII.

[13]There is plenty of documentation on this particular topic, but this is not the place to expound it.

havior of the faithful can only be that of respect and compliance, which should not inhibit the right of each faithful member to exercise his own judgment and discernment. At any rate, these kinds of norms, which truly speaking are *pastoral in nature*, should not be confused with matters *de fide et moribus*, for the latter fully fall within the jurisdiction of the Magisterium of the Church.

Be that as it may, it should be clear that every Catholic must profess obedience and respect to the legitimate Hierarchy of the Church; no one can consider himself able to establish a hierarchy on his own. If the Shepherds have been legitimately elected they must be considered as authentic Shepherds called to govern the Only True Church *outside of which there is no salvation*, even if they are accused of corruption or of not exercising the duties denoted in the ministry entrusted to them. It certainly could happen that, in a particular historical moment, a legitimate Hierarchy may impart to the faithful doctrinal teachings which clearly contradict the Traditional Magisterium of the Church. Notwithstanding this, the faithful must follow —regarding their judgment about and their compliance to those teachings— *what they gather from the guidance of the Magisterium itself.*

This statement may seem to contradict what has been said above. All becomes clear when one takes into account that the faithful do not have authority to set themselves as *judges* of the Magisterium; and, therefore, they must always proceed within the jurisdictional limits of the said Magisterium.[14] At any rate, the faithful always maintain the right, indeed the duty, to develop *their own criteria* about what they see or what they hear, for obedience does not preclude the ability to think. The true meaning of the *sensus fidei populi Dei*, as the Church has always

---

[14]Therefore. if the Magisterium assumes its character of infallibility. the faithful must accept it as infallible. Whereas if the Magisterium. for example. declines that prerogative. or refuses to constrain the acquiescence of the faithful as their duty. or is merely open to dialogue. it is then evident that the faithful are free to give their firm assent to other teachings. *namely those which implicitly or explicitly compel them.*

understood it, is exercised within the limits of the true Faith, is grounded in Tradition, nourishes itself from Scripture, and, above all, *takes on its full legitimacy from its subordination to the legitimate Magisterium.* Thus, it should be emphasized, infallibility rests, first and foremost, with the legitimate Hierarchy of the Church —with the conditions set *ad casum.* And it is based on this Magisterium, and always *a posteriori*, where the veracity and accuracy of the *sensus fidei fidelium* acquires legitimacy.

The progressive theology of the New Church, contravening Catholic doctrine of over twenty centuries, proceeds in the opposite way: it argues that infallibility rests, first and foremost, with the People of God, whence it is received by the Hierarchy, whose corresponding function, thenceforth, is one of confirmation, unification, and clarification.

The painful truth about all this, however, is that when the *sensus fidei* of the People of God is given *a prior authority in preference to the Magisterium,* then it uses as a source of true nourishment the data fed to it by the Press Agencies, Television, and the other means at the disposal of the powerful Apparatus of Propaganda and Indoctrination that the System utilizes so efficiently.

It is clear, from what has been said above, that if a particular Magisterium does not claim to be infallible, nor does it want to commit or exercise the Authority of the Church, then the faithful are free to adhere to doctrinal teachings which, in turn, are *expounded with true authority* and proclaimed by the Magisterium of all times. Moreover, the Holy Spirit will never allow within the Church the coexistence of two contrary doctrines which claim to possess, simultaneously, the seal of authenticity given by the Authority of the Spirit. Therefore, there will never be an alternative choice between *two Magisteria*, for there can be only one; and the faithful will acquiesce to the only one which *presents itself* as true and commits its Authority. At the same time, of course, the faithful will respect the legitimate Hierarchy, even when one or some of its members may be corrupted. In this sense, no Catholic ought to ever feel confused; for God is not going to allow the existence in the Church of two legitimate Magisteria which are, in turn, different, while putting forth doctrines at variance with or even contradictory to each other, and both demanding total acquiescence on the part of the faithful.

Nevertheless, the respect and obedience owed to the legitimate Authority, in order to be effective and blessed by God, require, in turn, a *total fidelity to the principles of sound doctrine*, namely those contained in Holy Scripture, taught by Tradition, and confirmed by the legitimate Magisterium of the Church. The faithful cannot, under any pretext or by following a particular doctrine, doubt doctrines like, for example, the Real Presence of Jesus Christ in the Eucharist; the Supreme Authority of the Pope as the visible Head of the entire Church; the authenticity of the Scriptures and the historical reality of the Person of Christ —which are but some of the truths of Faith that are expressly being denied by the current Modernism, even within the Church.[15]

This places today's faithful Catholics in a position both delicate (Mt 7:14) and very uncomfortable to bear —but who has said that Christian existence is something easy...? Radical approaches, which oscillate from one extreme to the other, tread upon a road free of complications. The good child of the Church, on the contrary, is compelled to keep a constant and double fidelity: on the one hand, respecting the Hierarchy, to whom he owes allegiance and obedience, despite acknowledging that it has often fallen into corruption and dereliction of its duties; while, on the other hand, firmly maintaining the principles of sound doctrine —which, having been given by Christ to His Church through His Apostles, are, consequently, being continuously animated by the Spirit and, safe–guarded by the authentic Magisterium, have come to us and are as immutable as

---

[15]The truths of Faith enumerated here do not comprise an exhaustive list; they are merely an example. Modernism expressly denies them, as it does deny all the other truths of Faith, as Saint Pius X said; for him Modernism was nothing but *the sum of all the heresies.*

they are intangible. Following Jesus Christ has always been a matter for courageous people — *The kingdom of Heaven suffers violence,
and only the violent take it by assault*[16]— but today it should be
considered a task rather reserved for heroes and martyrs.

Christian [Maritain's] humanism attempts an exaltation of man
through man himself, although it does not dispense with Jesus
Christ. Atheistic humanism, on the contrary, pursues the same
exaltation, but without God. Consequently, both humanisms, the
one advocated by Maritain and that sought by Freemasonry, actually lead to the same end: the deification of man once he has gotten
rid of God. The means to achieve such an end is the creation of a
Universal Religion, *of* Humanity and *for* Humanity, which is purely
natural and for which the only god is man himself.

On a close analysis, it is not difficult to notice that what the various *humanisms* want is to definitively establish man in this World;
to build here our Paradise, since there is no reason that may support
our thinking of another —which, for all intents and purposes, would
be pure fantasy and daydreaming. Modernism does not pursue any
other objective. As for the Modernism which has infiltrated the
Church, it embraces two quite different factions: that of the naïve,
those convinced that a more *rational* religion, a religion more *within
the grasp of modern man*, will become a platform for the expansion
of Catholicism; and that group made up of those who adhere unre-
strainedly to the heresy of Modernism and have renounced the Faith
—although they do not always admit it openly. Both labour for the
same end, serving the same Lord of Darkness.

For Modernism, the Church is no longer the *Pilgrim Church*; she
has become the *Established Church*. By the same token, the *Militant*

---

[16]Mt 11:12.

Church has turned into the *Church of Peace*, which has been finally attained. But neither of these two new *Churches* has anything to do with the one founded by Jesus Christ; moreover, neither will ever be a reality, no matter how hard Modernism, Freemasonry, and *progressive* Theology may try, for they are mere utopias. And utopias, as everyone knows, are great deceptions designed to fascinate the gullible —a product of the Father of lies.

Utopias are always based on lies. And, to further confuse those who believe in them, are always projected into an imprecise future —Marxist Paradise, Universal Peace, Justice and Social Welfare for all mankind— which, of course, never arrives; hence the condition of being constantly postponed. When they do (seldom) venture to set a more or less determinate future moment for their accomplishment —the *New Pentecost*, for example, whose coming to the Church was promised for the beginning of the third millennium—, the results are often disappointing.

It is curious to note the differences between Utopia and Prophecy. The latter uses an arcane, ambiguous, and indeterminate language, anticipating grand and worrying events, often difficult to understand clearly... until the moments of its fulfillment; Utopia, however, always uses a bombastic, clear, resounding language announcing wonders —which is logical when you consider that its goal is to deceive the fools, the naïve, and the dim–witted, who, as everybody knows, are more likely to wait for the delights of Cockaigne (which they are sure they will get) than to believe in adversity (for they think with all certainty that they will never experience it).

The new progressive Theology eliminates one fundamental characteristic for Christian existence, namely that the Christian is a being that walks. The disciple of Jesus Christ is a *follower* of his Master and, therefore, he is called to constantly walk after Him. A *sedentary* situation would cause in a Christian his complete denaturalization: *And while they* [the Apostles] *were beholding Him going up to heaven, behold two men stood by them in white garments who also said: You men of Galilee, why stand you looking up to heaven...?*[17]

Christian existence, on the contrary, implies a constant march upon a path which is steep and rugged (Mt 7:14); consequently it demands, as any following of Jesus Christ would, one's determination to walk upon a road that must be trodden in total identification with Him and not merely as a going after His footsteps; after all, and according to His own words, He is the Way; as can be seen in His words spoken to the Apostle Saint Thomas: *'And whither I go you know the way.' Thomas said to him: 'Lord, we know not whither you go, so how can we know the way?' Jesus said to him: 'I am the Way, and the Truth, and the Life.'*[18]

Hence, the abundance of passages in the New Testament in which Jesus Christ gives the invitation to *follow* Him (Mt 8:22; 9:9; 19:21; Mk 2:14; 10:21; Lk 5:27; 9:59; Jn 1:43; 21:19). After all, the essence of Christian existence is precisely this, and nothing else. In the Gospel, *imitating* Jesus Christ is synonymous with *following* Jesus Christ.

The neo–modernist progressivism assumes that man is already established in his final destination; he does not need to walk towards an unknown Goal which, in reality, does not exist. For the progressive theologian, this current world is man's real homeland; he need not rely on false promises about a *Better World*; nor is he going to

---

[17]Acts 1: 10–11.

[18]Jn 14: 4–6.

enjoy improvements other than those which he himself contributes to the environment of this final universe in which he lives.[19]

As we can see, there are here two planes with quite different perspectives: the perspective that is founded on Faith, and that which is based on disbelief; there is no middle term. Hence the absurdity of *Christian humanism*, in that it seeks to raise man solely upon the values of man, which in themselves are totally insufficient. This approach, far from merely implying that man is left without God, ultimately and inexorably leads man *to be also left without man*. Thus, in this sense, the atheistic Masonic humanism has greater consistency than Maritain's humanism.

If this life is a *valley of tears* for man, with more sufferings than joys, the disciple of Jesus Christ can always resort to the Christian meaning of suffering, which is much more than merely a hope and includes the joy of knowing that he is merely *on his way*, never at the finish line.[20] Those who think otherwise, especially the *progressive* theologians and all who doubt the Resurrection of Jesus Christ,[21] ought to remember Saint Paul's words: *If our hope in Christ has been for this life only, we are of all men the most pitiable.*[22]

---

[19]It would be quite difficult to appreciate the nuances of distinction between that which Modernism advocates and Marxist doctrines. The only novelty here is the strange garb of verbiage with which the heresy of Modernism clothes itself. If Marxism claims to be the liberator of man by destroying all Religion, Modernism presents itself as ennobling man by creating a New Religion. However, the result —which is all that really matters— is the same in both cases.

[20]The saying of Saint Teresa of Avila, according to which *life is a bad night in a bad inn*, is well known.

[21]The doubt about the Resurrection of Jesus Christ, and thus His divinity, is usually parallel to the questioning of the historicity of the Gospels; both seem to be taking root in the Church, Senior Members of the Hierarchy included.

[22]1 Cor 15:19.

The Christian finds his joy and his hope in the certainty that this life is a journey that leads to a goal and in the knowledge that he is not called to walk alone:

> *As you walk towards hills above,*
> *Allow me to walk with you, Pilgrim, my friend,*
> *And see if he whom I love*
> *Gives us his wine to drink of,*
> *In reaching together our long journey's end.*[23]

In this sense, the certainty that life is a journey, an itinerary, a route is a source of joy for the Christian in a double, or rather triple, sense. First of all, the fact that charity, or love of neighbor, provides the possibility of making the journey accompanied by loved ones, from whom he receives help and encouragement (one heart and one soul, united in the Spirit) is for him a cause of unspeakable joy, surpassed only by the second: his knowing that Jesus Christ Himself is leading him by the hand throughout the journey.[24] The third sense referred to above is this: once we have defined Christian

---

[23] Alfonso Gálvez, *Los Cantos Perdidos*, Segunda Edición, Shoreless Lake Press, NJ, 2011, n. 1. In the Spanish original:

> *Si vas hacia el otero,*
> *deja que te acompañe, peregrino,*
> *a ver si el que yo quiero*
> *nos da a beber su vino*
> *en acabando juntos el camino.*

[24] Charity, or love, is the first source, or *sine qua non* condition, from which all the gifts and feelings of joy rain down on human beings. Saint Paul named it as the first fruit of the Spirit, even prior to joy (Gal 5:22). This suggests that if we take into account this Pauline order, it is easy to deduce that joy is the first fruit of love, which becomes, in turn, a prerequisite for joy.

existence as a journey to be walked, upon a road which is by and large rough, difficult, and painful, we can conclude that there is an arrival at the end of the journey, along with the joy caused by capping an undertaking or earning a well–deserved rest after having overcome a whole series of hardships:

> *To the snow–capped heights and mists*
> *Of the white mountains we will climb, you with me,*
> *Overcoming valleys and the deep abyss;*
> *We'll arrive there finally,*
> *And intone together love's sweet melody.*[25]

The journey implies indeed the arrival at the end of the road and the conquest of what can be called the Christian *Mount Horeb*; a long steep hill which, precisely for that reason, makes its climbing a wonderful adventure. Saint John of the Cross spoke of the *Ascent of Mount Carmel*, while Saint Teresa of Ávila described the difficult and thorny way to be trodden as a series of *Mansions*, ending with the seventh, where the spiritual betrothal with God is consummated; and before them, Saint Bonaventure wrote his captivating *Itinerarium Mentis in Deum*. Hence the song of the poet:

---

[25] Alfonso Gálvez, *op. cit.*, n. 47. In the Spanish original:

> *A las nevadas cimas*
> *de las blancas montañas subiremos*
> *salvando valles y profundas simas;*
> *y cuando. al fin. lleguemos.*
> *los cantos del amor entonaremos.*

> *My Love, our climb goes steeply*
> *To hills with rosemary–rockrose covering.*
> *There we two will drink deeply*
> *From the pure abundant spring*
> *And taste waters fresh and clear and murmuring.*[26]

But, as we have said, the Christian has the joy of having reached the end of the road, after having traveled in loving company and overcoming so many incidents:

> *If then together we follow the pathway,*
> *Let me arrive sooner, the first one, I pray.*
> *And there at the end of the road we will find*
> *Our toils and hard labors are left far behind.*[27]

Modernism did not want to return to the pots of Egypt; it desired to stay in the desert. Or, in any case, it would not have left the lands of the Pharaohs, but rather would have pitched its tents definitively

---

[26] Alfonso Gálvez, *op. cit.*, n. 53. In the Spanish original:

> *Mi Amado, subiremos*
> *al monte del tomillo y de la jara,*
> *y luego beberemos*
> *los dos, en la alfaguara,*
> *el agua rumorosa, fresca y clara.*

[27] Alfonso Gálvez, *op. cit.*, n. 89. In the Spanish original:

> *Si pues seguimos juntos el sendero,*
> *deja que me adelante, yo el primero,*
> *allí donde se acaba la vereda*
> *y el duro trajinar atrás se queda.*

in that land, ultimately making it the only Paradise to which man could aspire. Its alleged inactivity is merely the result of its refusal to seek another unknown Homeland, which has been imagined on an idealized supernatural level that is alien to the full capabilities of a self–sufficient being like man. In doing so, Modernism deprives the Christian existence of any meaning, for it is committed to erasing all vestiges of Christian life, which is the only thing capable of making any sense of this earthly existence of man. Experience of the Faith, by contrast, is inexorably a faithful following of Him Whose feet went through all the roads of Palestine and Whose life remains forever as the model to be imitated by everybody.

The words of Jesus, addressed to the young man with an invitation to follow Him, may provide useful data for a better understanding of what Christian existence consists of: *If thou wilt be perfect, go, sell your possessions and give them to the poor, and thou shalt have treasure in heaven. Then come, follow me.*[28] The argument that we are going to present here concerning these words, even if it seems somewhat pliable, may lead us to some practical teaching, given the serious challenge posed by the following of Christ by His disciples.

According to the exhortation to the rich young man, the renunciation of one's property is a prerequisite for following the Master. To this degree of generosity is promised, in return, *a treasure in heaven.* After that, namely the invitation to surrendering one's own things and the corresponding promised reward, an invitation to follow Him is uttered, which crowns, like the capstone, the whole speech: *Then come, follow me.*

Thus it would appear that this following is like the culmination of a generous and heroic act which finds its full meaning, as could not be otherwise, in the love which animates it and makes it possible. Is this following then, perhaps, even more important, apparently, than the treasure waiting in heaven...? Certainly this should not be regarded as the correct meaning of what is being said here; *but it seems appropriate, however, to believe that following Jesus Christ is like the culmination and the epitome of the whole act of love regarding Him.* This is true insofar as the renunciation of things only makes sense when it is being done out of love: as we have said, things are not abandoned because they are bad, but because,

---

[28]Mt 19:21.

being good and beautiful, they are entitled for that very reason *to be offered to the Beloved.* Following Jesus Christ, sharing His life and destiny to the death, is the supreme act of love that brings about the renunciation of things —even one's own life— as well as the acceptance of any other suffering that may lead to participation in His life (Lk 14:26). The Bridegroom of the *Song of Songs* speaks:

> *The mandrakes yield their fragrance,*
> *The most exquisite fruits are at our doors;*
> *The new as well as the old,*
> *I have stored them for you, my love.*[29]

The modernist heresy wants to build a church made by men and for the deification and exaltation of those same men; her scope would only cover this earth, which is the one place where this heresy recognizes that all human existence begins and ends. For Modernism and *progressive* theology there is only this world, for they reject any reference to the supernatural realm. By denying the Faith, placing themselves on a level contrary to any data from Revelation, they reject the idea of a Pilgrim Church that is merely a transient place. The absolute opposition of this heresy to the Christian vision of reality is easily seen when one checks some passages of Holy Scripture, like this one taken from the Second Letter to the Corinthians: *For we know that when the tent that houses us on earth is folded up, there is a house for us from God, not made by human hands but everlasting, in the heavens.*[30]

If the Christian is able to bear the iniquity and injustice by which he rightly feels constantly overwhelmed while on this earth, it is only because he lives on Hope; encouraged as he is by the belief that where he lives now is not his Homeland, let alone his home:

---

[29]Sg 7:14.

[30]2 Cor 5:1.

There is no permanent city for us here; we are looking for the one which is yet to be.[31]

The certainty of feeling himself a stranger and a foreigner constantly accompanies the Christian —as something essential to his nature— throughout his earthly pilgrimage. Modernism, on the contrary, feels at ease and comfortable in this world; hence it does not want to wait for or believe in any other which could have a supernatural character; its hope is purely human, with no other explanation to turn to except those which its own possibilities can provide. This heresy certainly wants a better world, and even looks for it passionately, but because its dreams do not reach beyond this earth, it may be said that its chimeras merely lead to a utopia and have nothing to do with the Christian virtue of Hope. Modernism maintains its frantic search through the strength that the Lie provides, but there is not the slightest possibility of achieving the desired Goal —which exists only in the twisted imagination of those who, having renounced Truth and Goodness, have opted for the Lie and Iniquity.

It happens, however, that the Lie is not even *nothing*; it actually is only a counterfeit reality —or, at best, that which would like to *oppose being* and whose nature seems to escape the scope of the power of the created intellect.[32] Hence, whoever voluntarily accepts and endorses the Lie is necessarily led to *despair* of the spirit and *emptiness* of the soul, which are, at the end of the day, the living

---

[31] Heb 13:14.

[32] That is why the nature of the Lie refuses to be grasped by the human mind. It would not even be accurate to describe the Lie as something *contrary to being*, which, logically, would simply be nothing and fool no one. It seems more reasonable to say that it is a hunchback reality, a burlesque, a reeking caricature of reality, whose connection with being and truth could be compared —to say something— to the connection between praising God and blasphemy.

environment into which the modern World has plunged, despite its
refusal to admit it: sex lowered to the level of aberration; the search
for happiness and escape from the vacuum, which has turned into
an agonizing anxiety of drugs; the horror of the certainty of feeling oneself at some point diminished to a wretched condition, much
worse than any understanding could imagine —a feeling which tries
to drown itself in pursuit of Power and in the worship of money; the
mocking of God and Religion, which manifests the urgent need men
feel to quell the relentless foreboding —a veritable predestination to
Hell— that induces them to acknowledge the certainty of the near
and eternal damnation... these are just some of the ways of expressing the horror caused by a life based in utopia. To which you may
add the attempt, otherwise useless and vain, to turn what is but a
valley of tears and a transitory place into what they would have as
a final earthly Paradise and definite Home. However, no wretched
situation can be compared to the condition of those Christians who,
constituting the Hierarchy of the Church —Priests, Bishops, Cardinals, and other clergy in positions of high responsibility— have
renounced their Faith: *As for those people who were once brought*
into the light, and tasted the gift from heaven, and received a share
of the Holy Spirit, and tasted the goodness of God's message and
the powers of the world to come and yet in spite of this have fallen
away —it is impossible for them to be brought to the freshness of
repentance a second time, since they are crucifying the Son of God
again for themselves, and making a public exhibition of him.[33]

Christians, on the other hand, contrary to what Modernism postulates, feel themselves aliens and pilgrims on this earth, while they
keep walking on their journey to the definitive Homeland: *All these*
[the Patriarchs] *died in faith, before receiving any of the things that*

---

[33]Heb 6: 5–6.

had been promised, but they saw them in the far distance and wel-comed them, recognizing that they were only 'strangers and nomads on earth.' People who use such terms about themselves make it quite plain that they are in search of a homeland. If they had meant the country they came from, they would have had the opportunity to return to it; but in fact they were longing for a better homeland, their heavenly homeland.[34] As is clear from these words, therefore, they felt no nostalgia *for the country from which they came*; that is why *they were in search of a new homeland.*

If we have no objection to taking advantage of the ironies of language, we could say that the *New Church*, or if you will, *the Universal Church of all Mankind* does feel nostalgia for *the land she has never entered*, after having accepted the promises of the Father of Lies —promises that, of course, will never be fulfilled. Anyone who dares to consider this topic (which usually goes unnoticed) would soon realize that the definitive fall into the Place of Eternal Lamentation —the second and real death, in the words of Scripture— already begins its first stage here on earth: the loss of the mind in the precipice of madness and the transformation of the heart into a bottomless pit of corruption. Therefore, nobody should be surprised that we speak of a predestination to damnation —parallel to the predestination to salvation—, for, indeed, *those people who were once brought into the light, and tasted the gift from heaven, and received a share of the Holy Spirit... it is impossible for them to be brought to the freshness of repentance a second time, since they are crucifying the Son of God again for themselves, and making a public exhibition of him.*

It is true that the Christian person lives in the world but *does not belong to it*; rather the opposite, for he will always be considered

---

[34]Heb 11: 13–15; cf. 1 Pet 2:11.

by the world as something so alien to it that the world cannot accept
or welcome him except as its enemy. So much so, that the enmity of
the world is a guarantee of authenticity for the true disciple of Jesus
Christ, and its friendship and benevolence are signs of the absence
of Christian spirit as well as of membership to the mundane realm:
*Blessed are you when people abuse you and persecute you and speak
all kinds of calumny against you falsely on my account...*[35] And
in another place, in the opposite sense: *Alas for you when men
speak well of you! This was the way their ancestors treated the false
prophets.*[36]

The doctrine that the true disciple does not belong to the World
because he is in it as if passing through was clearly and categorically
taught by Jesus Christ Himself: *If the world hates you, you must
realize that it hated me before it hated you. If you belonged to the
world, the world would love you as its own; but because you do not
belong to the world, because my choice of you has drawn you out of
the world, that is why the world hates you...*[37] *I passed your word to
them, Father, and the world hated them, because they belong to the*

---

[35]Mt 5:11.

[36]Lk 6:26. It is curious to note Jesus' warning (which also ordinarily goes unnoticed) about the false prophets, who usually are held in great esteem and extolled
by the world: Could someone figure out any parallels with the current situation?
Indeed, because if anyone has any doubts as to the Word of God being alive and
active (Heb 4:12), here he would find an example of Its perennial relevance. A true
disciple of Christ, endowed with the spirit of discernment, would be suspicious of
those whom the world does not hesitate to acclaim and unanimously praise. The
era in which the Saints were proclaimed *by acclamation* belongs to the early days
of the Church, already definitively gone and with no possible return.

[37]Jn 15: 18–19.

world no more than I belong to the world...[38] *They do not belong to the world any more than I belong to the world.*[39]

The difference between the modernist doctrine, which advocates that the Christian should settle in this world because there is no other he can wait for, and the Christian doctrine, which proclaims that we are in the world as pilgrims passing through on our way to the heavenly Homeland, is exactly the same as that between Faith and Unbelief. The garb with which Modernism is often disguised with the sole purpose of becoming accepted as Christianity —*Integral Humanism, Christian Humanism, New Christianity,* and the *New Pentecost...*— only seduces those who, having lost their love of Truth, have agreed to negotiate with the Lie.

Against all appearances, this is not a book of denunciation, as I first stated. It responds to a painful state of mind and has been written for those people of good will who do not want to be deceived. In modern times in which the smoke of Satan, in the words of Pope Paul VI, has entered the Church, we must understand that such a thing has been made possible by the modernist heresy, which is now relevant in the Boat of Peter; a boat which has also been invaded by a multitude of false christs and prophets, who, from key positions in the Hierarchy, spread error and confusion among the faithful through their teachings and their actions. This opinion will be rejected by many as false, while others will consider it has no evidence. They will argue that it is not possible to speak of such false characters as operating here and now, as the moment for their occurrence is known only to God. But the Apostle Saint John would not agree with this objection, judging by what he said: *Children this is the final hour; you have heard that the Antichrist is coming, and now*

---

[38] Jn 17:14.
[39] Jn 17:16.

many Antichrists have already come; from this we know that it is the final hour. They have gone from among us, but they never really belonged to us.[40]

Anyway, he would not read this book with a Christian mind who walks through its pages with the tormented spirit of discouragement. For the disciple of Jesus Christ, as we have noted many times, lives on Hope, finds comfort in Joy, and firmly believes in the promises of his Lord. It is proper to Christians to live in the assurance of victory as the only possible ending of a life spent in fidelity. Moreover, as Saint Augustine said, there can be no crown without a victory; neither are laurels of triumph possible if there has been no previous battle or if trials have not been overcome: *And the world, with all its disordered desires, is passing away. But whoever does the will of God remains forever.*[41]

---

[40] 1 Jn 2: 18–19.

[41] 1 Jn 2:17.

THE GREAT APOSTASY

It seems reasonable to think that all the evils that the Church is suffering nowadays are caused by her fearful attitude towards the modern world. But it is not difficult to conclude that at the bottom of this attitude there is something much more serious, namely a crisis of faith, which has also caused charity to grow cold.

In view of what is happening, everything points to the existence, on the part of the Church, of an overvaluation of the world of technology, of the power of ideologies, and of the strength of totalitarian systems. Parallel with this, and as a consequence of it, the Church has fallen into the simplistic attitude of undervaluing her own treasures: having lost faith in the supernatural content of her Message of salvation, she is now making an effort to fall in behind the World, begging for acceptance. And it is not that we underestimate the power of the System; we can concur with what Revel said[1] about falsehood having made itself the master of the world because the System needs it in order to survive. But the Church had no need to be afraid or to let herself be influenced by the Powers which the Kingdom of Lies possesses. What she ought to have done was continue to believe in her own supernatural values because, in the last analysis, good will prevail over evil; and the Church knows that. But, as we have said, when love grows cold it leads inexorably to falsehood. Not in the sense that the Church has become a liar, but in the sense that many of her children have either moved away from

---

[1] Jean–François Revel, *La Connaissance Inutile*, Paris, 1988.

the truth or else silenced it or, in their cowardice, hidden it, allowing error full rein. And here one must also include many Shepherds,
however sad it makes one to say so.

If it is difficult to understand those who openly tell lies, it is
harder to figure out the mere cowards. Some of the latter have
adopted the policy of not denouncing error, fearing, as they themselves say, that it would only make things worse. They argue that it
is much more positive and practical *to teach the doctrine* because the
truth will thereby prevail by itself. Perhaps they are right, although
there are reasons to doubt it. The Lie has such an ability to permeate, given the present state of human nature, that it needs to be
denounced and stopped. It is the duty of the good shepherd not only
to lead his sheep to good pasture, but also to protect them from the
wolf. At least that is how the New Testament seems to think; which
is why it is filled with instructions to Shepherds to guard their sheep
and to keep them away from error (one can read, for example, the
pastoral Letters of Saint Paul and Chapter 10 of the Gospel of Saint
John). If today's doctrine of well–intentioned tolerance had always
been followed, heresies would have had *carte blanche* throughout
the history of the Church: Saint Athanasius would not have put an
end to Arianism, or Saint Augustine to Pelagianism, nor would Saint
Bernard have unmasked the errors of Abelard, nor would Pope Saint
Pius X have severed Modernism. But all this is talking for the sake
of talking, for modern Christians are not even willing to comment
upon this issue.

There are grounds for believing that the true content of *The
Third Secret of Fatima* was manipulated, falsified; that, according
to sufficiently serious testimonies, it actually referred to the Great
Apostasy that the Church would have to undergo towards the End of
Time. To claim, as has been done, that the prophecy alluded to the

murder attempt suffered by Pope John Paul II —*A Bishop dressed in white*—, and to make it public twenty years after that attempt took place, seems to be not only a heavy–weight and tasteless joke, but also a real insult to the intelligence of the common Christian People.

And yet, whether we acknowledge it or not, reality suggests that we live in a time of general apostasy in the Church, about which two things are evident.

The first evidence is that once the moment has come and the appearance of the Son of Perdition bringing History to an end is near at hand, *there will be an apostasy which will encompass nearly the whole Church.*

Therefore, it will be a huge apostasy, for Sacred Scripture says it. For example, Saint Paul, in his *Second Letter to the Thessalonians,* Chapter two, verse three: speaking about the moment of the last Times the Apostle says that *first the great apostasy must come*; and about its being a widespread one, Jesus Christ Himself explicitly affirms it with disturbing words: *When the Son of Man comes, will he find any faith on this earth?*[2]

The second evidence has to do with the present situation: *its symptoms in general look a lot like those described by Scripture as the ones which will immediately precede the End.* The wilderness the Church is becoming, and the ensuing paganism of Christians at large, along with the rebellion of the World and its persecution against every Christian value are realities out there, whether we want to see them or not.

And let us add to what has been said that the truly important and grave facts usually have profound causes generating them, *although very often one does not want to, or cannot, speak of them.*

---

[2]Lk 18:8.

Many skeptics will accuse us of being *alarmists*. The truth is that while we Christians are discussing whether or not these times will come, or while we are not even accepting any discussion about this matter, we could ask Institutions like the *Bilderberg Group* (that is, Freemasonry).[3] They will probably tell us, despite the secrecy with which they shroud themselves, how great their satisfaction is in view of what they have already accomplished and because of the certainty they have regarding their ability to fully achieve their world–wide objectives.[4]

---

[3]Daniel Estulin, *The True Story of the Bilderberg Group*, Trine Day LLC, Chicago, Illinois, 2005.

[4]Extracted from the book *The Importunate Friend*, pp. 87 ff.

THE INFERIORITY COMPLEX

Here is the sad reality of an obvious fact: the few Catholics who still attend Sunday Mass are bored by the homilies they listen to. One should say, though, that they are bored by the homilies they *hear*, since *listening*, really listening, always requires some attention on the part of the audience. But the faithful who attend Sunday worship, in most cases, feel completely uninterested about what is being said.

As for the reasons behind this phenomenon, after a careful consideration of this issue, there is no doubt that one can find many —but they do not absolve the audience from all responsibility: the crisis of Faith, the dominant paganism, the de–Christianization of society, the post–Conciliar liturgical reforms, etc., etc., all of which point in the same direction. But a superficial investigation as to a possible solution (or at least an amelioration) of the problem will not lead to any practical results other than drawing up an analysis useful for experts and for preparing statistics to be presented to the general public, which, in general, tend to be skewed.

Therefore, it is necessary to search for the profound roots of the problem; although, we must admit, it is probable that we will not accomplish anything other than a better understanding of the facts. The truth is that people do not listen because almost everything that is said is insignificant and does not interest anyone. The exhortations of preachers very frequently reach heights that stray far from reality (popularly known as *having your head in the clouds*) while the Faithful remain on earth.[1] It would be interesting to study those different planes (those parallel lines that never meet) where lie, on one hand, the inane ramblings of Pastors and, on the other, the real concerns of the People of God.

It cannot be denied that Preaching has deteriorated to the same measure as Christianity has become an anodyne. The guilty party, of course, is the entire body of the Christian faithful; it would not be fair to put all the blame on the ecclesiastical Hierarchy. But unlike the *Regulations of Charles III* for the army in Spain, which placed all the blame and penalization on the subordinates (*Those who are subordinate will always be punished* was the catch phrase that concluded almost every regulation), here it is impossible not to hold the Shepherds responsible for the greater part of this problem.

The first thing that calls our attention here is an important and apparent contradiction. According to the Epistle to the Hebrews, *The word of God is something alive and active: it cuts more incisively than any two–edged sword: it can seek out the place where soul is divided from spirit, or joints from marrow; it can pass judgment on the thoughts and intentions of the heart.*[2] And Jesus Christ is even more forceful when He says: *The words I have spoken to you are spirit and they are life. But there are some of you who do not believe...*[3]

Hence the question: According to what has been said above, what is the final verdict...? Is the Word of God *alive* or is it, rather, *boring*? The answer does not seem difficult to find; it would be

---

[1] People are willing to listen to, and even pay for, a conference on a banal or even phony topic, such as climate change; but, apart from the fact that these speakers know how to make their deception interesting, this type of situation has nothing to do with Christian pastoral work.

[2] Heb 4:12.

[3] Jn 6: 63–64.

something like this: *the reason is that all that is preached has very little or nothing to do with the Word of God.* On reaching this point, we must strive to the best of our ability to omit individual cases in order to honor Charity and also to avoid scandalizing the weak.

How did we reach this situation...? And precisely at a time when both the post–Christian West and the rest of the almost totally pagan world into which the former is integrated need, more urgently than ever before, the Word of God?

To facilitate possible answers and to center the problem on what interests us most, we will keep to Catholicism. In this regard the first consideration that comes to mind is the indisputable fact that *the present Shepherds of the Church suffer from an extraordinary inferiority complex*; or, at least, a great number of them do. This assertion, though, is still far from solving the problem entirely. And so, we will try to understand this problem by examining it on different levels, hoping to gradually close in on the root of the situation.

In the first place, we must point to the phenomenon of the *inferiority complex* itself; a reality whose existence cannot be doubted or denied.

It manifests itself in numerous and various ways, although they all coincide in spiriting away the Word of God, avoiding confronting problems. Therefore, they speak exclusively of banalities, never alluding to realities that could put those who dare to denounce them into a compromising position.

The Apostle Saint Paul proclaimed that he did not feel any shame in proclaiming the Gospel (Rom 1:16), while Saint Peter also insisted that nobody should be ashamed of being a Christian (1 Pet 4:16). However, after so many centuries, the Catholic Pastoral practice seems to be bent on sidestepping those problems which could become thorny or demand a personal commitment. It uses the strategy of talking about indifferent or various topics that are more or less interesting but which never remotely contemplate the possibility of making anybody uncomfortable because those issues have been touched upon. The preaching of the Gospel is avoided, limiting the themes of sermons or homilies to merely talking about insipid things.

So, the inferiority complex that afflicts Catholic Pastoral practice uses the well–known custom of *throwing the ball out of bounds*, or avoiding the real problems —and even more so when the need to face them is greatest; in any case, since it is necessary for them to preach, they talk of trivialities, banal things, or false *problems* that do not affect or concern anyone.

The theme of the *Christmas Message* for the year 2009, signed by all the Bishops of Patagonia, was focused on the theme *protecting the environment.* After this, we can only suppose that all the faithful would envy the situation of Christians in Argentina, a happy Arcadia where there do not seem to be any problems that affect the life of the Faith.

In the U.S., there is the very old practice of publishing joke books geared especially for Sunday homilies. Of course the homily must be adapted to the prefabricated joke so they *fit together* well, which is what usually happens with products prepared beforehand; in other words, the funny part is adapted to the content of the homily —or is it the homily that has to be adapted to the sense of the joke? Either way, undoubtedly the *industrially manufactured* joke, prepared to fill up the homily, is the clearest expression of the lack of value relegated to preaching and the dearth of ideas and feelings on the part of the preacher. Meanwhile, the poor attendants to these liturgical functions laugh at the jokes —what else should they do! After all, it is better to laugh than to cry.

This inferiority complex fears everything: angering those in Power; opposing the world's criteria (new dogmas that need no definition); the negative reaction of the *media*; being called conservative or traditional; not pleasing their listeners; possible reprisals that may compromise the *status* the preacher in question enjoys; etc., etc. Evil has much more power than good, at least in the present History of the World —actually, Good seems to have no power; and it has always seemed more fashionable to belong to the more secure side. On top of this, a large part of the Hierarchy suffers a strange sub–complex: a reverential fear towards all that the Left in general says or decrees. In effect, with things the way they are now; if the Left were to proclaim one day that the Pythagorean Theorem is false, many would start to think that this wise Greek, along with those who have applied his principle for centuries, has been wrong. That is why when some believed that Communism had achieved a definitive victory in the world, the Catholic Hierarchy was quick to assure the Colossus, through an official Agreement, that the Church would not raise her voice against it.

The inferiority complex of the Church is convinced that nothing can be done against the growing power of the World. That is why Maritain spoke of *kneeling before the World*.[1] And that is why what was announced in the Apocalypse about the end of times seems to be coming to complete fulfillment now:

And all the earth followed the beast in wonder. And they worshipped the dragon because he gave authority to the beast, and they

---

[1] What is odd is that he said this when he had already prostrated himself before it. Mainly his *Integral Humanism* (and his entire philosophy) may be summarized as an exaltation of man, valued *in himself* for the first time, in an independence that turned aside a world view centered on God (though it didn't explicitly deny Him, in theory) that, until then, had considered man as a creature.

*worshipped the beast saying, 'Who is like to the beast, and who will
be able to fight with it?'*[5]

And a little afterward it adds:

*It forced all the people, small and great, rich and poor, free and
slave, to be given a stamped image on their right hands or their
foreheads, so that no one could buy or sell except he who had the
stamped image, either the name of the beast or the number that stood
for its name.*[6]

Hence the use of logomachies which are constantly brought up to
date. Words and words without ever getting to the heart of any real
problem: who would dare confront the World and the Powers? We
are touching here upon a grave problem that was mentioned by Jesus
Christ Himself: the necessity of preaching the gospel (Mk 16:15).
And we cannot consider it sufficient to be concerned about secondary
questions that have little or nothing to do with His doctrine; in
other words, we are concerned here with *the necessity of preaching
the truths of the gospel* without restrictions or disguises.

The Master already warned against those who would be ashamed
of Him; and not only of Him as a Person, but also of His words: *For
if anyone is ashamed of me 'and of my words,' of him the Son
of Man will be ashamed when he comes in his glory.*[7] This leads
us to some especially serious aspects of the problem that deserve
particular consideration; until now, we have only touched the introduction without reaching the most worrisome part of such a decisive
question.

There should be no objections to a Shepherd of the Church
(whichever office he holds in the hierarchy) giving a conference,

---

[5]Rev 13: 3–4.

[6]Rev 13: 16–17.

[7]Lk 9:26.

speech, exhortation, or the like, about an indifferent, even banal, topic such as Art, History, Philosophy; or, say, about any of the many themes that human Arts and Sciences comprise. In this particular case, the important thing to take into account would be the need to not confuse such behavior with the proclamation of the Christian message. However, the normal course of action of the ecclesiastical parenesis is to try to instruct the faithful in the Christian Message —a purpose that becomes *compulsory* when the objective of that instruction is the *specific* truths of Christian Existence (as is the case of the homilies offered at weekday or Sunday Masses, or sermons on the occasions of various festivities or liturgical events).

It is also convenient to remember, if we want to understand better the issue we are speaking about, that Christian parenesis (which, for simplification purposes, we have identified here with preaching) may take on diverse expressions: exhortations, speeches, conferences, sermons, homilies, funeral orations, etc.

Let us consider, for instance, the theme of an exhortation of Pope Benedict XVI which we had the opportunity to listen to a few weeks ago: *European Cathedrals as a compendium of art and religious spirit.* If we strictly confine ourselves to the objective at hand, it would be difficult, if not impossible, to consider this theme as *specifically Christian.* Certainly, any speculative activity of the human spirit, to the extent that it is truly scientific, that is, true, belongs to the patrimony of the absolute Truth and is, consequently, *Christological.* But we are speaking here in terms of Pastoral activity; therefore we add *specifically.* The difference in nuance is often overlooked, when in fact it should be taken into account by both the Shepherds and the Faithful.

In effect, the statement acknowledging that European cathedrals are a compendium of art and religious spirit, although truthful, does

not correspond to the tradition of the Christian Deposit of Faith.
This thesis cannot even be regarded as an exclusive feature of the
Western or Christian world, for it is a verification that is valid in
all cultures. Indeed, the same could be said about Greek sculptural
and architectural art, for instance. The abundance of cults, as well
as the collection of Greco–Roman gods and goddesses, is part of the
framework of a religion. The same could be stated about the presence of the Pyramids. They are impressive millenary monuments
of Egyptian art and of belief in mythological gods and divinized
Pharaohs. The fact that these two cases are *false* religions does not
deprive them of the category of religion —or what the world regards
as such— as was well established at the Meetings of Assisi convened
by Pope John Paul II and then continued and evoked with great
praise by Benedict XVI. It is worth noting that at those *Meetings*
there were no distinctions among the religion of the true God, religions of false gods, and religions with no belief in any deity. And
let us not forget the historical importance that such an event had,
for it made it quite clear that the millenary idea of *paganism* has
been transcended ever since the Second Vatican Council: from now
on, all religions are recognized by Catholic Theology —if not on the
same level as the authentic one, at least as possessing enough value
to attain salvation, according to the new Ecumenism.[8]

As stated above, a Shepherd may give a dissertation about any
cultural theme. However, if he speaks to his faithful *as their Shepherd*, he must focus his dissertation on the spiritual needs of his
sheep and the problems affecting them, which may either lead them
to or separate them from salvation. If the Shepherd does not act

---

[8]This fact is grave enough to raise other problems that can be serious; for there
are difficulties even with considering other *religions* at a level below that of the
Catholic Religion. If all are valid for salvation, the alleged difference in status,
even if it is accepted, becomes a trivial matter.

accordingly within these parameters, and if this lack of acting accordingly becomes his habitual conduct, then he is giving ample reason for anyone to suspect that he has fallen victim to an inferiority complex.

If what has been said so far is accurate and right in that it points to the bottom of this issue, then we may conclude that we are facing a true problem: an inferiority complex in the eyes of the World, and the fear of announcing the Gospel. Nevertheless, it seems that we have not yet reached the true and ultimate cause of this phenomenon.

Internet news sites published the following news when this was written (December 10, 2009): *Eight married couples from Salzkotten, Germany decided not to send their children to sex–education classes that are compulsory in that country's schools. As a result, first they were ordered to pay large fines, and finally they were sentenced to prison... The President of the International Christian Institution 'Human Rights Group,' that is defending these families, has declared that the German authorities 'consider that the children belong to the state, at least while they are in school.'*[9] On that same day, the commentator Pérez Bustamante, in his blog *Cor ad cor loquitur*, made the following remarks about this news: *It seems unbelievable that a country that suffered the Nazis and the Communists would once again commit the same sin. I would emigrate before staying in such a country. And it is unbelievable that the German Catholic bishops look the other way, for, to this day, we still have not heard that any Bishop has come out in support of these families; and the same may be said about the official Lutheran Evangelical church. Perhaps they fear that the State will decide to take away the religious tax and leave them without financing. But I prefer a thousand times*

---

[9] *Infocatólica* webpage, December 14, 2009.

more a poor Church, faithful to its mission, over a rich Church imbued with the spirit of Judas Iscariot.

In short, fear is always haunting the Institutions of the Church; and the object of that fear is diverse: fear of opposing Power; of losing financing; of not being considered by those who decide who gets promoted...; perhaps of being called conservative or reactionary or an enemy of dialogue, alien to the *spirit of the Council,* etc. And there may be other reasons for that fear, like fear of the alleged advances of science, of scriptural hermeneutics, of historiography, of the fluctuations in Politics and of the campaigns organized by mass media..., and fear of so many other things. Meanwhile, the sheep of the Flock of Christ are being deprived of good pastures, on one hand, and on the other, they are left abandoned before the wolf that disperses them and devours them.

If someone asks the reason for such events, he can obtain the response from the mouth of Jesus Christ Himself: *A hired man, who is not the shepherd and whose own the sheep are not, sees a wolf coming and leaves the sheep and runs away, and the wolf scatters and catches them. This is because he works for pay and has no concern for the sheep.*[10] The importance of the content of this statement becomes clearer if we analyze its parts:

He acts like this who *is not the shepherd.*

Because he is not a shepherd, *the sheep do not belong to him.*

He flees when the wolf comes *because he only cares about his own life.*

He is a hired man: that is, he will only fulfill his duties for material interest and to seek his own gain, normally money and power.

In the last analysis, *he does not care about the sheep.*

---

[10] Jn 10: 12–13.

These statements may seem harsh, but we must not forget that Jesus Christ Himself uttered them.

Moreover, if it is admitted that one of the roots that feeds the inferiority complex is cowardice, then it is expedient to remember the words of the Apocalypse about the destiny in store for those who, out of whatever fear, neglect to fulfill their duty —which is even more serious when we are talking about duties that have to do with the saving of souls: *But as for cowards, the unfaithful, the depraved, murderers, the unchaste, sorcerers, idol–worshipers, and deceivers of every sort, their lot is in the burning pool of fire and sulfur, which is the second death.*[11]

If we continue our study of the causes that lead to the ecclesiastical inferiority complex, we find that lack of Faith is another possibility; something that Jesus Christ Himself seems to have confirmed:

—*Why are you so frightened? Have you still no faith?*[12]

Faith is the sister of Love and is actualized by Love (Gal 5:6), therefore it is licit to conclude that Love (or the lack of It) is the most profound cause of the ecclesiastical inferiority complex: fear, according to the Master, comes because Faith has been lost. At the same time, and conversely, one has faith in a person to the same measure —and only to that measure— that one loves that person.

We have seen that the abandonment suffered by the sheep of the Flock of Christ because the Hierarchy of the Church does not fulfill its duty in preaching the right Doctrine is mainly due to an uneasiness caused by an inferiority complex.

This complex is rooted in fear, which, in turn, is brought about by a weak Faith and Charity that has grown cold. Therefore, we

---

[11]Rev 21:8.

[12]Mk 4:40.

can conclude that this last reason —the cooling of Charity— is the deepest reason for fear and, by the same token, for the inferiority complex.

The lack of Love being at the root of cowardice or fear is not a matter of personal opinion; it is the Apostle Saint John who states it: *There is no fear in love; but perfect love casts out fear.*[13] Therefore, if, according to the Beloved Disciple, love casts out and is incompatible with fear, then the presence of the latter is a blatant proof that love has disappeared.

Therefore, narrowing the reasons for the lack of spiritual sustenance suffered by the faithful down to a mere inferiority complex on the part of the Hierarchy would be tantamount to staying on the surface of the problem. In the brief analysis we have made so far, we have seen that this phenomenon presents certain characteristics and a plurality of causes; the deeper and more determined these causes are found to be by this investigation, the more serious and worrying they become.

According to Jesus Christ, the abundance of iniquity is a concurrent cause of the cooling of charity (Mt 24:12). The deplorable phenomenon we have been talking about —and from which today's Church is so virulently suffering— cannot fully be explained by the fearful attitude of the Hierarchy. Its cause must be attributed to an Evil who is fully displaying its Power and whose activity is totally unchecked. This Evil is pulling the strings of its multiple henchmen (secret Societies, Governments, Political Parties, Institutions, Mass Media...) with apparent deadly effectiveness and total success. The cancer of Iniquity is progressively spreading all over the world, even penetrating and infecting the Body of the Church; so much so that the Bride of Christ is experiencing the worst attack ever in all

---

[13] 1 Jn 4:18.

her history, which has plunged her into a crisis more serious and dangerous than the ones once caused by the Arian and Protestant Heresies.

Yet, Christians must always trust in the promise made by Our Lord, for they know that the Gates of Hell will never prevail against the Church (Mt 16:18); that the Church, therefore, cannot disappear. Nevertheless, in view of the seriousness of the above–mentioned events and of the almost total anarchy and widespread confusion in the Church, today's problem is how to search for her. We know that the Church is out there because she cannot have disappeared; but where is she exactly...? The silence of the numerous sectors of the Hierarchy; the diversity of doctrines, often contradictory among themselves, preached here and there or discussed by theologians; the fact that the Magisterium prior to the Second Vatican Council has been questioned; the almost total disappearance of the principle of authority; the *de facto* schism of some countries from Rome; the questioning of almost all dogmas by the New Theology and its *discovery* that all men are Christians from the very moment of their existence —*Anonymous Christianity*— and that all religions are valid for achieving salvation... etc., etc. All these things seem to indicate that perhaps the moment has arrived to make ours Saint Peter's question: *Lord, to whom shall we go?*[14]

Nevertheless, in spite of all the appearances and the seriousness of the facts and despite the numerous arguments that one calls upon to the contrary, Christians can always count on the supreme truth enshrined in the triumphant shout of the Apostle Saint John: *This is the victory that overcomes the world, our faith;*[15] or even more so on the promise of Christ Himself: *I will be with you all days,*

---

[14] Jn 6:68.

[15] 1 Jn 5:4.

even unto the consummation of the world.[16]   And so it will be,
otherwise the promise about the final defeat of the Gates of Hell
will go unfulfilled. Regarding the justified hope that someday the
Church will be able to enjoy an abundance of Shepherds willing
to bravely lead the Flock, there is the assurance of an instruction
given by Our Lord: *Pray the Lord of the harvest to send forth
laborers to his harvest.*[17] Recourse to prayer, therefore, will suffice —
if Christians finally decide to practice it—, always keeping Abraham
in their minds, who hoped against all hope (Rom 4:18); and he was
not disappointed.

---

[16]Mt 28:20.
[17]Lk 10:2.

ECCLESIAL SCHIZOPHRENIA

He who calmly contemplates reality cannot ignore that the Church is going through moments of great confusion. The Spirit of Darkness has worked very efficiently and has spread a dark cloak over the minds of multitudes of the Faithful.

Consequently, many Christians feel themselves confused about what they must do. On the one hand, we have the clear, categorical, and still–in–force *norm*. On the other, there is the daily, absolutely contrary *practice*. Shepherds tolerate ways of behavior —sometimes even advising them— which are totally opposite to the norm. It is not surprising that many sheep of the Flock of Christ feel themselves disoriented, to the extent that they have ended up, not infrequently, abandoning the norm and consigning it to oblivion.

These statements, which undoubtedly must seem exaggerated to many, are totally true. To prove it, a few accessible examples will do:

In the field of economics, the principle known as Gresham's Law dictates that bad money will drive out good money. When two different currencies are available, one inflated and the other holding its value, people will always choose to pay their bills with the less valuable currency, until the better money gradually disappears from circulation. Since the late 1960s the same general principle has been at work in the Catholic Church: lax pastoral practice has driven out sound spiritual formation. Yes, the Church still bans the use of contraceptives. But for the past forty years, at least, a married Catholic has rarely had difficulty finding a priest who would tell him that in 'his' particular case, the use of contraceptives could be morally justified. Similarly, a Catholic who was troubled by the Church's teaching on divorce or on regular Mass attendance has generally been able to find a sympathetic cleric who would salve his conscience. In practice Catholics have found that it is possible to flout Catholic teachings, with the tacit blessing of someone who represents the Church.[1] These words of Philip Lawler, a well–known, accredited American journalist and author —and very knowledgeable of his country's Church— were written with the North American Church in mind, but they can be perfectly applied to the Spanish and many other Churches.

Let us consider first the contraceptive pill issue.

Almost everyone uses it, and countless are the priests who advise this practice in confession.

Nevertheless, the Encyclical *Humanae Vitae*, the validity of which offers no doubt, contains a clear and condemning teaching about this subject.

And practically all Christians know it. It is difficult to allow here a case of held–in–good–faith erroneous conscience. Normally, if erroneous conscience truly exists regarding this issue, it has likely been generated through trickery: by giving and receiving counsel, knowing it to be contrary to the teachings of the Magisterium. As for a doubtful conscience, it is known that *one cannot licitly act* upon it, for, according to the Apostle, *all that is not faith is sin*[2] — which is congruent with a traditional interpretation (which nobody has ever denied) about how to proceed in different situations with respect to moral conscience.

---

[1]Philip F. Lawler, *The Faithful Departed*, Encounter Books, New York, 2008, p. 125.

[2]Rom 14:23.

Be that as it may, it is difficult to dispel the idea that a schizophrenic conscience is being generated among Christian people: one thing is believed, and something different or contrary is practiced. One starts by willingly trying to forget the norm and ends up ignoring it totally. Therefore, only God knows when our consciences are justified.

Unfortunately, one must acknowledge that it was Pope Paul VI himself who, with good will but also with hesitation, contributed to creating this problem. Several years went by before his Encyclical was published; throughout this time, it was always said that the issue of the contraceptive pill was being studied, similar to being subjected to *ad experimentum.* Human nature, though, has its own ways, according to rules whose recurrence is well known. Therefore, the Encyclical came out too late, when nobody was willing to abandon the contraceptive pill.

I remember at that time that my then Bishop —Most Reverend Roca Cabanellas, a good Bishop otherwise— ordered us priests to attend a workshop in order that we could *become aware* of the new moral doctrine whose publication seemed imminent to everybody. Truly speaking, that was what Bishop Cabanellas thought in good faith, and many other people with him. I was a young priest at the time, but I had already studied *Natural Law* in depth; consequently, the very first day I left the workshop rather scandalized. It was clear to me that something that breaks the natural laws of the human organism, and therefore goes against Natural Law, could never be approved by the Magisterium of the Church. In effect, shortly afterwards, the Encyclical saw the light in clear continuity with the traditional Magisterium and doctrine, as could not have been otherwise.

The most delicate issue here —which gave rise to another much more serious problem— is that the controversy surrounding the contraceptive pill and the papal Encyclical triggered the appearance of a flood of ideas questioning the Magisterium of the Church.

Before continuing our reflection upon a possible *schizophrenia of conscience*, we should clarify an important point. We are not questioning the pastoral policy of the Church; even less any of her teachings that have to do with her Magisterial activity; for a Catholic, the legitimate precept of the Church should be obeyed. The matter now focuses on concerns aroused in the minds of some people about certain aspects of ecclesiastical policy, alien to multi–secular praxis, which do not fall under the infallible Magisterium (taking here the term *infallibility* in its rather widest sense).

Having said this, it is time to affirm that the second issue to deal with in connection with this problem is even more serious than the previous one, since it affects the survival and stability of the Christian family: *the indissolubility of the marriage bond.* Established as such by Divine Law (Mt 19: 1–11), it has been proclaimed and taught without hesitation by the Magisterium for centuries, confirmed through the practice of twenty centuries, and considered an immutable truth even at the very Second Vatican Council.[3]

But the so–called Western World abandoned its religious roots founded in the Gospel —which had given it firmness and foundation— and converted to paganism. Even Catholicism itself, besieged by a materialist and choking milieu, has yielded on some points. Thus divorce appeared, now embraced as a veritable triumph of civilization. Everything seems to indicate that many members of the Hierarchy of the Church were frightened and overcome by a world

---

[3] *Gaudium et Spes*, n. 48; cf. before, for example, Pius XI, *Casti Connubii*, Denz. 3706.

that, apparently, was getting out of hand. And that is how one of the most alarming, devastating, and intriguing phenomena, which had already affected the Church throughout the last two centuries, emerged again: *The fear of being considered as strange and foreign to the world, which, in turn, leads to a paralyzing inferiority complex.*

Of course the Church cannot abolish or modify Divine Law, nor can she contradict her own Magisterium. But, what happened then...? The Hierarchy of the Church wanted to get in line with the world even in this critical issue of marriage.

Finally, a gimmick was devised to address the inviolable wall of the indissolubility of marriage: the declaration of the *nullity of the marriage bond*. Of course it is not a proclamation that divorce is licit, which would have scandalized so many; it is just an official declaration that there was no valid consent at the origin, and, therefore, neither was there a real marriage.

That is how the problem was definitively fixed. From that moment on, any Catholic married couple can go to their parish to request an annulment, with the certainty that they will be amiably taken care of; as if it were a travel agency, where the clients are given various accommodations. Any pretext, no matter how small, is now accepted as valid, including, for example, *emotional instability*, which, it is said, can invalidate consent. In this way, filings for annulments are resolved favorably at a rate close to 100%. And in the extremely rare occurrence that some cases are rejected, there always remains the instance of a superior court (the Archdiocese, for example) to rule definitively in favor of the applicants.

Of course there will always be those who will tend to think that this process seems a lot like a trick used to legalize what, in itself, cannot be legalized. At any rate, the issue will never amount to much: people tend to think and admit what they like, even though, deep down, they suspect that it is a deception.

That is how it is possible, in this new order of things, that a married Christian couple, who have lived many years as man and wife and have been blessed by several children, may suddenly find that they have lived all the time in concubinage, although they cannot be accused of having acted in bad faith. As for the children, since there was not a true marriage, should they be now considered illegitimate or merely natural?

One may ask: where does the power of a mere Diocesan Curia come from to invalidate such situations and to establish them as officially valid in their new *status*? Consequently, Christian spouses can separate in this way whenever they wish it and without any type of difficulty. Besides, it is completely normal that it is the priests themselves who advise this type of *declaration of nullity*.

But then, very grave and serious problems have only started, as we will try to expound now.

Camouflaged divorce represents a much graver danger for the Faithful than what one might imagine, despite the fact that those affected by this problem do not clearly perceive its danger; but their eagerness to not perceive it does not absolve them in any way from their responsibility.

I am referring here to the schizophrenia of conscience, leading to a situation in which the Faithful are getting used to living with a *torn conscience*: that is, they are surely aware, at least in a more or less conscious manner, that things are not at all clear.

The indissolubility of Christian marriage has been a patent truth for the Catholic faithful, unquestionably admitted for centuries and too deeply rooted in everybody's mind for it to be now so easily eradicated. In spite of the many deficiencies that may have existed in their education, it is practically impossible for Catholics to claim *total ignorance* about this issue. Consequently, once the alleged divorce (now called *nullity of the marriage bond*) is obtained and the potential new marriage has taken place, peace of conscience becomes impossible for the rest of their lives for those who have welcomed this practice. Like the mother who has consented to aborting her son: regardless of how protected she may feel by the law, she will not be able to avoid that murder staying branded in her like an indelible seal corresponding to the perpetrator of a veritable parricide.

The problem is not difficult to understand. On the one hand there is the norm, which is clear and categorical. It is a norm of Divine Law, according to the words of Jesus Christ Himself: *What therefore God hath joined together, let no man put asunder.*[4] On the other hand there is the fact: the separation of two persons who have been united in marriage, perhaps for many years and with children, *who are guaranteed that their separation can be obtained legally.* Is there room here for a right conscience regarding a mere Diocesan Curia being able to grant legal status to this situation? Possibly only God knows; but it is difficult to dispel the idea that consciences will be forever torn apart by the specter of doubt, along with a latent remorse which will never go away. And even in the hypothetical case (very improbable, by the way) that somebody would acquire a conscience, certain and in good faith (although erroneous), about the legality of his situation, the Damocles Sword of an action which has broken Divine Law will always be somehow hanging over his head, as the Apostle Saint Paul warns: *Be not deceived; God is not mocked; for what things a man shall sow, those also he will reap.*[5]

---

[4]Mk 10:9.

[5]Gal 6:7.

The strangest thing about this issue is the fact that, when confronted with this categorical contradiction between the clear norm, on the one hand, and the practice of a camouflaged divorce, on the other, the Hierarchy has nothing to offer but *silence*. Undoubtedly we are dealing here with a situation serious enough to warrant, from the Magisterium, a definite clarification of the matter which would bring peace to consciences. Since the salvation of souls is the specific mission of the Church, the quandary we are dealing with is a much more serious problem than those of globalization, the warming of the planet, the world financial crisis, the convenience of a universal Government, etc., none of which falls under the direct *competency* of the Hierarchy.

All this could lead to a situation in which Pastoral activity, through established practice, would be producing Catholics suffering schizophrenia of conscience for the rest of their lives. If that were the case, then, what...?

Besides, the argument *since the Church permits it...* does not seem very convincing. For such an argument to be entirely valid, it also has to explain *why they are doing now that which has never been done before for twenty centuries and about which they have always said that it could not be done.*

When I was a young priest, for some years I did pastoral work in the city of Cuenca, which lies in a wonderful valley of the Ecuadorian Andes. At the time, Cuenca was not too large a city, rather quiet, beautiful, and with extremely kind people. There was a large Salesian School in the area with many students. And among the educators of that School there was the famous Father Crespi, a good–natured old man, rather eccentric, apostle of the children, and quite an accomplished social worker. This kind friar had the habit of confessing the children in groups of six or seven each; he placed the children at the same time before his confessional and somehow listened to them, whom he finally *dispatched* with a general absolution. I had the chance of hearing the confession of many of those children who had already received this sacrament from him on previous occasions; they invariably started their confession by saying: *I went to confession so long ago…, but it was with Father Crespi!* This suggests that those little ones possessed enough discernment to suspect that those confessions in groups were not clear at all. And now, one can draw his own conclusions when it comes to adults who are in different, though similar, circumstances.

As for me, this problem is greatly worrisome; for I sometimes even doubt that it was fear of the World which moved the Church to ingratiate herself with it.

From its inception, marriage has always been a natural institution and has remained so for centuries before our Lord Jesus Christ elevated it to the category of Sacrament. From that moment on, the *bill of divorce* which Moses had permitted was abolished, definitively abrogating divorce and declaring as adultery any new bond established after the attempted nullity of the first and legitimate one (Mk 10: 1–12). Consequently, a new and permanent stage for the Family was begun.

Since then, the *indissolubility of marriage* has been an undisputed patrimony of the Christian People who kept it for centuries up to the present time, as an incontrovertible institution, without any possible exceptions or wavering regarding its inalterable character and its permanence until death. Although Protestantism began to discard the indissolubility, the same did not happen in the Catholic Church; after all, she is the sole guardian and depository of the legitimate teachings of her Divine Founder. There are very rare cases contemplated in Canon Law through the so–called Petrine or

Pauline privileges, unconsummated marriage, etc.; apart from the fact that their determination was always reserved to the Apostolic See, their rarity and special exceptions make them issues that do not belong here. The fact remains that during twenty centuries, Catholics lived their Faith without even so much as thinking about divorce.

Logically, as it always happens in any type of human coexistence, there is always a possibility that discrepancies, dissentions or disputes may arise, some more important, the majority of them banal. But the normal thing was that the spouses always managed their differences and went on. Above all, because love ultimately understands, forgives, and forgets. When two persons love each other, as it normally happens in the marriage bond, all problems associated with their coexistence are solved. In connection with this, one must take into account that the Sacrament also provides extraordinary graces, which, in this case, consist of supernatural help to keep peace and happiness and strength to put up patiently with adversity; supernatural help also to assist the spouses in their sublime duty as parents and educators of their children.

We can add here that the clear certainty that their union was indissoluble and with no possibility of disappearance (except by death) was firmly rooted in the spouses, as well as unanimously confirmed by society at large. This conviction provided the couple with extra help to overcome any problem, turning it into a minor and passing incident. Who can doubt that such solid conviction, also confirmed without any hesitancy by the Church, provided the marriage bond with an extraordinary stability?

But then the new doctrine of the *annulment of the marriage bond* appeared —for that is the name since given to such a novelty, although nobody has ever harbored any doubt as to its true meaning.

Thus Catholic divorce became a reality. In the beginning, the numbers of divorces were few, but soon they grew to truly exponential quantities. In this new situation, husband and wife did not encounter any problem in getting an annulment of the bond, other than walking the distance to the parish. Any *reason* put forward was, and still is, considered valid; if it did not seem very plausible, the ecclesiastical setting helped find another, either a *founded* reason or a purely imaginary one.

But marriage is the foundation of Family, and Family is the primal cell and the main School of Formation, merely human as well as supernatural, in the life of the new human beings that come into this world.

Consequently, the System has made an effort to undermine the foundations of the Family. In Spain, for example, the Socialist Government has unleashed a campaign to destroy the Family, which is undoubtedly the most unrestrained offensive ever carried out in a civilized country in the last two centuries. Parents are deprived of the right of having their children academically instructed in their mother tongue; children are being indoctrinated and introduced to sexual life from their most tender childhood years; the teaching of atheism is compulsory in the Schools, through special *ad hoc* subjects; minor girls are authorized by law to abort without the consent or the knowledge of their parents; homosexual and lesbian unions have been declared legal marriages and are exceedingly promoted, giving them the right to adopt children; the promotion of prophylactics and information about using them is a normal and compulsory subject in the School; abortion is a legally protected procedure (the right to conscientious objection is not recognized to doctors); at the same time, euthanasia is beginning to be accepted and promoted, etc., etc.

And yet, in Spain, as incredible as it may seem, the powerful means employed by the System have not been the greatest contributors to the destruction of the Christian Family. The tremendous and painful reality, although nobody dares to admit it, is that *it has been the camouflaged divorce which has introduced confusion inside the Catholic world*; it has been the most effective contributor to the dissolution and gradual disappearance of Catholic families as such. These families, had they been encouraged and instructed by the example and teaching of their rightful Shepherds, would have undoubtedly held back (at least most of them) the onslaught of the System, as has always happened in times of persecution. Unfortunately, it could not be so in this case: The Hierarchy has been busy with its numerous tasks of different natures; for example, preparing some *International Encounter of Youth with the Pope*.

At this point the question becomes mandatory: How have we come to this situation of admitting the so–called *declaration of nullity of the marriage bond* as a normal procedure in ecclesiastical praxis?

It is the task of Philosophy to study the profound reasons for things and their ultimate causes. Doubtless, the case we are now commenting upon would be one whose study would surely lead us to astounding conclusions. To be sure, such a study would have to go beyond the intentions of those who have somehow intervened in the operation of *loosening* the ties of the marriage bond.

We must remember first and foremost that any ideas which may include limited situations, such as provisional character or partial giving, lead to concepts which are incompatible with the concept of Love. Love with a predetermined deadline, for example, is not true love, which, because of its very essence, understands neither conditions nor limitations of any kind. He does not really surrender everything he has, who gives his love for a fixed term. That is why such an attitude has nothing to do with Love, whose essence implies *totality.* To express it more clearly, a love whose nature implicitly contains temporality in the form of an expiration date, *is not true love.*

The love that does not include totality as its central axis is not love. We can hear it in Jesus' own words, Who, when asked about the most important commandment, answered: *You shall love the Lord your God with 'all' your heart, with 'all' your soul, with 'all' your mind and with 'all' your strength;*[6] wherein it is to be noticed the repetitious insistence of the word *all.* In this regard, it is interesting to recall the curious case narrated in the *Acts of the Apostles* regarding Ananias and his wife Saphira who sold their field with the intention of handing the profit over to the Christian community, but secretly kept part of the money for themselves, which earned them a sharp rebuke from Saint Peter: *Ananias, why has Satan tempted your heart, that you should lie to the Holy Ghost and by fraud keep part of the price of the land?... You have not lied to men, but to God.*[7] Similarly, in the *Song of Songs*: putting love on a par with any other thing, including all of one's property, deserves only contempt: *If anyone should offer all his property in exchange for love, he would only be despised.*[8]

To admit temporality in love relationships, which in this case is nothing but a form of partial self–giving, is merely the result of the degradation of the most sublime of realities, namely, love.

Marriage is founded upon and explained through Love and by Love; for it presupposes the unconditional surrender of a man to

---

[6]Mk 12:30.

[7]Acts 5: 3–4.

[8]Sg 8:7.

a woman and *vice versa*: *In sickness and in health, in good and bad times, in triumph and in disgrace...* until death.[9] If the Apostle equates marriage to the surrender of Christ for His Church — *This is a great mystery, but I am applying it to Christ and the Church*—[10] it then becomes impossible to admit in it temporality, which is, after all and as we have already said, one more variation of partial self–giving.

The idea of a possible dissolution of the marriage bond has become commonplace in the world, introduced even into the Church herself, because the concept of Love has become *lukewarm*. This expression, although strong, belongs to Jesus Christ Himself, who announced that a *general cooling of charity* would take place as the Final Times are closely approaching: In those days —these are the Lord's own words—, *because iniquity has abounded, the charity of many shall grow cold.*[11]

And that is not the worst. Since, as the Apostle Saint John says, Love is an indispensable condition, or *sine qua non*, to knowing God (1 Jn 4:8), we are brought to the conclusion that Christians who would no longer believe in Love, will have stopped loving, believing in, and knowing God.

Is this the situation and moment in which we find ourselves...? This is perhaps the worst and most important danger of all that we have enumerated, a possible consequence to be derived from the fact of having given a green light to that which in truth is opposite to the indissolubility, strength, firmness, and holiness of Christian Marriage.

---

[9]This end is subordinated to the primary end, the procreation and education of children, but it is not less fundamental.

[10]Eph 5:32.

[11]Mt 24:12.

THE CHURCH OF FEAR

The issue of this chapter pertains, above all, to the Hierarchy of the Church, especially to what one might call the *High Clergy* — since the *foot clergy*, or simple Priests, depend entirely on the other and necessarily have to keep the pace set by them.

As for the simple faithful, they have barely been directly affected by this phenomenon of fear. A very small minority courageously and faithfully continue to show their fidelity to Jesus Christ and the Church, despite the crisis affecting the latter. The vast majority, in contrast, have either opted decisively for desertion, leaving the Church (apostates), or taken the most complete indifference as a rule of life (non–practicing Catholics).

With regard to the Hierarchy —the segment of the Church most affected by this phenomenon—, it can also be divided, for this analysis, into several groups. The first group, the minority once again, is made up of those who have remained faithful to the Church and to their office and duty as Shepherds. A separate category must be given to those who, in a more or less concealed manner, have declared themselves to be against their own Church, with full awareness of their rebellious attitude. Finally, we must take into account those who have simply allowed themselves to be dominated by panic: they are the majority of the Shepherds.

It should be noted that we are going to refer here almost exclusively to Europe and the United States and, to a greatly lesser degree, Hispanic America which has been punished much more by the Marxist doctrines introduced by *Liberation Theology* than by Modernism.

Those who have not remained faithful have fallen victim, more or less consciously, to the nets laid by Modernism. We must not forget that the Modernist or Neo–modernist movement has been the source of ideas adroitly exploited by Freemasonry in its attempt to destroy the Church.

Fear, indeed, is a phenomenon that in recent times seems to have profoundly affected the universal Church, particularly the Hierarchy. This fear is founded upon and implies a wide variety of things: the ideologies that have imposed themselves on the world; the progress of technology; the Political Powers; the mass media; the opinion of the world (especially its accusation that the Church is intransigent or intolerant); fear of being branded as conservative or enemies of progress or anti–democratic; fear of the great *Lobbies* (such as the homosexual lobby) that have managed to exert a great and strong pressure in Society; fear of losing influence or *subsidies*...; and other fears.

These fears have led to the fact that both the Preaching and the numerous Documents emanating from the Hierarchy often avoid any reference to issues that may seem unpleasant or disturbing to the man of today. Hence the interest, on the part of the Hierarchy, in appearing as *being in line* with the present times; as well as the nature of the great Speeches and Pastoral Documents which, unfailingly, always speak of *wild flowers*; namely: speeches about pompous topics that never come to the point..., and never mention the real problems and needs that affect the faithful.[1]

---

[1] As an exception to what we have said, we must refer to important and numerous Documents, issued by members of the Hierarchy in high positions of authority, which spread Modernism in a more or less covert way.

As for the causes of this phenomenon, they were already provided by the Apostle Saint John: *In love there is no fear, because perfect love casts out fear.*[2] As anyone can see, this statement cannot be more categorical: when charity diminishes, fear appears. In effect, it is obvious that love, or the fervor of charity, has cooled in the Church. Jesus Christ already announced that this cooling of charity would reach its culmination in the last times of History: *And because iniquity has abounded, the charity of many shall grow cold.*[3] The same Apostle John adds also, in the verse just quoted, that *he who fears is not perfect in love*; which can be completed with the statement that he makes in another place, according to which *he who does not love does not know God; because God is Love.*[4]

As painful as it is, we must acknowledge that the Fear felt by modern Catholicism is nothing more than the extreme degradation from a weakness that man has suffered since the Fall. In effect, Fear became man's constant companion after his expulsion from Paradise. This fellowship, though, was less rude and crude than the current one, which has a somewhat different character.

This is a fear that leads modern Catholicism to feel cornered by the World and to blush, for example, when it is accused of still believing in the historicity of the Gospels, in the person of Jesus Christ, or in the viability of the Beatitudes. These and similar allegations impel this Catholicism to turn its face towards man and its back on God. That is why it tries to take refuge in areas where it believes that it has found greater security once it has convinced itself that the idea of Man is gaining momentum at the same time

---

[2] 1 Jn 4:18.

[3] Mt 24:12.

[4] 1 Jn 4:8.

that the idea of God is fading into the fog of myths that Humanity
has already left behind.

Some people may call this Fear of the current Catholicism cowardice. Undoubtedly, Jesus Christ referred to it when He said: *For
he that shall be ashamed of me and of my words, of him the Son
of Man shall be ashamed, when he shall come in his glory.*[5] That
is why Saint Paul confessed openly his attitude with respect to the
words of the Lord: *I am not ashamed of the Gospel.*[6]

The History of Spirituality shows evidence that Fear has been
present, sometimes, within the very structure of Christian existence.

It is also true that Fear is a feeling that safeguards human life
under special circumstances, something like a sixth sense given by
God to man with the obvious purpose of keeping him safe against
certain dangers in particular situations. When this fear is assumed
with a supernatural spirit, it can even become an element of sanc-
tification. The fear of death, for instance, so connatural to human
beings, was accepted by Jesus Christ Himself and made sublime ever
since: *Precious in the eyes of the Lord is the death of his saints.*[7]
And we should not forget the reverential and justified fear so wisely
recognized by the author of the Book of Proverbs: *The fear of the
Lord is the beginning of all wisdom.*[8]

However, fear has to be regarded as cowardice when, brought on
by pusillanimity or by culpable ignorance, it leads to surrender in
the face of evil or of error.

Manichaeism left its imprint even on Christianity, despite everything, in the form of Fear of matter —and more specifically of

---

[5]Lk 9:26.

[6]Rom 1:16.

[7]Ps 116:15.

[8]Prov 1:7.

the body. This Fear appears in the Platonism of some Fathers who even considered the body as a ballast of or an impediment to the soul. Saint Augustine, for example, thought that the human body was the *jail* of the soul. It was a strange belief which, in one form or another, has come down to our days and sometimes has been shared even by the great mystics. To the point that it endorsed the idea that the Humanity of Jesus Christ is *an impediment that has to be dispensed with* once one has arrived at the higher degrees of the contemplative life or union with God.[9]

However, the Fear that afflicts the ecclesiastical world of today, whose deepest cause is the ravages done to the Faith by the heresy of Modernism —in full force today—, rather consists of a veritable *kneeling before the World* which Maritain spoke of. There are many who have embraced the positions and criteria of the world because they considered them to be more solid and reliable than those provided by the *refuge* of Faith. They have arrived, by so doing, at doctrinal conclusions which are strange and even contrary to Christian principles.

One of the more clamorous chapters of this policy of surrender held by the *new* Catholic Morality, elaborated on the basis of conceding to and accepting the criteria of the World, took place with regard to the problems raised by the possibility that the Church would legitimize contraception. During the first third of the last century people spoke with enthusiasm about something that was hailed as

---

[9]This trend which, as we have said, was shared by some of the great mystics, has nothing to do with the cry of Saint Paul in Romans 7:23: *Who will rescue me from this body doomed to death?* A little further, he speaks about his longings for having his body totally freed from the bonds of this world and glorified after the Lord's body: *...we are groaning inside ourselves, waiting with eagerness for our bodies to be set free* (Rom 8:23). In the New Testament, Saint Paul is the staunchest defender of the glorification of the body.

a great —even triumphant for some people— practical discovery in the field of Morality: *the natural method of birth control based on abstention during the fertile days of women*. They considered that this new method would definitively solve the problem for those who wanted to avoid the procreation of children but did not want to use contraceptive methods, which they rightly considered as clearly sinful. With the discovery of such a happy solution, Morality was, at long last, reconciled with the practical aspects of life. Or at least that is what they thought.

It often happens that man comes to believe himself cleverer than God. There were even people, in those times when Faith was abundant among the Faithful, who were convinced that they could *put the Gospel right*. Therefore, what had to happen came to be...

The natural method of birth control based on abstention during the fertile days of women was indeed hailed as a great discovery and as the solution for those Catholic parents who were afraid of seeing the number of their offspring increase. It was actually a method, as happens with these things, which suited believing but mean parents who had rather forgotten the doctrine of Providence and the spirit of generosity which stimulate confidence in God according to the teachings of the Gospel.

At the moment, it seemed that everything was going to be fine..., but the approach to the problem had forgotten one important detail; namely, that the precepts of Christian Morality, which are but an application of the principles of the Gospel, were not dictated with a view to a *practical life*. Especially if by *practical life* one means a comfortable life without problems. The Gospel is a Manual of struggle (Mt 10:16; Jn 16:33; 2 Tim 3:12), and its behavioral methods cannot fail to take into account the famous *narrow and difficult path* that only a few people truly follow (Mt 7:14). All attempts to reconcile the authenticity of the evangelical existence with an easy life have never been successful.

Therefore, and due to the fact that Nature does not seem inclined to be mocked, *this natural method of birth control* ended in failure. True, one cannot say that the method in question is in itself sinful. The Apostle Paul himself recommended temporal abstention if there was agreement between the spouses; but the Apostle understood that this joint decision was taken so that the couple could *devote themselves to prayer* (1 Cor 7:5), excluding, therefore, any type of *practical* intention. Moreover, as has already been said, while *this natural method of birth control* cannot be considered at all as contrary to the Natural Law —nor, therefore, as sinful—, one cannot say the same about the fact —which is not usually taken into account— that, in this case, the principles of the Gospel have been put aside, and most specifically the fundamental principle that one must trust in Divine Providence (Mt 6: 25–32; 7: 7–11; Lk 12: 27–30). In the end, the result was a disappointing failure in too many instances; perhaps as a consequence of the known vengeance of Nature.

This natural method of birth control was followed by others; all of them were, more or less, of the same kind and with equally uncertain results.

All those methods had their origin in the seminal idea —also considered at the beginning as an impressive finding— of *responsible parenthood*. According to this idea, and following clearly the directives given by the Theology that has acquired full rights within the current Church, the determination of the number of children rests solely with the spouses. In their deliberations, the ideas of generosity and trust in Providence were placed in the background in order to give way to the ideas of calculation and consideration of welfare.

The concept and the terminology, as well as the ideology that supports *responsible parenthood*, were aimed at indoctrinating fearful —and not so fearful— parents who were facing the *risk* of a possible increase of offspring. The parents were encouraged to consider whether they had the necessary means to face the obligations that would arise from that possible increase: upbringing and sustenance of children, their education, etc.; with no other intention than to induce the parents to practice abstinence if they did not have those means. And it can be safely assumed that, after careful consideration, the lack of those means *was always determined to be the case*; for human beings often tend to behave like that. It should also be noticed that this *responsible parenthood* emerged at the time of the fever for *social justice*, when the problems concerned with economic well–being seemed to have acquired a place of pride among theologians, moralists, and Catholic pastoral practitioners. In the end, the same old struggle: the material well–being versus the evangelical principles of generosity and trust in Providence.

An old Spanish adage says that *God does not usually punish with blows*. As it could not happen in any other way, the final result was not very pleasing. *Responsible parenthood* immediately became an *irresponsible behavior*. It is not very difficult to understand what resulted. It is a well–known fact that, once the spillway has been opened to let the waters run, it is not uncommon that the waters eventually break into a broad overflow. After all, one can never expect too much from human nature. The truth is that this new *discovery* suffered from the same defects as the previous one: it lacked trust in Divine Providence; it had forgotten the context of the teachings of the Gospel. In the end, what happened is what usually occurs when one puts a new cloth on an old one (Mt 9:16): a breakage was all that was left. Today, almost no one remembers the *responsible parenthood*, now that the use of contraceptives has become widespread —a logical consequence which was bound to be reached, but which was not the only or the most serious one.

What the vast majority of Catholics ignore, however, is that it was Cardinal Wojtyla, later Pope John Paul II, who came up with the doctrine of *responsible parenthood*. He first expounded it in his work *Uomo e donna lo creó: Catechesi sull' amore umano* (Man and Woman He created them: Catechesis on Human Love), which he completed before he was elected Pope in 1978. Later, when he was Pope, and *Theology of the Body* was the final title given to his work (originally provided by him too), from the Fall of 1979 until the Fall of 1984, he had the opportunity to fully develop his doctrine through his Wednesday Catechesis. The consequences of this *Theology of the Body* were decisive:

First of all, his theory in which he modified the primary end of marriage (by placing procreation and education of the children at the same level[10] as that of mutual help and love between the spouses) was introduced into the Conciliar Doctrine and the New Code of Canon Law; this theory and the theory of *responsible parenthood* introduce the idea that the procreation of children and their number depends primarily on the *decision* and the desire of the parents rather than on the designs of Providence.[11] A logical sequence of consequences and derivations followed those premises: a blurred

---

[10]The phrase *at the same level* is a euphemism. When procreation and education of the children is deprived of its category of primary end, the logical consequence —as imposed by the reality of facts— cannot be other than its being considered as a secondary end. That is the way human nature operates.

[11]In his definitive doctrine about the *Theology of the Body*, the notion of *necessity* for applying the theory of *responsible parenthood* does not appear.

sense of the Faith, diminished confidence in Divine Providence, elevation of the decisive will of parents to the level of definitive criteria, introduction of the distinction of already conceived children between *wanted* and *unwanted*... If we add to this that *responsible* parenthood was too much to ask from the weak human nature, that the chemical and mechanical contraceptives fail all too frequently..., then only one way was left to be followed regarding the *unwanted* children, the very one that Humanity has trodden: abortion, with all its past and present consequences.

Human beings will never be convinced of something that is quite obvious: nobody laughs at God with impunity.

At any rate, fidelity to the teachings of the Gospel was definitively ruined, the very teachings that for many centuries had influenced the lives of countless Christians of good will. We can specifically mention here the doctrine stating that Christian marriage has its origin in a sublime Sacrament whose main end is the procreation and education of children. To which we can add others: the meaning of Sacrifice and Love for the Cross, which impels us to consider the difficulties suffered due to the upbringing of children as heroic and glorious work; the teaching that considers children as a blessing from God and not as a burden that we must endure; the teaching about our trust in the Paternity of God, whose Providence will always give, together with the children, the means to bring them up; the conviction, amply proven, that children are raised up better in the bosom of a large family, which is aided by the mutual love of the two spouses and their spirit of generosity, along with the certainty that they are collaborating with God in the task of providing Him with new children.

But the secularizing wave also reached the Church: the New Times and its courtship of *Novelties*: the *New Age*, the *Springtime of the Church*, the *New Pentecost*, and Neo–Modernism —more concealed and disguised now, but embracing everything.

Along with so much *aggiornamento*, fundamental doctrines like fidelity to the Cross, the spirit of Sacrifice, Trust in God, and, in the end, Love for Jesus Christ, were definitively confined to the shelves of oblivion. The road of the *narrow gate*(Mt 7:14) was abandoned far behind to yield to the eagerness for comfort, the desire for welfare and things of this world... and, in short, *the Fear of everything that implied sacrifice and effort.*

Because of abortion, millions of human beings have become parricides, that is, killers of their own children, with the scourge of a curse which will endure into Eternity. Abortion has also led to the alarming decline in the birth rate; the decadence of Europe and America; the fact of Western Civilization being in danger of and about to be soon disappearing, to be supplanted by other non–Christian *Civilizations*. In addition to these evils, *the horror of a world without children* has already appeared.

And all of this happened because many were determined to believe that the *wide path* (which, according to Christ, leads to perdition), once it has been converted into a modern highway and duly marked, would equally lead also to Heaven; but, what kind of Heaven? So it happened that men, having committed themselves to living according to the inventiveness of their own nonsense, their faith having been weakened, despised Jesus Christ and allowed Fear to manipulate them.

TRUE FEMINITY OR WILY FEMINISM

God created the nature of the human being under the form of two sexes, male and female: *Yahweh God said: 'It is not right that the man should be alone. I shall make him a helper'...*[1] *God created man in the image of himself, in the image of God he created him, male and female he created them.*[2]

From this moment on, many centuries passed during which woman was subject to man. This was a peculiar situation that gives cause to study three points in depth: whether such submission has the character of punishment; whether it should be considered as a demand of nature itself; or whether it is rather a mere disposition of the divine free will. Here, however, we intend to avoid this problematic line of thought to focus on the question of the authority of the man over the woman; and more specifically, about the situation of oppression which, according to some, that authority implies for women.

At first sight, Scripture seems to indicate that submission of the woman to the man has a punitive character. In effect, after the fall, God said to the woman: *Your yearning will be for your husband, and he will dominate you.*[3] Saint Paul, for his part, also seems to indicate that it should be this way: *It was not Adam who was led astray but the woman who was led astray and fell into sin. Nevertheless, she*

---

[1] Gen 2:18.

[2] Gen 1:27.

[3] Gen 3:16.

will be saved by childbearing, provided she lives a sensible life and is constant in faith and love and holiness.[4]

However, Tradition has been unanimous, firm, and constant in affirming that the submission of woman to man does not have a punitive character.

The declaration in Genesis, according to which man *will dominate* woman, should not be interpreted in a necessarily punitive sense; although, in the final analysis, one must recognize that it is one of the consequences of sin. The assertion and pronouncement that the man *will abuse* his authority over the woman does not signify a disqualification of authority as such, attributing to it, for example, a character of punishment and oppression. Authority is a condition which answers the need for norms that regulate the functioning of any society, be it large or small, referring in this case to matrimony and the family. That the possibility of abusing authority exists is another thing. Genesis is merely showing that from then on the abuse of authority will be a constant in the existence of human beings; but, after all, it is nothing other than the result of the disorder introduced into human nature as a result of the original fall, and that affects both of the sexes. It is evident that this has happened *de facto* throughout History. Even in modern times, the supposed *Feminist* Movements with their claims of women's rights, contrary to what is normally believed, are usually thought up and promoted by men, and are nothing, in reality, but another subtle form of manipulation of women.

Christianity contributed effectively to solving this situation. It affirms the offering of some resources, freely granted by God, which, in His turn, must be accepted and taken advantage of by man. In this respect, it would be a good idea to remember that Catholic Doctrine has always attributed a *potential* nature

---

[4]1 Tim 2: 14–15.

to the means of salvation, in the sense that they need to be *actualized* by man, that is, freely accepted and used by him, if you prefer to frame the topic in these terms. Progressive modern Theology, on the other hand, closer to Protestant belief, insists on the theory of *universal salvation* (the Anonymous Christian) through the mere act of the Incarnation of the Word. Thus it abolishes the need of human cooperation and leads to the conclusion that there is a love freely offered on the part of God which does not need, in its turn, a free acceptance on the part of the human creature. The progressive theory attacks directly the concept, as much as the reality, of love; which, freely offered on one part, and accepted (or rejected) freely on the other, is essentially freedom. An *involuntary* love (indicating that either it does not proceed from the will or it was originated by a coerced will) would not make any sense, for it would both proceed and not proceed from a free will at the same time.[5] God is infinite Love because he is Infinite Freedom: *Ubi Spiritus Domini, ibi libertas.*[6]

The *prophecy* of Genesis that man will *dominate* the woman, in the sense that he will abuse his authority over her, is not a declaration of something that would have to happen until only a precise moment in the History of Humanity, which would be the twentieth Century with the advent of *Feminism.* Such an idea, far from being merely ridiculous, is also a utopia, an illusion, a pipe dream, and, of course, an excruciating falsehood. The truth is exactly the opposite: the more effort made by the feminist woman to emancipate herself from the authority of the man, the more she ends up by falling under his control, finally becoming a mere instrument.

The reality of *Feminism* is nothing but an ideology invented by someone and picked up, fomented, and extended by Masonry; with the only end being to destroy the Family, beginning, as a first step, by turning the woman into a manageable instrument of the man. The Mafia that directs the large international business of brothels (and the related and associated drug business) is directed and managed by men and not by women. Also not to be forgotten is the propagation and extension of Islam around the world —with such an increasing intensity that it has already overtaken Christianity in the number of its followers, and with the odds more in

---

[5]God loves a cheerful giver (2 Cor 9:7) and not someone who gives because he has no alternative. In the act of loving, the factor of *freedom* would be more important than the factor of *will.* It happens, however, that whereas there can be a will without freedom, it is impossible to imagine a free act without will. In ordinary language, however, the concept of a voluntary act comes to be synonymous with a free act.

[6]2 Cor 3:17.

its favor every day. However, it is a firm and unshakeable belief in Islam that the woman is, and always will be, an instrument in the hands of the man.

The voluntary ignorance of these facts is leading to the ruin and destruction of millions of women, thanks to *Feminism*. The *convinced* feminist woman acts in such a manner as if her capacity of understanding had reached a degree of absolute emptiness. Such a state could not be thought of as mere ignorance since, in reality, it leads to a situation of living continuously in the Lie. A situation, however, that does not deserve to be excused, since those who fall into the Lie do so because they first loved it (Rev 22:15).

And yet, we still have to speak of other more serious, if possible, consequences that *Feminism* is causing for woman and, indirectly, for all of human society.

On the other hand, as far as the constant testimony of Tradition is concerned relating to what is deduced from Scripture, there has never been any doubt as regards the essential equality and dignity of both sexes.

Certainly, Saint Paul insists on the authority of the man over the woman. (Rom 7:2; 1 Cor 7:39; 11: 3.9–10; Eph 5: 23–24; Col 3:18; 1 Tim 2: 11–12). However, it is clear at the same time that *woman is the glory of man*;[7] and a little later on he adds that *neither the woman without the man, nor the man without the woman*.[8] Also, do not forget the comparison that he establishes between marriage (the surrender and belonging of the man to the woman and *vice versa*) and the love and surrender of Christ to His Church; see, in effect, Ephesians 5: 21 ff., where he also speaks expressly of the love, reverence, and respect that each of the spouses ought to profess to the other.

Anyway, as regards woman's relationship with man, God has given the woman more than enough qualities and gifts to allow her to maintain her place with honor and even to prevail over the man's will rather frequently.

---

[7] 1 Cor 11:7.

[8] 1 Cor 11:11.

The true problem began, above all, during the twentieth century, when modern ideologies, intending to destroy Christianity, understood the need to start by attacking the Family. In order to bring it about, nothing worked better than to imbue in the woman the idea that she needed to emancipate herself from the man, so that she could find *fulfillment* and in order to achieve the freedom and independence that she had been deprived of for so many centuries. That is what gave birth to the *Feminist Movements*, whose true objective was none other than to obliterate the Family, and above all the Christian Family. In order to achieve that, it was necessary to turn the woman, in every way possible, into an instrument, through the process of thoroughly exploiting the ideas of her freedom and her emancipation.

To tell the truth, the *woman does not need to emancipate herself nor free herself from anyone or anything.* The woman is simply The Woman (Rev 12:1), with all the dignity that this implies —to the elevated degree of excellence in which God has created her.

The fact that the man frequently has abused his authority is nothing but a consequence of the lack of control introduced into human nature by original sin. This disorder equally affects man and woman, since both sinned, and also influences other aspects and situations of the human existence, in one sex as much as in the other.

Feminism, for its part, has taken good care to jealously hide two important aspects of the problem. In the first place, the fact is that the bad treatment, the lack of consideration, or the failure to remember the respect owed to the other sex are not attitudes to be attributed exclusively to the man, since they are also practiced, although with less frequency, by the woman. In the second place, it also ought to be kept in mind —although this fact cannot be admitted as justification— that at times it is the woman who first causes and is guilty of domestic violence.

As we have indicated before, the question of the *identity* of the woman, together with the question of the ideal model to which she ought to aspire, do not really exist as problems. In reality, these questions are nothing but one more invention of the progressive leftist ideology.[9] The Christian woman that truly wants to *find fulfillment* as a woman has the Virgin Mary easily at hand as the perfect model to which she could aspire as the norm for her life and as an example of the ideal woman.

The Virgin Mary is the Mother of Christ and the Mother of the Church, and therefore has to be considered also the Mother of all Christians. If it is kept in mind that the supernatural sense supposes a greater bond than the purely natural or carnal, the person and virtues of such a Sublime Mother ought to be recognized as an example and norm for all, as much for men as for women. However, her condition as woman is a determining and decisive element for the feminine sex, no matter how much this circumstance goes unnoticed. The Virgin Mary is the perfect model that a woman can and ought to observe: the possibility of understanding from Her the best way of living the virtues of the Christian existence, *as a woman*; or, said in another way, *as they ought to be lived by a woman*. The character and the feminine psychology are distinct from the masculine, apart from the different tasks, obligations, and proper offices of each one of the sexes.

---

[9]Here we should note the enthusiasm of the progressive modernist thought for creating a *crisis of identity*; most probably, it has discovered how instrumental these made–up crises are, being capable of destroying anything that possesses a Christian character.

The problem that is usually posed regarding the *identity* of the woman, and which is preferred by *Feminism* to wield it as a weapon, centers on the alleged *submission to the husband.*

But what underlies this belief deep down is nothing but contempt for the Christian virtues and, more specifically, for obedience. And delving into the problem even more deeply leads us to the sin committed before the beginning of time, which is pride.

Obedience has been considered at one time as one of the *passive* virtues (obedience, docility, humility, simplicity, naïveté, purity, simplicity, the strength or capacity for suffering, etc.) without realizing that passive virtues do not really exist. The true meaning of the term *virtus* is *strength.* And indeed, it is no small strength that is needed, together with a great capacity for heroism and generosity of heart, to practice Christian virtues.

But even admitting, for the sake of hypothesis, the characteristic of passivity in this type of virtue, we would end up discovering a *peculiar charm* proper to these virtues that is as seductive as it is unknown; which, in its turn, is characterized, among other things, for its capacity to attract over itself an extraordinary energy: *Strength is perfected in weakness,*[10] as well as a shower of blessings. In this way, the alleged weakness may contain marvelous possibilities which, in their turn, can be actualized in a wealth of graces and possibilities, whose understanding and scope escape human knowledge and feeling (Mt 11:25; Lk 10:21).

Those who attribute to obedience a character of passivity, or of humiliating submission, fail to recognize the greatness of spirit and heroism that are necessary to practice it. And we will soon see that such ascription is far from making sense. Apart from the well–known fact that charity is the queen and the guarantor of all the virtues, it could even be said that obedience stands out above all the

---

[10]2 Cor 12:9.

others. To attribute to it, therefore, as *Feminism* does, a discriminatory character, or one of humiliation and baseness, when dealing
with women, supposes an absolute ignorance: about God, of human
nature, of life, of truth, of uprightness, of the nature of things, of the
world in which we live, and even of the exercise of common sense.
But if such an attitude, as usually happens, goes beyond the state
of ignorance and is based in a deeper feeling, it is necessary then to
conclude that it answers a voluntary twisting of reality, motivated,
in the last analysis, by a heart dominated by evil.

To understand the meaning of obedience, as well as the high dignity granted to those who practice it, it is necessary to contemplate
Jesus Christ. It is fitting to remember that in the Incarnation, living as true Man among us and as one of us, the Scripture says that
Son though he was, he learned obedience through his sufferings.[11]
Therefore, according to Scripture, true Man that He is, after all, it
was necessary for Him *to learn* obedience. And, what is more, in the
same way that men learn it and make it part of their lives, namely:
at the cost of their own *sufferings.* In this way, there remains clearly
established, on one side, the character of strong virtue that belongs
to obedience; and on the other, the need of a generous and great
heart, replete with a courageous spirit, on the part of those who dare
to set off on the adventure to practice it. It would be very difficult
to recognize in this virtue the air of baseness that *Feminism* tries to
give it when it is the woman who practices it.

Keep in mind that the divine will of Jesus Christ is the same as that of the
Father (*numerically one*); the text of Hebrews highlights indirectly the human character of His will as Man. In fact, contrary to the theories advocated by Monothelitism, there exist two wills in Jesus Christ, one divine and one human. At the
same time, a path has been left open for man to get to know the greatness of the
possibilities that the human will, animated by grace, is capable of reaching. Even
in the actual state of fallen nature, once the human will has been restored, helped

---

[11]Heb 5:8.

and elevated by grace, it becomes the second cause (the first is grace) of the most sublime state to which man could aspire: nothing other than sanctity. The human will also is the faculty of the soul that has been granted the gift of responding with a *yes* to the offering of love that God freely makes to him.

According to the content of this text from the Letter to the Hebrews, the virtue of obedience needs, in order to be practiced properly, a certain ascesis and discipline of *training*. It is the only virtue of which it is said that it has to be *learned*.[12] As far as concerns immolation, which is the basis of the virtue of obedience, it appears that compliance of the will is more difficult for people than compliance of the intelligence.

The climax of Jesus Christ's heroic obedience appears clearly at the moment of His Agony in the Garden: *My Father, if it is possible let this cup pass me by. Nevertheless, let it be as you, not I, would have it.*[13] There has never before been, nor will there ever be again, an act of obedience of such perfection and elevated heroism. Given the deep knowledge of the evil of sin that Jesus Christ had, the *negation* of His own will, in order to submit Himself to the Father's will (Jn 4:34) in the unfathomable generosity of His human Heart, required a degree of immolation impossible to be understood by man. Indeed, the fact that a Heart entirely removed from other hearts that are not animated by Pure Innocence and Perfect Love —although at the same time knowing the infinite evil of sin— assumed the guilt of all human misery accumulated after millenniums is something whose depths will never be reached by the understanding of any creature.

---

[12] The infused virtues also have to be practiced in order to mature to the measure of the life of those who receive them. Despite everything, obedience appears to require a certain degree of depth regarding the self–denial or *immolation* of those who exercise it; therefore the need of an elevated degree of maturity and strength in the obedient subject. In short, as we have been saying, it is a virtue for strong souls.

[13] Mt 26:39, Mk 14:36.

According to the Letter to the Hebrews, the Word was made Man and came into the world through an act of obedience (Heb 10:9) with the will to exercise it *to the end.* However, the text that best expresses the will of Jesus Christ to arrive at the peak of immolation through total obedience is contained in the Letter directed by the Apostle to the faithful of Philippi: *Being in every way like a man, he humbled himself and became obedient unto death, even to death on a cross.*[14] It is important to point out separately the elements contained in this declaration:

He accepted for Himself obedience.

To a degree of total immolation: *up to death.*

And death on the gallows.

The obedience of Jesus Christ is not merely one virtue lived to perfection. *It presupposes a fundamental character of His existence, on which depended, moreover, our salvation.* On the other hand, it is the most forceful *epiphany* or revelation (demonstration) of an act of perfect love. If such love requires, as it does, surrender in totality to the beloved person, the first thing to be surrendered and subdued, as the indispensable condition for bringing about such a donation, is one's own will.

Even before the intellect. It is not likely that the Virgin at the foot of the Cross, principal witness and the one most closely linked to the death of her own son, Jesus Christ, totally understood the designs of the Father. But undoubtedly, and in those moments in which a sword of sorrow pierced Her soul, *She accepted fully the ways of God that led to the death of the Son Whom She herself had given birth to and Whom she recognized as Her God*; another clear case in which the will forces the intellect to kneel.

Another important text from the Letter to the Hebrews is fundamental for this topic: *That is why he said, on coming into the*

---

[14]Phil 2: 7–8.

world: "You wanted no sacrifice or oblation, but you gave me a body. You took no pleasure in holocausts for sin." Then I said, "Behold, I come;" in the scroll of the book it is written of me, that I should do your will, O God.[15] As you can see in the text, sacrifices and offerings have been displaced, to be substituted by another more perfect sacrifice: that of the will, by means of the surrender of obedience.[16] We are, once again, at the foundation to which Revelation goes back again and again, namely that the most perfect act that a rational being can perform is one of love —nothing other than the oblation of one's own will (which entails all of the being of the person who loves) to the beloved person. What stands out in obedience as most sublime and noble is this: it is an act of love.

As regards women, it ought not be forgotten that the Incarnation of the Word was the point of departure in the History of Salvation, and fundamental to it; and *it depended on a perfect act of obedience carried out by a woman.* The young virgin of Nazareth, faced with the message and summons of the Angel asking in the name of God for her consent, answered with the words that brought about the reality of God made Man and His presence among Men: *Behold the handmaid of the Lord; be it done to me according to thy word.*[17] It is the moment in which that humble and unknown young girl of Nazareth not only granted her absolute conformity to what was

---

[15]Heb 10: 5–7.

[16]Here distinction between the sacrifices of the Old Law and that of the New does not have consistency. If the Sacrifice of the New Law, which is that of the Cross, can be considered as the greatest and most valuable of all sacrifices —to the point that it annuls all those that came before— it is because, in the end, it is a perfect act of the most perfect Love. All the rest of the sacrifices of the New Law make sense and receive their reason for being from this One Sacrifice, and not from any other nor from any other thing.

[17]Lk 1:38.

proposed to her but did not consider herself diminished when she described herself as the *slave* of the Lord.[18]

Such an act of obedience would suppose an intimate participation in the immolation to which Her Son was destined. This obedience reached its highest point for Her —through the fulfillment of the will of God, not always understood but at all times accepted— in the sword of sorrow that would pierce her soul at the foot of the Cross, as had been announced to her years before by the old man Simeon (Lk 2:35). It is not to be supposed that the Virgin understood, at the very moment of the Annunciation, the plan of God in all its depth and in all its derivations. But we can definitely believe, as something absolutely certain, that She personally did not try to rule out even one of the contingencies, not always pleasant ones, which would undoubtedly occur. The expression *let it be done to me as you have said* signifies a total surrender, complete and unconditional, to whatever might be decided by Him Whose ways are absolutely incomprehensible and unpredictable (Rom 11:33).

After what we have said above, we can consider as established a double conclusion: In the first place, it is a fact that the virtue of obedience represents an important milestone, as *decisive* as it is *characteristic*, in the History of Salvation. And the second conclusion holds the distinctive feature that it was precisely *a woman* to whom was granted the role of practicing perfectly such a virtue in such a decisive way —by even accepting both the consequences that such behavior could give rise to and the weight of an unimaginable responsibility. It was a representative of the feminine sex who, by means of her obedience, contributed eminently to the Redemption of Humanity, crushing in this manner, entirely and forever, the head of the Serpent (Gen 3:15).

---

[18]The Greek δούλη contained in the text signifies literally *slave*, or in any case, *female slave*.

Things being so, having clarified that we are dealing with a virtue suitable for strong, stouthearted souls, it is then incomprehensible, even absurd, that *Feminism* attempts to remove obedience and submission from woman's existential condition as if they were too denigrating and humiliating. In reality, what this ideology proposes is to deprive woman of something intended to be the crown of her feminine condition, for it is one of the most valuable pearls that God desired to grant her.

This explains why God has bestowed on woman the virtue of Fortitude endowed with special characteristics. The designation of being the *weaker sex*, so often attributed to her, is but another *invention* of man with respect to woman. Of course, generally speaking, woman is *physically* weaker than man —but only physically; and let us not forget that, in the final analysis, strength is not the best or even the most important quality to value: physical strength is not precisely the attribute that distinguishes the rational animal as superior to the irrational animals. However, it is well known that women are superior to men from a *psychological,* or rather a spiritual or strength–of–soul, point of view. The proof is in her great capacity of endurance in the face of the sufferings and setbacks that life presents, such as illnesses, pains, failures, vexations, injustices, etc. It would be useless to deny what any man has experienced at some time, whether it be in him or in others: the greater capacity of endurance and strength of women in the face of illnesses in comparison with the greater weakness of men. Not to mention the multitude of sufferings and troubles associated with motherhood and the education of children that she faces, in general, with enormous patience and strength.

They forget something fundamental —or maybe they ignore it completely— who argue that the obedience of the wife is a detriment to the dignity of woman.

Surrender to the beloved, as a donation and total self–giving of the lover, is part of the essence of true love. If love, taken seriously, denotes the characteristic of total and unconditional surrender to the beloved, the conclusion is obvious: we are dealing, then, with a loving self–giving —that is, free and voluntary— of all that the lover is and possesses to the beloved. The purpose of this surrendering is so that the beloved may dispose, at his will, the lover who gives herself to the beloved as his entire property.

Regardless of the situation proceeding from the conjugal state, it is difficult to argue that obedience and submission are demeaning attitudes —or even humiliating— when it comes to women. They *could be*, in effect, if they were the result of a voluntary attitude of indignation and prostration, or the result of coercion by an oppressive force suffered involuntarily; *but never when they are the fruit and consequence of love.* Or put another way: when they are the expression of a free will that is inclined to obey after having felt itself seduced by the charm that emanates from the beloved.

We can focus the study of this issue, once again, on what is said in the *Song of Songs* in relation to the mutual love between the Bridegroom and the bride.[19]

---

[19]From one to the other, in a reciprocity which is another of the fundamental conditions of perfect Love. It is well known that the traditional interpretation, headed by the testimony of the Fathers, has been more often inclined to see in this Holy Book an exhibition of love and self–giving of Christ to His Church. However, you cannot marginalize the fact that such an interpretation, even being correct and the most common, *in no way excludes the interpretation which takes the narrative of the Book as referring to pure divine–human love*; or, if you prefer to say it more clearly, as referring to the love relationship between God and every man taken individually. And this interpretation is also maintained by Tradition. However, the doctrines that consider this Holy Book a mere epithalamic narrative are ruled out.

The opening verse, in which the bride expresses her desire *to be kissed* by the Bridegroom, is shown here in an active sense:[20]

> *Let him kiss me with the kisses of his mouth!*
> *For your love is sweeter than wine.*[21]

Here, everything seems to imply that the initiative belongs to the Bridegroom; and so it is, indeed, as the brides also thinks when she expresses her impatience. It is true that the kiss of love can be initiated by either the Bridegroom (the male) or the bride (the woman). Yet it is undeniable that general opinion has always regarded it more natural that the initial impulse finds its origin in the male. The Bible leaves no doubt about it; it always attributes the initiative in the act of love to the husband (God): *We love because He first loved us.*[22]

In the study of this problem, contrary to the opinion of those who ascribe to this holy Book a purely epithalamic character, and although it certainly seems to be confined to conjugal love, we must take into account that the love relationship between the Bridegroom and the bride narrated in the *Song of Songs* does not refer so much to those relationships between male and female persons as to the love of Christ for His Church, and more particularly to the love relationship between God and every human being. Customarily, treatises on Spirituality, as we know, often speak in this context of the relationship of love between God and the *soul*; but the use of the latter word in this context does not seem very fortunate. Nevertheless, the female gender has always been *attributed* to the human soul —abstraction made of particular details; in fact, the grammatical gender of the word itself is feminine, both in Latin and in the Romance languages, and even in other languages which

---

[20]The word φιλημάτω is the active imperative aorist, third person singular, of the verb φιλέω. This verb, meaning *to kiss*, is found in other passages of the New Testament, for example in Matthew 26:48; Mark 14:44; etc.

[21]Sg 1:2.

[22]1 Jn 4:19.

are not derived from Latin, like English. However, it must be assumed that *in the amorous story of the Book of the Song of Songs*, according to the true sense of traditional Spirituality that is connected to the dogma, the male character is assigned to God,[23] while the female character is designated to the soul. If we remember that, in reality, the *soul* is the whole human being, then the qualities that the *Song of Songs* attributes to the Bridegroom and to the bride —which we will use to distinguish male and female— are certainly valid.

A closer look to the female character will reveal that, along with her *femininity* —which is an endearing and charming characteristic proper to her sex—, there is another trait that seems to correspond to her: the passive attitude of *being kissed* rather than the active initiative of *kissing*.[24] Usually, although not always, profane poetry has considered that aspect of the relationship of love between man and woman as normal. Instead, that way is a commonplace in mystical poetry, as we can see:

> *My Love, if you should want me*
> *To look for you on mornings still fresh with dew,*
> *Near the stately balsam tree,*
> *Know when at last I find you,*
> *Kisses of your mouth will be my payment due.*[25]

---

[23]Modern attempts to attribute a feminine character to God the Father are blasphemous, to say the least; they are but a result of *Feminism*.

[24]Cf. Alfonso Gálvez, *Commentaries on the Song of Songs*, Vol I, Shoreless Lake Press, NJ, 1994, pp. 44 ff.

[25]Alfonso Gálvez, *Los Cantos Perdidos*, Segunda Edición, Shoreless Lake Press, NJ, 2011, n. 17. In the Spanish original:

> *Amada, si quisieras*
> *que en las frescas mañanas te buscara*
> *entre las balsameras,*
> *cuando, por fin, te hallara,*
> *con besos de tu boca me cobrara.*

Or in this verse:

> *I climbed heaven's starry stair,*
> *Aflame with love's burning fire and ardent sigh,*
> *Just to try to find you there*
> *To beg you with ardent cry:*
> *Please give me a kiss of love; then let me die...!*[26]

Something similar seems to be implied in the *Song of Songs* 1:4:

> *Draw me after you. Let us run!*
> *Bring me, O king, to your chambers.*

Nevertheless, these verses seem rather to stress the desire of the bride *to run after the Bridegroom* in order to *be led by Him* to His own chambers. Therefore, one can clearly see here that the bride — by placing herself in an inferior condition— recognizes His status as owner and as the one who sets the initiative in motion. Sometimes mystical poetry expresses the same idea even more emphatically, as we can see:

---

[26]Alfonso Gálvez, *Los Cantos Perdidos*, Shoreless Lake Press, NJ, 2009, n. 72. In the Spanish original:

> *Subí hasta las estrellas,*
> *de amor en llamas de su ardiente fuego,*
> *por si te hallaba en ellas*
> *decirte en dulce ruego:*
> *¡Dame un beso de amor, muera yo luego...!*

> *The fading of day is fleet,*
> *Dulcet brown goldfinch, your songs dwindle faster;*
> *As in a dream bittersweet,*
> *Night comes, we both sorrows meet,*
> *You without freedom, me without my master.*[27]

The idea is not difficult to understand because the pain that is shown in the stanza follows a well–defined principle: the day has passed in vain hopes, and the bird feels saddened because she must stay without regaining her freedom. And, at the same time, the soul also sings her own sadness, although apparently for the opposite reason: her Owner has not appeared, when all she wanted was to be a captive of the Bridegroom and His property.

Some verses of the *Song*, carefully read, clearly demonstrate the longings and the commitment of the bride who wants to consider her Bridegroom as her owner; at the same time, she expresses her admiration for Him and her desire to feel dependent on Him. She does this by distinguishing the Bridegroom as something singular and unique among all other beings, both in dignity and in beauty, to a degree impossible to be compared with anything or anyone else: *as an apple tree among the wild trees.* Therefore, she longs to rest next to Him, happily sheltered in the shade he provides:

---

[27] Alfonso Gálvez, *Los Cantos Perdidos*, Segunda Edición, Shoreless Lake Press, NJ, 2011, n. 28. In the Spanish original:

> *El día ya se aleja,*
> *dulce jilguero de color trigueño,*
> *y así otra vez nos deja,*
> *como en amargo sueño,*
> *a ti sin libertad, y a mí sin dueño.*

> *As the apple tree among the trees of the woods,*
> *So is my beloved among young men.*
> *In his delightful shade I sit,*
> *And his fruit is sweet to my taste.*[28]

That is why the bride dares, with as much boldness as longing, to call and invoke the Bridegroom to come to her side. The *Song of Songs* expresses this with beautiful poetry filled with metaphors:

> *Before the day–breeze rises,*
> *Before the shadows flee,*
> *Return! Be, my love,*
> *Like a gazelle, like a young stag,*
> *On the mountains of Bether.*[29]
>
> *Haste away, my love,*
> *Be like a gazelle,*
> *A young stag,*
> *On the spice–laden mountain.*[30]

The bride wants with irrepressible ardor to hear the voice of the Bridegroom that is for her so sweet and soft that without listening to its melodious and charming timbre she could not continue living:

---

[28]Sg 2:3.

[29]Sg 2:17.

[30]Sg 8:14.

> *My Bridegroom's voice is for me,*
> *Like the wake of a ship deeply furrowing*
> *Like winds that stir so lightly*
> *Like a gentle whispering,*
> *Like the solemn moves of a night bird on wing.*[31]

So far we have shown that obedience and submission of the wife to her husband —or the submission of women to men, generally recognized as submission and obedience by women— far from being an impairment or diminution of her dignity, rather become like precious pearls that adorn the already excelling female sex. They are key elements and part of the seduction and charm of the so–called —now quite properly— *fairer sex*; so much so that they could be considered as touchstones in terms of balance and equilibrium regarding the alleged —but entirely false— *inferiority* of women compared to men. We shall return to this important topic. But for now, we are concerned with establishing that, as we have already seen in our study of love, divesting women of such qualities would imply denying her the ability to love and to be loved.

But before going further, and in order to discuss this issue with the fairness and objectivity it deserves, two observations should be addressed that have surely crossed the reader's mind.

First: If it is said that obedience, submission, and self–giving —as positive aspects referring to the bride— are proper and fun-

---

[31] Alfonso Gálvez, *op. cit.* n. 87. In the Spanish original:

> *Es la voz del Esposo*
> *como la huidiza estela de una nave,*
> *como aire rumoroso,*
> *como susurro suave,*
> *como el vuelo nocturno de algún ave.*

damental elements of the concept of love, then it follows that those features should also be attributed to the male.

Second: To confirm what was just said, it is necessary to note that, throughout the entire Poem, the *Song of Songs* depicts the submission of the bride to the Bridegroom, making it analogous to that of His surrender to the bride.

To which we must respond that both observations *are entirely correct and in keeping with truth.* How could it be otherwise?

Regarding the first, indeed, we must consider that if obedience and submission to the beloved are part of the concept and reality of love, these qualities apply equally to men.

As for the second, there is precious little to say. Simply read the contents of the Poem, and no further explanation is necessary.

Let us start with the Bridegroom's role, taking now the term in its general meaning: either referring to God, in keeping with the terminology of Mystical Spirituality, or simply to man, describing his role in the love relationship.

Clearly, as a lover, he is called to be in a position to *surrender* to the bride (woman), or to the soul (understood as the human individual). According to this, he is willing to accept in full, and even with the greatest joy, the feeling of knowing that he is her property, the *prey* captured by her (Phil 3:12). The *Song of Songs* expresses this reality in its usual poetic beauty:

> *You ravish my heart,*
> *My sister, my promised bride,*
> *You ravish my heart*
> *With a single one of your glances,*
> *With a single pearl of your necklace.*[32]

---

[32]Sg 4:9.

It is interesting to note the role of one's *gaze* in the art of love. It seems as if the eyes fulfill their mission of being the illuminating, burning flash through which a person, in a mysterious and inexplicable way, conveys to another his loving message of unconditional surrender. The three Synoptic Gospels tell of the encounter of Jesus with the rich young man who wanted to attain eternal life:

—Good Master, what must I do to inherit eternal life?
Jesus said to him: —Why do you call me good? No one is good but God alone.
You know the commandments: 'You shall not kill; You shall not commit adultery;
You shall not steal; You shall not give false witness; You shall not defraud; Honor
your father and your mother.'
—Master, all these things I have I kept from my youth— he replied.
And Jesus looked steadily at him and was filled with love for him.[33]

And indeed, what mysterious power lies hidden in the eyes of the human face? *A kindly glance gives joy to the heart*, says the Book of Proverbs.[34] The *Song of Songs*, a Poem equally loving and divine, puts on the lips of the Bridegroom the expression of His feelings before the mysterious beauty of the eyes of the bride:

> *How beautiful you are, my love,*
> *How beautiful you are,*
> *Your eyes are doves!*[35]

It is to be understood that God, moved by His kindness and by His desire to demonstrate the inadequacy of the human language in dealing with realities as lofty as that of love, wanted to endow the human gaze with a mysterious and silent power that mere language lacks; the same power through which the most beautiful feeling of all which springs from the heart is transmitted. In that sense, it could be said that the loving gaze plays a double role. On the one hand, it offers itself and calls imploringly at the door of the other person *—Behold, I stand at the door*

---

[33] Mk 10: 17–21.
[34] Prov 15:30.
[35] Sg 1:15.

and knock...[36]—; on the other, that gaze invites the beloved/lover to come and be master of the heart that is offered to him/her in surrender. Therefore, it can be said that the silence of the eyes that look amazed and dumbfounded before love, is immensely more expressive than the words uttered by a mouth that speaks. This is not at all surprising when we consider that the human face was purposely modeled by God to be, in itself, quite eloquent; hence, it is able to express, through the eyes, feelings and emotions that go far beyond the reach of words. The following verse eloquently shows these two functions that the loving gaze is able to express:

> *My sweet Lover came to me*
> *As the morning sun rose over the hillcrest.*
> *When he gazed on me gently,*
> *I felt in his eyes keenly*
> *That one thing which only a kiss can cure best.*[37]

When it comes to the highest and most perfect form of love, divine–human love, the mystery of the eyes that transmit it will be forever hidden to man, at least in this life. The explanation may be found in the *eloquence* of the enamored silence that speaks so deeply without words: the *silent music*, or also the *sounding solitude* of Saint John of the Cross. Poetry strives, again and again, to understand its mystery, but in vain:

---

[36] Rev 3:20.

[37] Alfonso Gálvez. *op. cit.* n. 45. In the Spanish original:

> *Vino hasta mí el Amado*
> *antes que el sol naciera por el teso,*
> *y, habiéndome mirado,*
> *sentí en sus ojos eso*
> *que sólo amor lo sana con un beso.*

My bride, my fair one, my sister, come:

You asked me if I could tell you about four
Of all things beautiful, those that I love more.
Since you asked me to decide, my choice is clear,
In ascending order these I love, my dear:

The silence of the forest wrapped in summer,
The soft rippling sounds of the gentle river,
The morning dew drops gleaming as they linger...

What holds, above all things, my dear, most beauty...?
Those sweet glances, pierced with love, you send to me.[38]

And the sacred Poem, indeed, tells us about the Bridegroom, submissive, even pleading, again and again, before the bride. This indicates that he is yearning to feel close to her and to delight in her presence as soon as possible, to taste the Perfect Joy that is the consequence, as a ripened fruit, of those being together who truly love each other. In this case, the Bridegroom and the bride, God and man:

---

[38] Alfonso Gálvez, *op. cit.* n. 93. In the Spanish original:

Me pediste te hablara de las cosas
las cuatro para mí las más hermosas.
Pues bien, hélas aquí, mi bien amada,
en escala ascendente elaborada:

El silencio del bosque en el estío,
el suave borbotar del manso río,
las matinales gotas del rocío...

¿La más bella de todas, mi adorada...?
Tu mirada, de amores traspasada.

Come then, my beloved,
My lovely one, come.
For see, winter is past,
The rains are over and gone.
Flowers are appearing on the earth...[39]

Open to me, my sister, my beloved,
My dove, my perfect one,
For my head is wet with dew,
My hair with the drops of night.[10]

This surrendering to the bride out of love for her —this act of boundless love and abasement of God for the sake of man— has nothing to do with the *deification* of the loved woman as proclaimed by the Provençal minstrels of the High Middle Ages in their songs of courtly love; a love professed to the beloved woman who is often so exceedingly glorified that she is impossible to reach; a love which usually leads the lover to despair.[41] Such forms of being in love tend to generate in the reader the idea of an irrational idolatry, rather than a true love.

Cervantes mocked the crazy love of the Knights–Errant for their lofty and cruel damsels, more inclined to enjoy the practice of contempt than the practice of love for their desperate lovers. This Satire and mockery from the Prince of Spanish Literature takes aim at the lady who filled the dreams (and vigils) of Don Quixote: the incomparable Dulcinea del Toboso. In this regard, maybe the episode of the Letter, written at the beginning of the penance that our Knight in love undertook on the cliffs of the Sierra Morena, is one of the most satirical contained in the narrative of the adventures of the Ingenious Hidalgo. The Letter, which was to be carried to the lady by his squire, Sancho Panza, went as follows:

---

[39]Sg 2: 10–12.

[40]Sg 5:2.

[41]About *Courtly Love.* sung by medieval and renaissance minstrels. as portrayed in *Prison of Love.* by Diego de San Pedro. see Alfonso Gálvez. *Siete Cartas a Siete Obispos.* Shoreless Lake Press. NJ. 2009. Vol. I. pp. 235 ff.

Sovereign and exalted Lady:

The pierced by the point of absence, the wounded to the heart's core, sends thee, sweetest Dulcinea del Toboso, the health that he himself enjoys not. If thy beauty despises me, if thy worth is not for me, if thy scorn is my affliction, though I be sufficiently long–suffering, hardly shall I endure this anxiety, which, besides being oppressive, is protracted. My good squire Sancho will relate to thee in full, fair ingrate, dear enemy, the condition to which I am reduced on thy account: if it be thy pleasure to give me relief, I am thine; if not, do as may be pleasing to thee; for by ending my life I shall satisfy thy cruelty and my desire.[42]

The exaggerations, the nonsense and folly of *Courtly Love*, in addition to the Books of Chivalry, Pastoral Literature, and the like are the best demonstration of how difficult —or even impossible— it is for humans to get to know the true reality of love without the help of Revelation.

We just saw that the condition of obedience, submission, and surrender to the beloved is representative of any person in love, man or woman. But then, where is the supposed uniqueness of women, and where can be found the discrimination and the inferior status that she suffers by accepting such situations or when they are imposed upon her?

To answer this, it is necessary to examine the issue calmly and get to the bottom of the matter with the certainty that we will find surprising and interesting discoveries.

First and foremost, if we accept the reality that those much maligned *passive* virtues or qualities are as proper and connatural to men as they are to women, since both equally are loving beings, then *the situation of inequality or disadvantage for women disappears.*

The famous liberation of women, much touted and trumpeted by *Feminism*, having less reality than the tale of Little Red Riding Hood, appears as what it is: a mere intellectual scam and nothing

---

[42]Martín de Riquer, in his critical edition of *Don Quixote*, offers a long list of fragments of amorous epistles contained in the books of chivalry (I, Chap. 25, p. 265). All of them are as ridiculous as they are funny.

more. Once again, we are coming across ideologies fulfilling their role, always willing to deceive the simple and pay lip service to their victims.

Actually, given the way things are and as we said above, *women do not need to be liberated from anything.* If women would somehow be deprived of such capabilities of obedience and submission —which is exactly what *Feminism* intends to do—, they would be deprived not only of their capacity for love, but also of the possibility of being loved. Thus, far from being elevated in her womanhood, she would be reduced to the level and category of an irrational being.

We have, therefore, solidly established that women are at the same level as men and equal in dignity. And if that were not enough, we found that what we agreed to call *passive* virtues —obedience being the most emblematic— not only lack the quality of passivity, but are characteristic of strong souls, willing to deny themselves and to take on the heroism necessary to practice them.

But then, from what slavery or humiliating condition must women be emancipated and liberated...?

In order to get to the bottom of this issue and to clarify certain points, some elucidation is still needed.

The duty of obedience and submission to her husband by the wife remains in force. The proclamation that the husband is the head of his wife, as Christ is the Head of His Church, as Saint Paul said (Eph 5:23), remains intact. And what follows from this?

It should be noted that the state of equality that exists between lovers for love's sake, being indeed a *reality* that surpasses any appearance of idealization, does not alter the fact that the *condition* of each one of them remains intact; even necessarily so, because we have here a fundamental paradox of love: the exchange of lives requires, indeed, that *each* lover remains being *each* lover, otherwise

love (which does not admit of any fusion or con–fusion) would not
be possible. Therefore, in the divine–human love relationship, God
is still God and the creature is still the creature. And as for love relations between creatures, something similar happens: the exchange
of lives does not lead to a confusion of persons or to some sort of
monistic or pantheistic fusion. Therefore, the husband gives himself
in and with his authority as husband, although he remains being
the husband; at the same time, his condition as husband is now
governed and ruled by love: *Do you know what I have done to you?*
You call me Master and Lord, and you are right, for so I am. If
then I being your Lord and Master have washed your feet...[43]

On the other hand, within the concept of true love —which we
have always and only been talking about— the loved person never
thinks about taking advantage of what she or he receives from the
lover. On the contrary, for what she/he really wants is to give everything she/he has received, along with what she/he is and has.
The bride in the *Song* never fails to consider her Bridegroom as
her Lord and King; so much so that she could never think otherwise. He who loves desires the beloved *as he or she is*; to the point
that the lover does not wish the beloved to be any other person or
to have a different personality. The Christian wife will see in her
spouse the loving husband and, of course, her head, as Scripture says
(1 Cor 11:3; Eph 5:23); this fact, accepted out of love, will become,
in turn, thanks to one of those paradoxes and mysteries of Christian
existence, *one of the main and most important reasons that she will*
be filled with joy.

Something also happens here which, unfortunately, has become
commonplace among Christians: they suffer from the tendency to

---

[43] Jn 13: 12–14.

easily forget the contents of Faith, including the most important ones.

But in the world of Christian Existence, with which all of our speculations are concerned, *authority* is the furthest thing imaginable from despotism or domination. Its essence is to have an attitude of love and service towards those who are under that authority: *You know that the princes of the Gentiles lord it over them, and they that are the greater exercise power upon them. It shall not be so among you; but whoever is the greater among you, let him be your minister. And he that will be first among you shall be your servant. Even as the Son of Man is not come to be ministered unto, but to minister and to give his life in redemption for many.*[44] The doctrine of Scripture is clear; although many try to forget it, to hide it, or to spirit it out. Jesus Christ Himself, while recognizing Himself as Master and Lord, immediately adds, however, that *He does not want to call us servants but friends* (John 15:15). And as for our topic about husband and wife, male and female, the Apostle speaks categorically: *Husbands, love your wives as Christ also loved the Church and delivered himself up for her.*[45]

The topic could now be definitively summarized as follows:

a) The virtue of obedience, as well as submission out of love to another person, is not an attitude of weak but of strong souls.

b) Taking personal circumstances into consideration and that each spouse maintains his or her proper role and functions, those virtues or attitudes are equally connatural to men and women.

c) Based on the laws of love relationship, the lover who is allegedly endowed with greater authority or dignity will see that such

---

[44]Mt 20: 25–28.

[45]Eph 5:25.

prerogative becomes an attitude of service and love to the other person.

d) There is, therefore, no reason for either party, which mutually surrenders to the other —acting by so doing according to the laws of love—, to believe that he or she is being discriminated against: *Whoever knows and feels loved, he or she feels dignified, exalted, and raised to the highest degree by the lover.* If things are not so for some people, that means that they have not understood what love is.

The virtues of obedience, humility, patience, etc., hitherto the subject of our analysis, can be practiced, just like any other virtue, by both men and women. The merit of each action, which ultimately depends on grace *and* the cooperation of each individual, deserves a separate consideration; however, some peculiar characteristics, typical of these virtues when practiced by women, ought to be noted.

When these virtues that we have agreed to call *passive* —for the purpose of a better understanding of the subject— are practiced by women, they get a special seal that characterizes them. Of course this is not an increase in merit based on sex —which could be construed as a case of discrimination against the male—, but a kind of *aura* acquired when such actions are carried out by the female. That aura results in a peculiar *charm*, a *spell* if you prefer, which makes the female sex especially enticing. It must be borne in mind that this particular *appeal* is not a mere subjective assessment; it really is an objective characteristic that inevitably accompanies the female sex as such. It is true that beauty, as an attribute of the human nature created by God, is manifested in one sex as well as in the other; however, it appears to be more *enhanced* in women.[46] To

---

[46]This has nothing to do with the mutual *attraction* of the sexes.

this enhancement contributes the charm of which we are speaking, as something exclusive of a *femininity* destined, after all, to balance —and in many cases even to revoke—, by its power of seduction, the alleged superiority of the male.

In that sense one could say that this attribute helps to balance the position of women regarding men. According to which, both the female charm and spell, along with special emphasis on physical beauty, cannot be simply considered as unique gifts or graces which God has given women, arbitrarily and as if by chance; God granted them with a particular and specific purpose, as He always does things. Although, in the end, as always, everything has to be judged according to the use to which one has put the talents received. Those who admit to a certain preeminence of man, in some aspects or under certain circumstances, can find here a compensation that brings things back to parity.

With more or less support —in fact, without any basis except when it comes to physical force—, man has always considered himself stronger than woman. But, once again, divine wisdom must be reckoned with, for it establishes the mysterious order of the reality of things. The alleged *weakness* attributed to woman is precisely her greatest *strength*. This is not surprising, since we already know that *power is made perfect in infirmity* (2 Cor 12:9). This *frailty*, coupled with the female charm and simplicity and purity of soul, contains a field of energy capable of overpowering man's physical strength and even, in too many cases, the vigor of an apparently iron will of a male. We should not forget that the Virgin Mary was able to *break* the will of her Son at the wedding at Cana (Jn 2) and He had to bring forward His hour.

One more thing about frailty: Those, if any still exist, who share with *Feminism* and its shady dealings the false notion that the wife

—or woman regarding man— is in a situation of humiliation for the wife *vis-à-vis* her husband... and, conversely, those whose love of truth urges them to want to insist on the fact that the particular frailty of women —like the *frailty* of china or a rare and delicate beauty— contributes to making her especially adorable, both groups of people may need to rely on the fact that God has always shown a preference for the weak, the poor, the little ones, and, in general, for all the children in the world. It was when He saw a humble, innocent virgin, forgotten and unknown, in one of those miserable hamlets of the ancient world, that He felt inclined to advance the time of the Incarnation of His Son; as some Fathers have declared, as well as many theologians and spiritual authors. Moreover, God once solemnly proclaimed this truth by the mouth of His Son Jesus Christ, *I thank thee, O Father, Lord of Heaven and earth, because you have hid these things from the wise and prudent and have revealed them to the little ones. Yes, Father, for so has it seemed good in your sight.*[47] And let us not forget that the Apostle proclaimed the woman as *the glory of man.*[48]

---

[47]Mt 11:25.

[48]1 Cor 11:7. The Greek term δόξα means brightness, splendor, radiance (Lk 9:31; Acts 22:11; 1 Cor 15: 40 ff.); glory and majesty when referred to God and celestial realities (Acts 7:2; Rom 1:23, etc.); magnificence and splendor attributed to Kings (Mt 4:8; 6:29), etc.; and so on.

THE YOUTH WITH THE POPE

We could have given this chapter a more suggestive title, possibly *The Popeboys*; but that could possibly risk appearing as discriminatory to *Popegirls*; and, frankly, this is not the moment to be unfair —even if it is an apparent unfairness; truly speaking, girls are *fans* of the Pope as much as the boys are. The word *fan,* as everybody knows, is an unfortunate and affectionate barb: short for *fanatic,* and can be used to describe members of either sex. We have taken into account, of course, the possible distress of the Feminist Movements; therefore, we have changed the epigraph. However, we want to note here that we would have very much liked to definitively incorporate into our cultural stock these and similar buzzwords —in order to get on board with the pile of simplicities that have been accumulating for quite some time in the so–called *Spanish Royal Academy of Language.*

Be that as it may, we are referring here to that motley and multitudinous Youth which, as the mass *media* reminds us with praiseworthy frequency, overflow with outpourings of love for and devotion to the Pope. In spite of being so numerous, this Youth has the prerequisite conditions for being considered as a compact elite, or, rather, a select group of praetorian guards (of both sexes, of course), whose profound sentiment for Catholicity and affection would even lead them to give their lives for the Pope —if it were necessary... and if it were true. Fortunately, it has never been necessary before now to go that far; therefore, our statement is based upon mere conjecture which, nevertheless, nobody in his sound mind would dare to doubt (except for us, of course).

The official Spanish Church, probably encouraged by the existing peace and the absence of problems toward which she could dedicate her attention, has given herself to the laudable task of making possible the *Gatherings* of Youth with the Pope. These are extraordinary events which, while propelling the Catholicism of the Youth with a newly infused spirit, at the same time provide the opportunity to engage in energetic and lengthy preparations, which consume time that otherwise would be difficult to find a way to utilize. Undoubtedly, many who spend their lives worrying about the situation of the Youth, especially the customary alarmists who think that the Youth at Large has abandoned the Church, see in this gathering a glimpse of hope and optimism looming on the horizon.

Those pessimists should expeditiously be reminded of other Youth *Gatherings* with the Pope. For example, the one celebrated in Sidney, Australia, in 2008. It was a tumultuous and spectacular concentration of young people, which was, nevertheless, itself outdone by the more grandiose event which took place in Cologne, Germany, in 2005, right after the election of Pope Benedict XVI.

It is always pleasant to call to mind some of the things that occurred there. For example, the spectacular arrival of the Pope at Cologne for the commencement of the Gathering; he came sailing on the Rhine in a beautiful vessel escorted by five smaller boats, each one operated by a crew gleaned from the five continents.

And how could one forget the no less crowded, raucous, and enthusiastic Youth gatherings that the charismatic Pope John Paul II had the gift to summon during his frequent travels? Or what about the hotheaded, strident feelings and exclamations, bordering on hysteria, that occurred at the Pontiff's death? We all remember the events of those days: *Santo subito, santo subito!* cried the young crowd, growing hoarse and filled with enthusiasm.

And so on... Where is it now, then, that quasi–apocalyptic vision of reality according to which almost the entire Youth has abandoned the Church...?

We agree wholeheartedly. Yet, notwithstanding what we have said, perhaps a calm and in–depth analysis of the real facts is called for here.

From the moment Catholic Theology abandoned the Thomistic philosophy of *being* —a historical event coinciding approximately with the death of Pope Pius XII— and replaced it with the Idealist philosophy of *appearing*, the World, and the Church along with it, has become accustomed to granting more importance to the *appearance* of things or to the *feelings* those things are able to arouse than to their *real content.* Consequently, the true or authentic nature of things does not matter *as much as what one merely decides (wishes) to think about them.* In the particular case of Pastoral activity — with which we are now concerned—, when it comes to preaching, for example, we will soon realize that the proclamation of the truth does not matter *as much as merely speaking about what people wish to hear.*

With these premises, and given the very real and dangerous possibility that perhaps we are in the midst of a new, propped–up spectacle or *show*, without even intending it, prudence seems to advise that we examine the results of this new pattern of ecclesiastical activity. For there is a possibility that, when all is said and done, the sole consequence of so much activity is simply the moving around of great masses of seemingly passionate and hotheaded people —young people in this case—, albeit devoid of any authentic Christian life or content... or, at best, with a merely superficial layer of it. Could it be possible that we are contemplating a case of Youngsters more inclined to having fun than to true affection and devotion for the Pope...? And perhaps it would be unfair to lay the greatest degree of responsibility at their feet.

The fact that diverse ecclesiastical projects and enterprises almost never elaborate what, in the financial and mercantile parlance, is called an *analysis of results* is something which calls our attention. Exactly the opposite happens in civil life where any firm, whether big or small, must make a minute study of results which can indicates profits or losses. All commercial endeavors must pay careful attention to the success or the failure of their projects: how and why profits and dividends, if any, have been obtained, or losses incurred; otherwise, any increase in productivity would be improbable; even more, the ruin of the firm would become possible.

Ecclesiastical activities never look for monetary profit —although there also are some who are *experts* at turning those activities into lucrative businesses. Their dividends pertain exclusively to the supernatural world: the greatest good and advantage for souls, with the spreading and increasing of Christian existence among men as their final result.

And this particular characteristic is what makes the analysis of the results much more important, for what is at stake here is not economic profit but the salvation of men. Hence, *it would be utter craziness not to examine this issue.*

We must take into account that, in this kind of venture, the level of success and good results cannot be measured based on the number of people taking part in the activity; nor on the coverage of the event by the *media*; nor on the magnitude and intensity of the shouts of enthusiasm and praise resounding during the activity in question —which would not be difficult to stir up, given the modern techniques used to manipulate the common masses; nor on the headings or catchphrases exhibited on banners or on the slogans enthusiastically chanted in unison; no, *the success can only and exclusively be measured by the increase, or the lack of it, in Christian life among the Youth.*[1]

**During the *Gathering of Youth* which took place in Sidney, Australia, in July, 2008, His Holiness, Benedict XVI, said in one of his speeches that *Australia has had the opportunity of knowing the young face of the Church.* It is a beautiful phrase, undoubtedly true, and deserving full acceptance, given the Person who pronounced it.

**Nevertheless, as everybody knows, no corporation, whether big or small, no company which takes on huge sociological enterprises normally takes into account either the content or the charm of beautiful sentences as the basis for its *analysis of results*; and, of course, it does not feel the constraint of being restricted by Literature or Poetry. On the contrary, the analysis is based on very thorough studies, detailed with the help of meticulous calculations of economical, financial, mathematical, and statistical data. These studies examine, in depth, the vicissitudes engendered by every last penny, in order to reach the final conclusion, vital for the corporation, as to whether or not management yielded earnings or losses.

**Undoubtedly, the *Gatherings* of Youth with the Pope, or *World Youth Day*, do not belong in this category of activities; but that is not an obstacle to their results being diligently examined. After all, they are a *business* —although referring in this case exclusively to the good of the Church and the salvation of souls. It is in this particular area where these *Gatherings* have given rise to some neg-

---

[1]The text marked with **, transcribed below, is taken from the book by the author *Siete Cartas a Siete Obispos*, Vol. I, Shoreless Lake Press, N.J. 2009, pp. 275–277.

ative criticism which, although possibly questionable, deserves to be taken into account because it also is based on evident facts which cannot be denied.

**It is known with all certainty, for example, that pro–homosexual and pro–lesbian activists were very dynamic in spreading their ideas among the gathered youth; that protestant sects and Jewish propagandists worked tirelessly among them, often with abundant fruits. It is equally evident that there was a profuse circulation of contraceptives, abundant sexual activity and drug use —there are graphic documents which leave no room for doubt. There also was more than a mere possibility of a mass profanation of the Body of Our Lord, given the custom in these tumultuous acts of worship of receiving the Eucharist indiscriminately. And let us add here that no positive results regarding an advancement in the Christian life of the youngsters could be appreciated, neither in this last *Gathering* nor in the previous ones; things have been exactly *business as usual,* once the youngsters went back to their respective countries. Even worse, a significant regression in their Faith has taken place, which even they themselves do not bother to hide.

**Yet everything seems to indicate that there is general satisfaction in the mere fact that these events took place; just that and nothing more, as if that and no other motive had been the sole objective. Truly speaking, all the negative data brought up here could be called into question by somebody stubborn enough to do it —something that always happens. But there is one totally indisputable fact: *The tremendous truth that nobody seems to have even cared enough to examine the outcomes of the Gatherings.*

**Was the mere celebration of the events perhaps their only purpose...? It stands to reason, logically, that there must have been enough pastoral incentive to justify them. If that has been the case, have the Pastoral analysts, once an event took place, meticulously examined its results —whether favorable or adverse, while also considering the negative elements that coincided with it? And if so, where and when have the results of such investigations been made public? The truth is that the few persons who have dared to formulate some objections have been silenced immediately; and, of course, they have been branded as pre–Vatican II, traditionalists, enemies of progress, and, above all, strangers to the *spirit* of Vatican Council II. And it is common knowledge that appealing to the *spirit of the Council* is the effective secret weapon brandished by *progressive* Theology to disqualify those who attempt to put up any objection to its teachings.

There is no doubt that the changes introduced by the New Theology, reflected, in turn, in the new Liturgy and the new Pastoral activity, have filled a lot of people with confusion. There are many sheep of the Flock of Jesus Christ that wander about aimlessly... although one cannot say exactly the same about the Youth.

But if what we have been saying cannot be applied to the Youth, then what are we talking about?

Indeed, it cannot be asserted that the Youth of the present generation are disoriented, *for the simple reason that they have never been truly oriented*; for nothing can derail which has not been previously set on rails.

They can shout from the rooftops that *the Youth is with the Pope*; announce slogans presumably improvised by the Youngsters, like *Totus tuus* and similar ones; proclaim *Manifestoes* elaborated at *Youth Councils* —which, in reality, rather seem to have been written by the adults— and addressed to a bourgeoisie *enemy of progress*, etc., etc. And many other things could be done, following the guidelines of a triumphal train of thought, which extends the ecclesiastical *Springtime* to the Youth as well.

But truth, which irrefutably asserts itself through the evidence of the facts, patently shows that *the Youth, at least in its majority, is neither with the Pope nor with the Church.* This could scandalize and grate on pious ears, which will insist on denying it, as usually happens. Nevertheless, the problem with those in denial is that they usually do not explain certain facts that are there: such as the total lack of vocations in seminaries, in novitiates, and to consecrated life in general; or the general abandonment by the Youth of the churches, acts of worship, and the use of the Sacraments. On the other hand, one can equally deny any aphorism, such as "the whole is bigger than its parts" or the simple numeric addition of *two plus two makes four.*

Nevertheless, it would be false, and unjust, to presume that all Youngsters and the entire Catholic Pastoral activity operate according to these parameters. There are still Youngsters and Catholic institutions of young people which keep the freshness and vitality of the Church of old; and the exhortation of Saint John the Apostle is still true: *I write to you, young men, because you are strong, and the word of God abides in you, and you have overcome the evil one.*[2] But they are in the minority. If we refer to the Youngsters whom we see every day, the analysis sketched above does not even reflect the entire magnitude of the problem.

At any rate, everybody agrees that a mere critique does not solve any problem, which is true. But we only intend here to call attention to the possible need for providing Pastoral care for the Youngsters with a new approach, since the current Pastoral endeavors possibly as some particular aspects which urgently need to be revised in order to face the questions outlined here. When all is said and done, these issues are the ones most strongly affecting the life of the Church.

---

[2] 1 Jn 2:14.

WINTER SPRING

This title looks like a contradiction, and possibly it is: Spring is not Winter and Winter is not Spring. And yet, we must not forget that we are living in an age in which contradiction, absurdity, and lies are the normal state of affairs in social life. Logic has been definitively banished; and, as for reason, everything seems to point to the fact that it has been mistaken for personal will —only *what I want* is now reasonable or true. The Modern world now accepts as normal behaviors which formerly would have been considered madness; hence, *normal* people —that is, those who would have been considered as such until recent times— are being rejected by a society which regards them as intolerant, eccentric, ignorant of progress and modernity, *conservatives* of a past which is obsolete and irrevocably banished to the lumber room; rare specimens who can only hope to be tolerated.

Consequently, the present profound crisis which is afflicting the Church has been termed —without any shame and as cool as you please— *The Springtime of the Church*. Any possible protests demonstrated against this term (although, to date, none has been known to exist) would be considered ridiculous.

The very few believers extant in the Catholic World who still want to remain faithful —Jesus Christ spoke of His *little flock*[1]— find themselves in a state of confusion and perplexity. They are harassed from all sides, branded as being strange to and rebellious

---

[1] Lk 12:32.

against a presumed *spirit of the Council*, marked as a grave obstacle
to the *New Order* and the *New Church* which are being implanted;
they wander, not knowing where to go —*Wandering in deserts, in
mountains and in dens and in caves of the earth*[2]—, aimlessly, *like
sheep without a shepherd*,[3] thinking that perhaps they are the ones
who are wrong or the ones who have betrayed their fidelity to the
true Church. Because of this anguished situation in which they
live, sometimes they are so perplexed that, in spite of their knowing
that the Church cannot disappear (Mt 16:18), they believe that
she cannot be found anywhere. They think, for they cannot help
but observe what is evident or to perceive what is all too patent,
that the Church in which they live is different from the One in
which they were baptized; and they can barely recognize her. People
around them rebuke them and try to convince them that nothing
has changed —unless it has changed in order to yield to the rising
of something infinitely better than the old, where the faithful have
found, finally, the true Church of Christ.

Nevertheless, *facts are solid brass*, as the experts in Sociology
like to say. Facts are always there and cannot be denied by anybody except by him who stubbornly calls the black white and the
white black. Indeed, things have changed too much for anybody
to think that a mere circumstantial transformation is all that has
taken place which, if nothing else, has caused, in turn, fundamental
improvements.

In distant times, similar circumstances were easily resolved. It
sufficed to adhere to the teachings and guidelines of the Magisterium. A Magisterium which was always firm, coherent, and in
line with the Tradition of the Church —*let no innovations be in-*

---

[2]Heb 11:38.
[3]Mk 6:34.

troduced; let us simply keep what has been transmitted to us, Saint Vincent of Lérins said already in the fifth century—, and he spoke with Authority. These days the problem is not so simple. There are many Shepherds in the Church positioned all over the world who hold varying opinions which all too frequently are contradictory and sometimes even clearly contrary to the Faith. In addition to this, the contemporary Magisterium tends to be concerned with social problems which, as worthy of consideration as they may be, are foreign to the supernatural realm and to anything pertaining to the wellbeing and salvation of souls. This Magisterium even uses a language which is evanescent, ambiguous, and twisted, in which the faithful, unfortunately, cannot find answers to their problems.

Then, is it true that we are in a *Springtime of the Church* and that nothing has changed except for the better...? At any rate, given the uncertainty of the present situation, what can the *little flock* do while it searches for the true way and yearns with longing for fidelity to the Church, for it knows very well that there is no salvation outside Her? This little flock is also convinced that the Hierarchy, whether faithful to its mission or not, is nonetheless the Hierarchy; consequently, they cannot do without it or replace it with another... if they want to remain faithful to the will of Jesus Christ. This is the poignant and painful drama of the conscious and faithful Catholics of our time.

We are going to try to shed some light upon this problem, especially by attempting to point out sure paths to walk upon. They do exist, for God never abandons His own, nor can He permit the boundaries of the true Church to appear as something blurred or too difficult to find for those who search.

Is it a fact that nothing has changed...? Is it true that an ample sector of the modern Church, the part which is most exposed to the contemplation of the world —*neither do men light a candle and put it under a bushel, but upon a candlestick*[4]—, does not look different from what it used to be? More yet, does it not give the impression of being even *another* Church?

The progress achieved by publicity and mass manipulation techniques is beyond belief. Through these means, people are barely allowed to think about this problem; at best, they are being convinced that we are in the most flourishing ecclesiastical springtime.

The following is a quote (introduced by asterisks) from one of Father Malachi Martin's books;[5] due to its length, it is fragmentary and incomplete but faithful to the original. It may seem a long extract, but it is more eloquent than anything I could say.

**...When the violence of the winds had passed and the new day dawned, people looked about and found that suddenly the universal Latin of the Mass was gone. Stranger still: The Roman Mass itself was gone. In its place, there was a new rite that resembled the old immemorial Mass as a lean–to shanty resembles a Palladian mansion. The new rite was said in a Babel of languages, each one saying different things. Things that sounded un–Catholic. That only God the Father was God, for example; and that the new rite was a *community supper*, not an enactment of Christ's death on the Cross; and that priests were no longer priests of sacrifice, but ministers at table serving guests at a common meal of fellowship...

---

[4]Mt 5:15.

[5]Malachi Martin, *The Jesuits (The Society of Jesus and the Betrayal of the Roman Catholic Church)*, New York, 1987, pp. 246–250. Father Malachi Brendan Martin, a former Jesuit priest, was a Roman Catholic theologian and a professor at the *Vatican's Pontifical Biblical Institute.* A very controversial character, in his life as well as in his works, he was considered to be too traditional by the supporters of the New Theology.

The devastation of those hurricane winds had not stopped there. Churches and chapels, convents and monasteries had been denuded of statues. Altars of Sacrifice had been removed or at least abandoned, and four–legged tables were planted in front of the people instead, as for a pleasant meal. Tabernacles were removed along with the fixed belief about Christ's Sacrifice being the essence of the Mass. Vestments were modified or laid aside completely. Communion rails were removed. The faithful were told not to kneel any longer when receiving Holy Communion, but to stand like free men and women and to take the Bread of Communion and the Cup of the Grape of Fellowship in their own democratic hands. In many churches, members of the Congregation were immediately expelled for *public disturbance of worship* if they dared to genuflect, or worse still, to kneel, for Holy Communion in the new rite...

In addition to what happened to churches and chapels, Roman Missals, brochures containing norms for the Mass, prayer books, crucifixes, altar cloths, Mass vestments, Communion rails, even pulpits, statues, and kneelers as well as Stations of the Cross were either consigned to bonfires and city dumps or sold off at public auctions where interior designers picked them up at bargain prices and launched an *ecclesiastical look* in the decoration of high–rise apartments and the elegant homes of suburbia. A carved oak altar made such an unusual *vanity* table...

Very many teaching nuns simply doffed their religious habits, quickly acquired lay clothes, cosmetics, and jewelry, said good–bye to the local bishops who had hitherto been their major superiors, declared themselves now constituted as ordinary, decent, straightforward American educators, and carried on their teaching careers...

Those who remained —lay and clerical— were not satisfied with the attempted abolition of the traditional Roman Mass, with the

overall changes of Catholic ritual and worship, and with newly exercised freedom to cast doubt on all dogmas. It wasn't enough. A
clamor arose in favor of the use of contraceptives, of legalizing homosexual relations, of making abortion optional, of premarital sexual
activity under certain conditions, of divorce and remarriage within
the Church, of a married clergy, of women's ordination, of a quick
patchwork union with Protestant churches, of Communist revolution as a means not only of solving endemic poverty but of defining
Faith itself.

A new form of blasphemy and sacrilege came into vogue. For
homosexual Catholics, the *disciple whom Jesus loved* took on new
meaning. Hadn't that beloved disciple *rested on Jesus' bosom* at the
Last Supper? Man–love–for–man was thereby consecrated, wasn't
it? Lavender–robed homosexual priests said Mass in the new rite
for their homosexual congregations...

Backing up this motley array of changes and changers and change-
lings, there came marching in a whole phalanx of feisty *experts*. Theologians, philosophers, liturgical experts, *facilitators, socio–religious
coordinators*, lay ministers (male and female), *praxis–directors* —
whatever their pop–up titles, all were looking for two things: con-
verts to the new Theology, and a fight with the battered and re-
treating traditionalists. A flood of publications —books, magazine
articles, bulletins, newsletters, plans, programs, and outlines— in-
undated the popular Catholic market. The *experts* questioned and
reinterpreted every dogma and belief traditionally and universally
held by Catholics. Everything, in fact, and especially all the hard
things in Roman Catholic belief —penance, chastity, fasting, obedience, submission— were subjected to violent, overnight change...**

And all this is just the beginning and the summary of an inventory which could continue almost indefinitely, a veritable tip of

the iceberg. And I did not want to delve into the theological and philosophical roots of the hurricane in the Church which have been merely sketched here. While everything seemed to indicate that Pope Saint Pius X had finished off the Modernist heresy, now it was patent that the heresy had been hibernating in order to reappear in our time with unsuspected strength. One must hope that Divine Providence provides His Church with a new Saint Pius X who will put a stop once and for all to the problem.

Experience shows that once madness has been unleashed and the human being is willing to behave foolishly, there are no limits to the manifestation of absurdities, aberrations, and lies. Scheeben considered sin to be a *mystery of iniquity* because it is a bottomless abyss of malice; after all, the offense inflicted by sin is infinite, for infinite is the dignity of the offended Person, God. Consequently, the list of ravings, the very ones whose sprouting has made possible the mild weather of the *Ecclesiastical Springtime*, seems to be endless.

One of them, for example, is the triumph achieved by *feminism* over *machismo*. At long last, women have *liberated* themselves from the oppression which they had been suffering at the hands of males; it is now that women have finally obtained the possibility *of fulfilling themselves as persons* and of *being themselves*. It is a victory worthy of being engraved in marble, quite capable of giving happiness to the (old) weak sex which (now) has finally become strong and emancipated. The only condition required to feed such euphoria, of course, was to not lay too much emphasis on the meaning of expressions such as *fulfilling herself as a person* or *being herself...*; the simple reason being that nobody has ever been able to find out the meaning of those absurdities. Absurdities which reached their acme when it was discovered —wonder of wonders!— that God is feminine and that the Church has become feminine...!

Consequently, if homosexuals have finally found their status as citizens within the present *Ecclesiastical Springtime*, why should that status not be granted to woman–love–for–woman? Let us here quote Malachi Martin:

Only Catholic women of the sixties generation were clever enough to perceive themselves as victims of *ecclesiastical sexism*; for them, a day of reckoning with the age–old sexist–minded Church had come at last. There now arose *Womanchurch* —one of those eerie, new pop–up words which meant meetings for women in private apartments where She (God the Mother) was worshiped and thanked for having sent her Child (Jesus) by the fertilizing power of the Holy Spirit (Herself the primo–primordial Woman).[6]

Obviously, we cannot continue enumerating the catalog of absurdities which is too long; besides, there is enough serious bibliography about the issue. Nevertheless, we need to mention here, at least in passing, the outrageous assault effected against the divine constitution of the Church.

The absurd winds which attempted to impose the *democratization* of the Church, as another fruit of the *Springtime*, almost finished off the authority of the Hierarchy in an unrestrained effort to replace that authority with governing by the laity. But this is totally contrary to the will of the Divine Founder of the Church; such substitution, should it be successful, would deal her a death blow: the Church is not a democracy but a hierarchy.

Let us consider, for example, the Bishops. They have full power to regulate their own dioceses, to the extent that they are directly accountable only to the Pope or to the Ecumenical Council (provided that it is also presided over by the Pope, as a condition for

---

[6]Malachi Martin, *op. cit.*, p. 248.

its legality and validity). Therefore no *Conference*, no matter how *Episcopal* it may be, has any jurisdiction over them. This fact becomes even clearer if we keep in mind that Episcopal Conferences are one of the rather unfortunate creations of the Second Vatican Council. In reality, they have restricted the freedom of Bishops in their sees, frequently imposing some form of coercion on their decisions (presuming that they have done so in good will). But there is, in addition to what has been said, the gravest of all the consequences: the Conferences have proven to be susceptible to the influence of special Pressure Groups, which never seemed to have been too worried about the true needs of the Church.

The same winds of democracy have appeared at the parochial level. Parishes have been changed into *agencies* led by laymen who decide everything through Liturgical and Economic Commissions, Pastoral Councils, Councils of Parish life, Administrative and Social Councils, etc., etc.; all of them governed and presided over by lay people. In this way, the pastor has been reduced to a mere employee operating at the dictates of the various Councils, without the power to dispose of anything without their approval. In short: the shepherd is now receiving orders and directives from the sheep.[7] In some of the new *Communities* that have arisen in the Church, even the direction and the principal roles in worship are reserved for the laity, while the presence of the priest is almost irrelevant. However, since Jesus Christ instituted the Church structured in the form of a Hierarchy and simple faithful, not even the Church herself can modify her configuration: *a Church that has been made into a democracy, thus abandoning her hierarchical structure, would no longer be the Church founded by Jesus Christ.* But in spite of this,

---

[7] This phenomenon appeared most starkly in countries like the United States of America.

as Father Martin says, alluding to the tornado which is shaking the Church.[8]

All hopes are now centered on the community. *The People of God* was now distinct and separate from the old, still–boned hierarchy of Pope, bishops, priests, and nuns in the tight coagulation of Roman discipline. More than that, this People of God —altogether, as well as in each little gathering of believers— was now said to be the real Church, the real source of revelation, the only legitimizer of morality, the sole source of what to believe. In matters of faith, morals, dogma, and religious practice, Rome, Georgia, had the same authority as the Rome of the Popes...

—*Lord, to whom shall we go? You have the words of eternal life.*[9]

As far as I am concerned, my birth into the supernatural life took place within the Catholic Church; the Only true Church founded by Our Lord Jesus Christ. I was ordained a priest in Her during the pontificate of Pius XII, and I hope to be granted the grace of dying in Her bosom. I am well aware that, according to the promise of Her Divine Founder, the Church cannot disappear, and, therefore, She *is there*; although sometimes it is difficult to recognize and even to find Her. I am also convinced by the grace of faith that the Church being the only way to salvation, no other salvation can possibly be found outside Her. I have not been mandated to found a new Church or to do away with Her Hierarchy or to change it for another: *Where Peter is* —whether he is the traitor who heard the cock crow on the night of the Passion or the hero who died on the cross, upside down and out of love and fidelity to his Master— *there the Church is.*

---

[8]Malachi Martin, *op. cit.*, p. 249.
[9]Jn 6:68.

And yet, Her metamorphosis is so patent and profound that it would be useless and not very honest to deny the fact that She *seems* to be another. Nevertheless, and in spite of all the evidence and the multitude of appearances, *this is the sole Church which lives in continuity with the Church of all times and, consequently, the only True One.* That is why this is the moment for us, the faithful, to actualize our faith, to put our trust in God, and, like Abraham, *to hope against all hope* (Rom 4:18); for God will finally come to our aid. How could it be otherwise? Can God by chance abandon His own? Can He stop watching over His Church and looking after Her...? The true disciple of Jesus is the only carrier of true Joy, and only he possesses true Hope: *But when these things begin to come to pass, look up and lift up your heads, because your redemption is at hand.*[10] The Good Shepherd will never abandon His flock: *He that gives testimony of these things, says: 'Surely, I come quickly:' Amen. Come, Lord Jesus!...*[11] And, *Be glad in that day and rejoice: for behold, your reward is great in heaven.*[12]

---

[10]Lk 21:28.

[11]Rev 22:20.

[12]Lk 6:23.

THE WRONG END OF THE STICK

Modern man has acquired a tendency for putting into practice the adage which admonishes against *getting the wrong end of the stick* in the social, political, and —which is most lamentable— in the religious sphere. This adage refers to a phenomenon which is motivated by a twofold fear. First, to always avoid calling things by their rightful names; and second, to never get to the bottom of the problem in order to always stay on the surface of the issues, either for vested interests... or for fear of the consequences (which some would call prudence and others cowardice).

The examples we could give are innumerable, so we must be content to examine some of the most obvious ones and address the others in more general reflections.

One example in the spotlight in the western world today is abortion.

It is a well–known fact that there is a fierce debate about this issue which involves every level of society, including, of course (it could not be otherwise), the Catholic Church. The debates almost always coincide in a common approach to which all seem to adhere: *getting the wrong end of the stick*; that is, no one dares to get to the bottom of the problem, even though this would really be the only way to confront it and solve it.

The Church, or at least a good number of the Highest Members of the Hierarchy, as the most important element in the debate —even though politicians do not want to recognize it— has been

advancing, unfortunately, feckless arguments: it is against the constitution (in countries where this supreme law contemplates issues
related to human life) or a crime against the right to life, etc. But
they do not have the courage to proclaim the truth openly: abortion is a crime with every possible aggravating factor, a sacrilegious
mockery of the Law of God, an unspeakable, abominable, and most
grave sin to which, sooner or later, God will apply His justice.

Instead of that statement we have the usual spectacle of the
Church defending the truth, but with *kid gloves*: with the typical intention to avoid offending or provoking the annoyance of the
System, of politicians, of the *media*, and, above all —and most
importantly— to avoid appearing conservative or against progress.

This has been, after all, the policy of the Shepherds throughout
the whole Church: the outstretched hand, the desire to avoid offending anyone, cessions and concessions to attract the lost ones...;
in the end, the result is that these compromises do not convince
anyone and, as if that were not enough, they tend to cause many
desertions. One must presume that the Shepherds have good intentions, although the Faithful as a whole would prefer that their
Shepherds were less afraid and more firm in their proclamation of
the Truth.

It seems as if openly proclaiming the Law of God or the Gospel of
Jesus Christ would inspire profound fear in the Hierarchical Church.
To use the name of *God* and even more so of *Jesus Christ* has become a taboo that everyone tries to avoid at all costs. That is why,
too often, only arguments based on purely human concerns are put
forward —with the thought, seemingly, that modern man will not
accept any others.

Even more shameful, if possible, is the attitude adopted toward
the issue of homosexuality; a topic that has gained enough force to

shake to its foundations a world that is already immersed in the lowest level of decadence.

The instance of homosexuality (both its masculine form as well as its feminine form, or lesbianism) is quite unique. Commentators and theorists, thinkers and *Catholic* politicians, including, of course, the Ecclesiastical Hierarchy itself..., everyone seems to have forgotten that homosexuality is a very grave sin and an abominable vice, something that constitutes an aberration which threatens what is most essential in human nature. And yet, this is the way homosexuality has always been considered by those with common sense, an unquestioned conviction formed over thousands of years throughout the History of Humanity, the clear doctrine of Natural Law, the Tradition of the Church, Patristic Doctrine, Ecclesiastical Magisterium, and, above all —and perhaps most importantly—, by the positive Divine Law, *which has explicitly condemned homosexuality in the most unambiguous and strongest terms,* in the Old Testament as well as in the New Testament.

In the Old Testament, we find the well–known narration of the tremendous punishment suffered by the cities of Sodom and Gomorrah, plunged as they were into this abominable vice (Chapter 19 of the Book of Genesis). In the New Testament, Scripture condemns and rebukes homosexuality with harsh and unsettling words and threats (Rom 1: 26–28; 1 Cor 6: 9–10; 1 Tim 1:10; Rev 21:8; 22:15).

True, the Bible does not pose a problem for the unbelievers...; and the same could be said about countless numbers of Catholics for whom the Bible is just an obsolete book concerned with moral conceptions pertinent to ages already past in Human History; a book, moreover, which is susceptible to multiple interpretations — but barring those meanings that are not metaphorical or allegorical, etc. Nevertheless, when all is said and done, it may be proper to remind everyone about other words from Scripture: *make no mistake: God is not mocked, for a man will reap only what he sows.*[1]

Everyone, including many Shepherds of the Church, agrees on one thing: homosexuals —the *Gay* community or lobby, as we say today— is a reality that exists and is significant, and is, *therefore something that must be taken into account.*

Thus, obviously, a momentous step has been taken in the history of the socio–political tenets of Humanity. We are referring here to the legalization of what exists out there, or the doctrine of the acceptance of consummated facts which is heralded as a Triumph of Progress. The problem arises when it is claimed that, thanks to this progress, soon we will also see regulated and structured, according to Law, terrorism, piracy, drug–trafficking, organized crime, human rights violations..., and a long list of related issues; for these also are realities that are already *out there.* As compensation, however, we will have the joy and peace of knowing that, though these realities will continue their doings (and probably will develop even greater activity), at least we can be sure that they will be *contemplated* by Law. Indeed, human beings have always been able to deceive themselves very easily.

And yet, it is not difficult to guess the collection of vested interests that make up this business. What carries weight for the political Parties, of course, is the number of votes they can garner. If the so–called *Gay Rights* lobby is a massive and coercive force, no one can afford to count it as an adversary. Additionally, because political parties do not give a hoot about Morality, welcomed are the *Gays.*

It is more difficult to explain the acceptance of homosexuality as a *bona fide* reality by the Shepherds of the Church. For some of them,

---

[1]Gal 6:7.

this whole issue boils down to the convenience of doing away with any lingering traces of the old philosophical *realism* of Saint Thomas Aquinas, which today, they maintain, is happily bettered by the doctrines of Idealism, Personalism and Existentialism, to the greater glory of these philosophies. Nevertheless, this explanation is difficult to accept; therefore, more truth seems to reside in the reasoning which is based in the inferiority complex of many Shepherds. Part of this complex is the fear of appearing as closed to the world or being labeled as conservative. But certainly a wavering Faith, along with a certain laxity in living the teachings of the Gospels, has an even greater weight in this complex.

The center of the problem is found in the fact that, from a Christian point of view, *it is impossible to accept the legitimacy of the regulation by Law of a reality that is intrinsically evil.* If the State is determined to enact *channeling* Laws about homosexuality that are not clearly punitive, and which consequently are plainly supportive to this reality, that legislation is radically null and void. Human Law that is opposed to Natural Law —the rational creature's participation in the Eternal Law— and even, in the end, to Positive–Divine Law, has no validity and cannot be considered Law at all: *Obedience to God comes before obedience to men*, said Saint Peter.[2] And if this argument is not accepted by unbelievers, it is clearly obligatory in its entirety for Christians. This turns the speculation and repeated attempts by a large part of the Hierarchy that tirelessly insists on the necessity of regulating the *reality* of homosexuality into pure nonsense.

The Apostle Saint John said that authentic Love throws out fear (1 Jn 4:18). Therefore, when men, blinded by the craziness of seeing themselves as gods, have rejected true Love, they necessarily become

---

[2]Acts 5:29.

slaves of Fear. The freedom they think they are enjoying is a farce and a caricature. When such a thing happens, one can be certain that the time of terror, slavery, and tyranny has arrived. As for Christians, such an attitude of cowardice is a betrayal to Him who said of Himself *I am the Truth*; adding —for all those who would hear it— that He is indeed the only truth that leads man to true freedom (Jn 8:32).

There are multiple and various ways of *getting the wrong end of the stick*. One of them involves focusing on one of the more insignificant aspects of a given problem while ignoring the most important part —or even missing it completely. The advantage of this *procedure* lies in the thought that it wards off all danger of complications for those who use it. The spirit that animates it is, of course, fear, a common denominator that is never lacking in this type of conduct. This procedure is proper among pusillanimous or not–too–smart or mostly selfish persons who are less than fond of setbacks and sudden shocks; although there are cases in which these three cowardly characteristics are simultaneously present.

At the same time as these observations are being written (2010), the press has published several statements issued by the Bishop of Cáceres (Spain) which were made in response to a campaign organized by the *Governing Body of Extremadura*, an organism which supposedly *governs* that autonomous Region in Spain. This campaign is called *Pleasure Is in Your Hands*, and its objective is none other than to encourage masturbation among children and to teach them how it is done. This will scandalize anyone who is unaware of the degree of degradation and corruption into which Spain is presently submerged, thanks to Socialism... and to the passivity and culpable silence of those who consent to these things or do not condemn them.

The Bishop of Cáceres, as could only be expected of him as a Shepherd, has issued some statements on the matter. He affirms that the campaign is *unwise* and involves an *excessive expenditure of money* (14,000 €) *in the current time of crisis.* This gives reason to believe that the *Governing Body of Extremadura* will be in an uproar after such an incisive reprimand on the part of the Bishop. One question remains to be answered, though: one could ask the Spanish Prelate if, in his opinion, that campaign would have been *wise* had it been more inexpensive or were we not in the midst of an economic crisis? At any rate, perhaps it would have been more opportune to remind the *Governing Body of Extremadura* of Jesus' words: *It would be better for him to be thrown into the sea with a millstone round the neck than to be the downfall of a single one of these little ones.*[3]

But, generally speaking, this propensity for *getting the wrong end of the stick* is an approach which is collectively adopted, encompassing multiple sectors of society. In the present Socialist Spain there is another case worth mentioning which is even more patent and heartbreaking. The terrorist attack that took place in Madrid on March 11, 2004, left in its wake almost two hundred dead and close to two thousand injured; its manifest objective was to bring about a change of government. And yet, after six years of numerous proofs and investigations, as well as of lengthy and controversial trials of the alleged material authors of the attack, nothing is really known about the true organizers of this quasi–genocide.

It is true that hidden vested–interest groups have gone to impossible lengths to impede the investigations. In spite of this, and of not knowing who the culprit is, and of the fact that *nobody dares* to say it clearly, suspicions are always pointing in the same direction.

---

[3]Lk 17:2.

Truly speaking, the procedure for finding out the complete truth would have been quite simple... had they really wanted to get to the bottom of the problem. It would have been sufficient to have read Agatha Christie's novels and observe the *modus operandi* of the famous detectives who appear throughout their pages: Hercule Poirot, the famous Belgium detective immortalized by the English writer, for instance. His method for finding the murderer in question was simply... to discover *the one who would benefit from the murder under investigation.* That was the beginning of the thread which would lead the hound–like detective to uncovering the whole plot.

When, moved by selfish interests and ultimately shackled by cowardice, men are bent on refusing to confront the stark truth and, instead, try to hide or disguise it, then they have made an agreement with the dark Kingdom of Lies, without much minding the logical consequences of such a deal.

And when the Shepherds of the Church, moved by the same reasoning and led by the same motives, behave likewise —that is, not facing the problems, galvanized as they are by their fear of confronting the System; when they rather trivialize serious problems in order not to commit themselves to solving them; when they only pay attention to minutiae, which are neither the key to the true threats nor do they matter to anybody... In one word: when the Shepherds abandon their duties regarding the Faithful entrusted to them, the Wolf arrives and, in Jesus' very words, *attacks and scatters the sheep.*[4]

---

[4] Jn 10:12.

IS THE SLOGAN "BE YOURSELF" TRULY EVANGELICAL?

The fact that a variety of philosophical principles of Idealism have burst in upon the Church, even at the highest levels of the Hierarchy, seems to endanger her subsistence; a collapse that would have already occurred were it not for the promise of her Divine Founder that *the Gates of Hell can never overpower her.*[1]

For, once the principles of Idealism have been conceded, it is only a matter of time before its logical consequences and offshoots appear. That is how modern man has come to the point at which he does not feel the need to come out of himself to follow someone else —and even less to do so by renouncing his own life.

According to this scheme of things, man considers himself a self–sufficient being, once he is convinced that the search for a Paradise outside of this world is nonsense. At best, he believes that this paradise is to be found only in the world in which he lives, since there is no other. Moreover, love, for him, is merely a physiological phenomenon in which there is little difference, when confronting it, between human beings and animals. That is why it no longer makes sense for man to come out of himself and search for the *other*, as the fundamental law of love dictates. Therefore, man realizes himself inside himself, without the need for external elements which would alienate himself.

---

[1] Mt 16:18.

The principles of Idealism and its philosophies —with its adhering excrescencies and by–products like Marxism— are far from
having disappeared from the modern world. The truth is that they
saturate the atmosphere in which man exists today —including, of
course, the Christian.   Therefore, it is not surprising that, even
within the Church, the emphasis has shifted from God to man, or
that Anthropology has occupied areas that formerly belonged to
Theology.

In the tremendous effort of today's Church to recover a de–
Christianized world, many Shepherds have convinced themselves of
the need to use the only categories that man is willing to accept today: his own, which because they are purely human are usually far
from the supernatural ones. That is how the task of concealing the
authentic content of Revelation started, without hesitating to use
purely natural categories and concepts..., and ended up forgetting
its true meaning. It seems incredible that simple dictates of common sense can so easily be forgotten. For example, that it is not
reasonable to adopt the policy of concealing or hiding merchandise
in order to sell it better.

Certain classical notions of Christian Spirituality, such as *as-
similating the life of Christ,* or *becoming another Christ,* have been
replaced by others like *being yourself.* The legitimacy of the latter
phrase perhaps cannot be questioned, but it evidently lacks all supernatural connotation. Even though this change is very radical,
nobody seems to have perceived the tradeoff effected; the ancient
and classic saying: *be another Christ,* for example, has been shelved
to make way for the more modern and more brilliant *be yourself.*

All told, some changes have an importance well beyond what is
perceived at first sight. Because it no longer is about coming out of
oneself to live the life of another but, on the contrary, reaffirming

one's own identity. Nothing further from our Lord's words: *Anyone who wants to save his life, will lose it; but anyone who loses his life for my sake, and for the sake of the Gospel, will save it.*[2] One must admit that any attempt at finding conformity between the new mantra and the revelation of the New Testament would be a difficult, if not impossible, task.

Nevertheless, contrary to what it could seem, man never knows himself completely nor can he even fully become himself when confining himself in his own self. Truly speaking, he must leave his own self to the point of total oblivion of self in an attempt to find *another* and abandon himself to him.

What has just been said has nothing to do with the theories held by Idealism and Personalism according to which, in a general way, man does not possess an already complete nature determined by God, but he is forming and becoming himself according to his relationships with the world and the others: man is not; he makes himself. In contrast, sound Catholic doctrine maintains that man is a complete being, as he came out from the hands of his Creator (even in his present condition of fallen nature, although repaired); he can certainly perfect his being through love, embodied in his self–surrender to others and in abandoning his selfishness.

Neither are the new progressive doctrines true, according to which the coming of Jesus Christ was intended to *reveal to man what he is*. The truth is that He came to *redeem* man, with all that this redemption entails: union with Jesus Christ, recovery of divine sonship, and so on. *Losing one's life* for Jesus Christ's sake implies that one already possesses a prior personal life that *belongs* to that individual (you cannot lose or give up what is not yours). Saint Paul, while asserting that it was Jesus Christ who lived in him, insisted at the same time that it was he himself who lived, according to his famous words: *I live, although it is no longer I, but Christ who lives in me.*[3]

The difference between what is said here and what Personalism claims is this: the latter refers to the constitution of human nature as such and to the mere

---

[2]Mk 8:35.

[3]Gal 2:20.

realization of man *on the natural level* (the supernatural approach is alien to Personalism, although it often tries to disguise itself). Here, on the contrary, we are talking about a perfecting and realization of the human nature which is already entirely constituted in its natural being; and about man's perfection and fulfillment *in the supernatural destiny that has been granted to him*, which does not dispense with nature as such (grace does not nullify nature but perfects it).

In the bosom of the Trinity, the Idea that the Father has of Himself is another Person, the Word; so much so that when *He looks at Himself he sees another*, identical to Himself in numerical identity of Essence, yet distinct from Himself as a Person.[4] When man focuses on himself without considering anything outside his own self, he can only know what he is able to be *negatively* —here one must take into account the mystery of fallen nature and of the infinite malice of sin—; whereas in order to know *positively* what he is capable of doing, he must forget his own self and look to Jesus Christ. Only then can he say in all truth: *Ecce Homo.*[5]

To make man believe that he is self–sufficient is to impede him from feeling the need to follow Jesus Christ; it would not make any sense, for what good would it do for a being that already has everything? Besides, what reason would now justify the demand to lose one's own life? To close man in on himself is nothing other than to destroy in him all possibility to love and to be loved and constitutes thus a direct and critical attack on the very soul of Love —an attack on that Love which would disappear from the world if, by some unfathomable madness, man should ever remain in the solitude of his own self.

---

[4] Needless to say, this doctrine is only applicable to the human being if one keeps analogy in mind.

[5] *Behold the Man* (Jn 19:5). We must take into account what has been said above: we are talking about a perfecting *within the supernatural order*.

As is easily seen, expressions that may sound pleasing to the ears of the modern times, but which lack any content, can become a dangerous weapon.

This saying, which tries to encourage young people to be *themselves*, runs the risk of not taking into account the ambiguity of the expression and the dangers which it contains; for the fundamental reality for a Christian is living the life of Christ, not his own (Gal 2:20).

Man can only be *himself* —since he has been given a supernatural destiny and God is his ultimate end— when, forgetting about himself, he surrenders his own life out of love. This Doctrine belongs specifically to Christianity; it is not a sort of truth evident in itself (*per se nota*). Therefore, if it is not adequately explained, young people are in danger of understanding the expression *be yourself* in a purely human fashion, without any of the supernatural connotations with which Revelation has enriched the concepts of love and man himself.

The approach of stressing more what sounds pleasant, because it is more fashionable, than what is the true content of the concept, whose supernatural content is silenced, perhaps tries to make more palatable to the world a doctrine which in itself is difficult. But, in doing so, they do not realize that the doctrine in question has been mutilated and, to the same extent, falsified; besides, not even then has that doctrine become more appealing. At first sight, it could seem that the System has been successful in presenting a doctrine as something now more easily accomplished. But the procedure is useless because it deprives that doctrine of both its content and, to the same extent, its appeal; and this is particularly important when dealing with Young People, since it has been established that only men of violence take the Kingdom of Heaven by force (Mt 11:12).

Catholic Pastoral activity must convince itself that the method of divesting the Gospel from its sharpness and its biting strength, so that the world may accept it, is ineffective and dangerous. Christianity is a veritable *novelty*, so much so that to the extent it is no longer a novelty, to that same extent it ceases to be Christianity. But when Christianity loses its most appealing characteristic, it no longer seduces men —especially young people, who are precisely the ones most attracted by *novelties*.

It is urgent, then, that the Pastoral activity with Young People is not led by the old in spirit, who, all too often, tend to have no faith in Young People. Certain slogans, like the ones used at the *Council of Young People* held in Taizé shortly after Vatican II, clearly demonstrate the manipulation that some adults have made of the Pastoral activity with Young People: it stands to reason that young people would have thought of many ways to describe their gathering, but *Council* would never have been one of them. This behavior of those adults can hardly evade accusations of being demagogical, for they seem to be convinced that their approach pleases the youth and that young people cannot understand or accept anything different. Those adults forget that, commonly speaking, young people do not like to *be themselves*; most of the time, they rather want to *be different* —including those who have accepted their own defeat (those without roots, drug addicts, those enslaved by alcohol or sex) as well as those who protest against the world by taking it as a joke.

Progressive Pastoral activity does not understand that what really seduces young people is searching for *someone other* (with upper or lower case letters); they think that finding him will make them different and quite capable of changing the world. It is simplicity to believe that the rebellion of the Youth only refers to the world in which they live; one must realize that the Youngsters have always included themselves among the things they complain about. The True Youth, that is, those who, precisely because they are young, are truly rebellious, has never been happy with itself; hence the first thing it has brought into question has been its situation and its way of life. We should never forget this, lest we approach Young People with rather naïve ideas more suitable for older and rather mediocre people totally estranged to the way Young People think. To believe that Young People are not able to accept an unmitigated, completely supernatural–in–content Christianity is to do them no justice; rather, it underestimates them. It seems as if some people, feeling themselves withered with age and quite hopeless, are unable to believe in a young and resolute Faith, notwithstanding their public claims to the contrary. Their attitude is very different from the stance taken by the Apostle Saint John, who firmly believed in the Young People: *I write unto you, young men, because you are strong, and the Word of God abides in you, and you have overcome the evil one.*[6]

---

[6] 1 Jn 2:14.

THE GREAT TRIBULATION

No person without prejudice will venture to deny that the Church of today is in the midst of a *great tribulation*: a serious commotion which is being facilitated by the fierce campaign that is being waged —from inside as well as from outside the Church Herself— against Her, most especially against the clergy.

Nowadays, most of the dogmas are called into question or doubted. The ties of continuity with the traditional Magisterium have been severed. The demands of Christian Morality have been relaxed to bring them up–to–date and to conform them to the criteria of the World. Liturgical anarchy has become the order of the day throughout the entire Church. Esteem for the Hierarchy has reached the lowest levels ever seen in all her history. The sacraments have been divested of practically all their content and meaning; consequently, their practice by the faithful has been reduced to almost a vanishing point. The indissolubility of Christian marriage, which had been admitted throughout so many centuries as a condition demanded by Divine Law, has yielded ground to a *de facto* divorce which in vain tries to disguise itself under another name. Mass attendance of the faithful has plummeted to a negligible, minimal number. Members of the clergy are being attacked with such an unheard of, never before seen, intensity and malice that it seems to be rather the work of the Devil than something of this world. Religious Orders, Congregations, and Institutes have reached such an alarming state of disintegration that they are on the verge of total extinction...

Most of the sheep of the Flock of Christ are confused and disoriented, not knowing most of the time where to go or what to do. To top it all —and along with the internal divisions that have emerged within the Church of today—, there is the looming danger of a grave schism hanging over her like a threat; although apparently nobody sees it or tries to dispel this possibility.

The words that Saint Peter wrote in his *First Letter* seem to be more relevant today than when they were written: *Dearly beloved, do not be surprised at the fiery ordeal which comes upon you to prove you, as though something strange were happening to you;*[1] though, if we consider the exhorting context in which these words appear, they sound more like a cry of hope than a voice of alarm —as we shall see in greater detail later.

Be that as it may, and in spite of what many people stubbornly say to the contrary, it is evident that Catholicism is immersed in the state of a *great tribulation* which the Book of the Apocalypse speaks about in reference to those faithful who, having overcome terrible and painful trials, are already before the throne of the Lamb: *These are they who have come out of the great tribulation and have washed their robes and have made them white in the blood of the Lamb.*[2]

One cannot say that this text is exclusively referring to the final moments of History, since Christians have suffered persecution and put up with sufferings and tribulations all throughout her History: *And all that will live godly in Christ Jesus shall suffer persecution.*[3] As for the present moment, everything seems to indicate that the Enemy of Humanity, as if he had a feeling that the end of Time is

---

[1] 1 Pet 4:12.

[2] Rev 7:14.

[3] 2 Tim 3:12.

near, is putting the Church to a severe test, the likes of which she has never known before.

Does this mean that we are in the Last Times and that the Second Coming of Our Lord is imminent?

Only God really knows the moment when all the things predicted will be fulfilled: those things which will bring History to its end and which will coincide with the judgment of all Men who have ever lived, thus inaugurating the starting point of the New Heaven and the New Earth (Rev 21:1). Therefore, one cannot affirm that this decisive moment is here nor can he, for the same reason, state categorically that it has not yet arrived.

Within these parameters, therefore, either of the two possible options seems legitimate, so long as one's conjecture is advanced as a *hypothesis*: the End of Times is already here; or the Final moment of History has not arrived yet, and it is not even possible to determine when it will.

Undoubtedly, the first hypothesis will have the fewer number of supporters and the greater number of detractors; and yet, it is perfectly realistic, for two main reasons:

In the first place because, although it is true that the moment of the Second Coming of Christ is known only by God, the New Testament contains —especially from the mouth of Jesus Christ and through the Apostle Saint Paul— enough prophetic *signs* whose fulfillment must precede His Second Coming. They are veritable prophecies which contain abundant and various numbers of *indicators* which, according to Revelation, will bring the attention of men to the imminent arrival of that moment. One must assume that the revealed Word has been written down to say *something* whose exact meaning is unknown to us, but whose objective undoubtedly is to provide us with *clues* or guidelines for our knowledge; for God is not fond of using literary grandiloquence or of deceiving people. These announcements of events are indeed shrouded by a certain vagueness, typical of prophetic language, but they are a sufficient warning to those who want to use them.

In the second place —and this is more telling— because some of the events proclaimed in those prophecies are either fulfilled or about to be fulfilled; thus the Great Apostasy announced by Saint Paul (2 Thess 2:3) and by Jesus Christ Himself (Lk 18:8): the wars and rumors and dangers of wars, along with hunger and earthquakes in various places (Mt 24: 6–7). As for the mysterious *abomination of desolation standing where it ought not to be,*[4] it may suffice to quote a passage written by Pope Benedict XVI, then Cardinal Ratzinger: *We are referring to many other phenomena typical of our times which are a real threat to Christians; that is, paganism within the Church herself, 'the abomination of the desolation standing where it ought not to be' (Mk 13:14).*[5]

Things being so, one seems compelled to ask: What can we Christians hope for in the near future? And above all, what attitude must we adopt before the serious events that are currently shaking the Church?

In order to somehow answer such delicate questions, we will have to resort again to the two–hypothesis theory; therefore, some clarifications are called for:

First of all, one must say that if we were near the Last Times — and let us here stress the fundamental assumption that these times are known only by God— then what the future has in store for us seems to be very clear: no possibility of improvement in regard to the present situation will be there to be seen; more yet, things

---

[4]Mk 13:14.

[5]In his book *The New People of God.*

will gradually tend to get worse, even very grave, in an accelerated progression. The prophetic signs contained in Revelation as the announcements preceding the imminent Second Coming will necessarily and indefectibly become real, despite the fact that practically the entire human race will refuse to take notice of the warnings: *For when they shall say: 'Peace and security' then shall sudden destruction come upon them, as the pains upon her that is with child, and they shall not escape.*[6]

Thus, another calamity, which is part of the number that make up the Last Tribulations, will come to pass: Men, being more blind than ever before, will not in the least want to see what is happening or to repent from their sins; much less will they want to turn their lives around so as to somehow placate the wrath of God. Rather, the contrary will occur. Humanity will go on sinking deeper into the mud of its abominations: declaring legal and legitimate the most horrible aberrations; considering all possible kinds of mockery of God and His Christ as triumphs of Progress and heralds of the New Age; disowning the Faith and increasingly spreading and deepening the universal Apostasy. And because there will be no sign of admitting the mistakes made, no minimal sign of desire for turning back to God, the terrible events that mark the End of History will inexorably continue in their course. Thus, the perdition of vast multitudes will be sealed and sentenced: *And the rest of the men, who were not slain by these plagues, did not do penance from the works of their hands, that they should not adore devils and idols of gold and silver and brass and stone and wood, which neither can see nor hear nor walk; neither did they penance from their murders nor from their sorceries nor from their fornication nor from their thefts.*[7]

---

[6] 1 Thess 5:3.

[7] Rev 9: 20–21.

As for the Church, we know that She cannot disappear because She enjoys the promise of Her Founder (Mt 16:18) which will infallibly be fulfilled; notwithstanding the Great Offensive against Her and against the Faithful of Christ which Hell, taking advantage of the Last Times, will unleash.

Nevertheless —and this is another point of maximum importance but which, inexplicably, usually goes unnoticed— it is also true that *the Church will be reduced to a minimum*; which is something that we know with absolute certainty based on the very words of Jesus Christ (Mt 24:22; Lk 18:8).

Therefore, it is true that the Church will not disappear; but it is equally certain that the number of Faithful will be reduced to the lowest point in all Her History. Truly speaking, and no matter how painful it is to admit it, according to the clear statements of Revelation, *not many will be chosen* (Mt 22:14).

In the meantime, as incredible as it may seem —human nature often is mysterious and inexplicable— false Christs and self–proclaimed *true* saviors of Humanity will accumulate everywhere (Mt 24: 4–5). And all will be accompanied with an abundance of great signs and wonders and *definitive* revelations which will seduce many people. At the same time, Men, jubilant, will celebrate the birth of a New Age and the advent of New Times for the Church...but, in reality, they will be pledging total submission to the Liar: *Whose coming is according to the working of Satan, in all power and signs and lying wonders, and in all seduction of iniquity to them that perish, because they receive not the love of the truth, that they might be saved. Therefore God shall send upon them a strong delusion, to make them believe lying, that all may be condemned who have not believed the truth but have pleasured in iniquity.*[8]

As for the second hypothesis, the one which believes that we are not yet in the Last Times —which most people consider as the most probable—, what seems reasonable to think as to what is going to happen?[9]

Since, within this approach, one can only anticipate events merely based on the authority given by one's personal opinion, everything seems to indicate that the tribulations which currently afflict the Church will continue, with a clear tendency to worsen with time.

Since the Church cannot disappear, this hypothesis implies that her eagerness to survive will impose the need for an authentic Reform. A Reform that will take place by the rising, perhaps, of a holy Pontiff; and, most probably, by the calling of a new Council, one endowed with a strong spirit of responsibility as well as with sufficient determination to reestablish and to live again the true principles.

Unfortunately, however, this perspective does not seem to be anywhere on the horizon, within either a short or a medium period of time; neither the Faithful, as a whole, nor the Hierarchy show the least desire of initiating such a Reform. Therefore, we will have to wait for an uncertain future, totally within the mysterious plans of God, Who, undoubtedly, will take care of His Church.

---

[8] 2 Thess 2: 9–11. It is typical of the heresy of Modernism —which is currently in force *within* the Church— to consider that the *New Church* is the only one which, finally, keeps the key to the true Revelation. The more or less implicit consequence of this approach is that the Institution founded by Jesus Christ has remained in error throughout twenty centuries.

[9] Truly speaking, this hypothesis, far from being considered as probable, is admitted as the only true one by the great majority of people. In stark contrast to what happened among the first Christians, nobody nowadays is willing to think about the Second Coming of Christ.

In the meantime, the short–term prospects for the future seem to be rather tragic. Triumphant slogans like *The Springtime of the Church, The New Pentecost* of the Church, the beginning of a *New Age* will continue to be proclaimed to the four winds, along with the new *dogmas* discovered after the Second Vatican Council: universal salvation, validity of all religions, religious liberty understood as full autonomy of the human conscience to determine itself, and, in one word, a whole new Religion of Man which will try to replace what is already considered to be the obsolete Religion of God.

As a complement to this scene, the parade of Gatherings, Conferences, Declarations, and Documents —which will deal with numerous issues, none of them essential— will continue. They will be accompanied by a number of *Shows* and spectacular *Parades* which will vainly attempt to disguise and to hide the tragedy of an unstoppable Decadence and of a heart–wrenching and deplorable Apostasy which becomes more patent with the passing of time.

> Everything suggests, at least at first glance, that the *shows* and the *parades*, which have reached such an extraordinary boom in the Church since Pope Paul II, are the result of an attempt to disguise the current era of decadence and decomposition of Catholicism.[10] There is no evidence that this is the intention of their promoters, although the objective reality corresponds to that idea. Rather, it seems that the pursuit of the show is simply the inevitable consequence of a terrible *emptiness*. For the *New Church*, since she knows nothing about authentic spirituality and is ignorant of interior life, the excitement of the scene is a need that tends to conceal (even unconsciously) the horror caused by nothingness with the appearances provided by fiction.

Some might think that with the blueprint we have drawn, in which we have briefly outlined the trials being endured by the Church today, we have reached the heart of the matter. Nothing, however, could be further from the truth.

---

[10]See *The Decomposition of Catholicism* by Louis Bouyer.

First of all, the aforementioned inventory is no more than a *superficial summary* of the entire problem. It is but the tip of the iceberg in the sense that we can go no further if our intention is to avoid shocking the faint of heart. We have purposely tried not to detail all the symptoms of the malady that is affecting the Church; consequently, we also sidestep reaching the core of the issue.

Let us examine the second of these points, for it illustrates the more worrisome aspect of the problem.

As we have said above, it could seem that the account of the previously described misfortunes —a list which, as we have made clear, is not exhaustive— contains a complete analysis of the ordeals faced by the faithful members of the Church in our day. However, we have already said that this is not exactly so. As anyone can understand, such symptoms, namely liturgical anarchy, a general lack of discipline, the questioning of dogmas, the placing in parenthesis —rather than a simple "forgetting"— of Christian morals, the shortage of true Pastors, the abandonment of the Sacraments, the continual increase in desertions, etc., etc., are but the *consequence* of a deeper and much greater evil.

This evil, in turn, reveals several facets. One of these facets contains a special peculiarity: the habit, which is embedded in the hustle and bustle of Church life, of almost never facing the real problems at their true depth. This is a serious wrong that, having lately extended itself with ferocious intensity within the ecclesiastical sphere, has become yet another cause of the misfortunes now besieging the Church.

Let us consider, for example, one of the most severe problems afflicting the Church of today which involves preaching. If anyone has doubts about how banal sacred oratory currently is, he can freely ask any of the faithful who still go to Mass on Sundays and hear, amidst yawning —since we can no longer say that they actually listen to it— the homily of the day. He may be sure that, once he has done this and obtained an answer, any further clarification will be unnecessary.

With reference to this topic, and as a confirmation of the reality of what we have said, we can recount a recent example. Not long ago, a certain number of Rules, whether official or unofficial I cannot say for sure —the bureaucracy and the ecclesiastical laboratories of Pastoral work do not neglect their duties— appeared which contain guidelines to be observed for a good Sunday homily. Taking into account the fact, which these Rules openly recognize and try to solve, that the faithful are bored with today's sermons, these Rules counsel priests not to exceed a limit of eight minutes in their homilies. This regulation —no doubt the fruit of profound consideration— has somehow failed to realize that *an exceptionally boring fifteen–minute sermon* becomes, thanks to such clever advice, *an equally boring eight–minute sermon.* As for the faithful, who are not versed in grammatical digressions, the *boring* part is more substantial and of greater importance; while the *length of the sermon* is more a secondary concern.

Of course, this problem demands a more profound inquiry in terms of remote causes which are, in the end, the ones that give birth to this particular issue. Such causes could be, for example, the meager formation of the clergy, the lack of an interior life, the absence of study... and —worst of all— the example given by a great part of the Hierarchy when carrying out its Magisterial duties; for this Hierarchy tends to never address the true problems suffered by the faithful. It frequently and cautiously avoids pointing out behaviors and situations which, precisely because of the damage they cause to the faithful, should necessarily be denounced. On the other hand, the Hierarchy rarely tenders solid doctrine, since its exhortations try to focus on *exciting* topics... *so exciting* that all they can obtain from their unfortunate listeners are open mouths.

As for the doctrinal anarchy and the utter confusion in which the faithful often find themselves, the causes of these problems are complex and of a very delicate nature; therefore, we can discuss them here only with the brevity and discretion that circumstances allow.

We often hear complaints from the faithful about the heterodoxy of many publications, as well as about serious doctrinal errors which are profusely being spread —with impunity, as a matter of fact— through preaching. Because of this, a shadow of doubt and confusion is being cast everywhere; a shadow which, with ever waxing strength, is shape-shifting into a universal indifference, abandonment of all religious practices, and even loss of Faith.

Concerning this issue, we must take into account the following briefly itemized observations:

There is often a lack of appropriate guidance which should be offered by a clear and forceful Magisterium.

It is also undeniable that official recognition of the validity of all religions, in terms of salvation, has alarmingly spread indifferentism and distrust among the faithful: *If all religions are valid to attain salvation...*

Another fact, also obvious and easily seen by anyone, is the disquieting truth that in practically all the Faculties of Theology in the Church, starting with the ones in Rome, *the teaching of true Catholic Theology is not provided.*

If it is true that although the deep chasm in Theological Doctrine, with respect to the Magisterium before the Second Vatican Council, has had little *speculative* repercussion on the bulk of the

Christian people (who, logically, remain unaware of the problem), nevertheless, it did have *practical* consequences. These have, naturally and as could be expected, somehow managed to infiltrate the faithful and give rise to a general feeling of insecurity among them with respect to the Faith.

The alarming scarcity of priests urgently demands a true Reform, as much in the Seminaries and Novitiates as in all other ecclesiastical Centers of Formation. This Reform must be undertaken with regard to doctrine as well as to discipline. Above all, it must concentrate on fostering a serious spirituality, one founded on the love of Jesus Christ and the Priesthood; and it must dismiss, without preambles or delays, those who are incapable of carrying it out.

In the Great Offensive being led against the Church at this very moment by the Devil himself, the position that is most heavily besieged is the Priestly State. This maneuver undoubtedly is the greatest of all the Tribulations that the Church is now suffering. It is also, at the same time, the fiercest and more serious attack that the Priesthood has undergone since Jesus Christ established it.

There is nothing strange about such an assault if we consider the times that both the Church and the World are experiencing, the role of the priest during such times, and how much there is at stake for Hell.

This stage of the Campaign against the Church —specifically against the Priesthood— consists of a combined attack that is simultaneously taking place on two fronts: inside as well as outside the Church herself.

Meanwhile, the Christian People as a whole remain unaware of what is happening. In fact, the Faithful know neither the core of the problem nor the ends sought by such a maneuver. However, we cannot say that their condition is entirely passive or indifferent, for once they have been brainwashed and manipulated by the Machinery of the System, they are effectively, although inadvertently, contributing to the aggravation of the situation. For example, many lend their voices to the chorus of those baying for the blood of the guilty.

The Offensive is being simultaneously carried out on two fronts: in the sphere of civil society... and, strange as it may seem, also in the ecclesiastical realm.

Before we continue, we wish to clarify that it is not our intention here to acquit those who are truly guilty in this matter; much less to justify the unjustifiable. We simply want to point out some principles derived from the fundamental demands of Justice. Thus, for example, no one may be condemned without considering all the facts and circumstances of the case (which is not the same as exonerating from guilt those who are truly culpable). Neither is it licit to cast the burden of the entire responsibility onto someone — normally the weakest one— without taking into account those who have collaborated by their conduct —through action or omission— in the commission of the crimes attributed to others.

Concerning the sphere of civil society, we must begin by saying that the brutal Campaign unleashed upon the Church, especially the Clergy, because of the perpetration of certain crimes of which some of the clergy members have been found guilty *is one of the greatest displays of shameless hypocrisy, on a social scale, that History has ever known.*[11]

---

[11]What follows makes reference to all those crimes of pederasty that took place throughout the Church from the second half of the twentieth century up to the beginning of the twenty–first, approximately. The facts, properly magnified and universalized, were used by the System to stir up a wave of campaigns against the Church, most particularly against the Clergy. Nevertheless, hardly anything was reported about the serious crisis affecting the Church at all levels: doctrinal, moral,

First of all, these crimes which have been denounced —as morally grave and, therefore, as condemnable as they are— are of no concern to those laying blame. The actions they denounce as crimes *are the very ones that they themselves commit, the very crimes they proudly flaunt as achievements and triumphs of Progress, giving them grandiloquent names (Gay Pride)*. In the last analysis, certain forms of homosexuality —the ones these accusers deplore— are merely derivatives of that abhorrence that homosexuality itself is. Besides, in many cases, those deplorable crimes are just plain homosexuality, which the accusers, with the worst of intentions, have deliberately classified within the category of a more specific crime.

Secondly, certain crimes that the Clergy are accused of are also committed outside of this group, and in a proportion so much greater as to be terrifying. In Germany alone, for example, of the more than 200,000 cases declared and recognized as pederasty, only 94 were attributed to members of the Clergy. Though this fact certainly does not justify those few cases, one must take it into account when the time comes for weighing human conduct, which can be attributed to society as a whole, on the scales of Justice.

Thirdly, the majority of the stone throwers, apparently so filled with zeal about Honor and Righteousness, *could not care less about purity as a social virtue*; most of them take great pains to avoid practicing it.

Let us now examine, more specifically, the Campaign against the Pope whom some want to involve also in the *conspiracy*:

When all is said and done, and contrary to what most of the naive people who inhabit this Planet believe, this Campaign, as such, is not directed against the person of Benedict XVI. After all,

---

liturgical, and disciplinary, which was the determinant cause of the degradation of the Clergy.

this Pope, thanks to his ecumenical policy of openness and reaching out; his official recognition of all religions (following in the footsteps of Pope John Paul II, whose conduct reached its height at the Meetings of Assisi); his drawing nearer to the other Christian Confessions and to Judaism, so as to consider them on a level equal with Catholicism; his opened mind concerning pre–Conciliar and post–Conciliar mentalities... the Pope enjoys the rapport of Jews, Protestants, men of Modernist tendencies, as well as the favor of other Circles more or less related or loyal to Freemasonry. The truth is that the Campaign has been launched *directly against the figure of the Pope*, hated as such by all the enemies of the Church. These enemies have always considered the Pope as the incarnation of the Antichrist and Rome as the Great Babylon spoken of in the Book of the Apocalypse. Their purpose is none other than to terminate, once and for all, the hated Institution of the Papacy.

We must examine the far worse facets of this assault —which we will speak of next. The goal pursued here, with a malice which seems to belong to the Powers not of this world, is to destroy those who, for love of Jesus Christ and of souls, sacrifice their lives in spite of a World that will not only never thank them, but which will never stop hunting them down in hatred. Jesus Christ Himself told us: *...But because you do not belong to the world, because my choice of you has drawn you out of the world, that is why the world hates you.*[12]

The Campaign launched against the Catholic Priesthood, *apropos* the scandal which certain sexual crimes have produced, has reached an intensity never seen before.

We should insist here on the high level of hypocrisy in a society that lodges such accusations. Not only does that society contribute,

---

[12]Jn 15:19.

with its conduct as the most important component, to promoting a favorable environment for committing such crimes, but it is also guilty of committing such crimes itself —sometimes even far more serious and more widely spread crimes.

To unmask this firsthand we feel it necessary to highlight certain occurrences which, no one knows why, are never objects of accusation and have not been taken into consideration by anyone.

The Movie Industry tends to use, shamelessly and up to now without protests from anyone, children of young ages to star in pornographic movies or in movies of a clearly scandalous sexual nature. How this affects children, as well as infancy in general, can be guessed by anyone. This is a matter in which, as far as we know, the Clergy has not been involved.

In Spain, within the Movie Industry itself —subsidized by the Government with taxpayers' money—, cinematographic rubbish is almost the only thing produced, whose content is distributed within the following ratio: approximately sixty percent of the movies are exclusively concerned with bedroom scenes; the remaining forty percent, also approximately, is reserved for spreading the ideologies connected to Marxism. Fortunately, almost no one goes to contemplate such *works of art*; after all, Providence, as well as common sense, protects and cares for the people in any way It can. The Clergy has had nothing to do with this either.

The dissemination, via a great multitude of means, of the most abject sexuality among children and youth in general has become something widespread throughout the entire world.

In Spain for example, the Socialist–Marxist government currently in power has imposed in *all* the schools of the country, as an *obligatory* subject for children and adolescents starting from the age of six or seven, the teaching of all kinds of sexual practices (with themselves, with persons of the opposite or of their own sex, and even with animals); not to mention the use of every kind of contraceptive and device designed to procure pleasure. This is the same *subject* whose objective is to imbue Marxist ideologies in children, as well as to uproot from their minds any trace of Christianity and, in general, all the values that have, for centuries, been the foundation and support of Western Culture.[13] These are all matters in which, as far as we know, the Clergy has not participated.

Television programming in Spain, generally speaking, is systematically bent on flooding all the homes of the country, almost twenty–four hours a day, with pornographic garbage of the worst kind; especially *targeting* Infant Children and the Youth. Again, this is another affair in which, at least from what we know, the Clergy has had no part.

Examples could be multiplied *ad infinitum.* Aberrations that are *contra natura* —and considered as such since the beginning of Humanity— are now praised, paraded, and fostered throughout the whole World as a triumph of *Progress.* These aberrations have reached their most degrading levels with activities —like *homosexual marriage*— that would cause any who had not previously lost every trace of modesty to blush for shame. Never has the Family, this time–immemorial Institution, been more degraded and debased. Once again, the Clergy has neither directly nor indirectly taken part in this matter.

In fact, the firm opposition by the Clergy has provoked severe reactions, as to be expected, from the supporters of the *New Civilization.* Concerning the specific topic of these aberrations being pro-

---

[13] At the very moment that these lines are being written, we have just been informed by the press that the Town Hall of Segovia (Spain) will impart special courses whose purpose is none other than to teach 13–year–old girls how to *get laid* with boys.

moted to the category of *institutional rank*, it is possible to suppose that, if Providence had given animals the ability to express their feelings in the form of laughter, it is probable that entire species would have already disappeared: killed, of course, by the continuous bouts of laughter roused in them by their observation of human behavior. None of this, however, has any bearing on the campaign against the Priesthood: the priests are still the *bad guys*, the ones to blame for everything, the ones whom the *good guys* of the movies feel compelled to hunt down and exterminate.

The Devil's greatest weapon is the Lie, which, in his hands, takes on a multitude of shapes. One of the most frequent of these is hypocrisy, which consists of looking at the sins of others so as to exhibit and magnify them at leisure, while, at the same time, with despicable cynicism, hiding one's own.

As for the Tribulation that the Clergy suffers, but this time coming from within the Church herself, it is in a way more worrisome than the former, due in great part to the complexity of a problem which presents itself as particularly delicate and which, precisely because of this, deserves special treatment. What is unbelievable in this state of affairs is the inescapable conclusion that the responsibility for this occurrence must be attributed to the Hierarchy of the Church itself, which would have been unthinkable in former times.

In reaction to the Great Campaign unleashed throughout the World against the Church, this time aimed specifically at Priests concerning certain crimes committed by some of them, the Church Hierarchy in general, even among her Highest Officials, has undertaken severe measures against those guilty of such crimes. These measures have inevitably splashed on to the reputation of the Clergy in general and have damaged their credibility in the eyes of the faithful.

As a first consideration, it must be said that such measures are worthy of general applause. After all, it is the duty of the Church to look after the spiritual welfare of the faithful, as well as to keep watch on the virtuous behavior of her own Ministers by applying even the harshest sanctions when necessary. In the end, it is all about caretaking and zeal for the House of God, which the prophet Hosea and the Book of Psalms spoke about in words quoted by Saint John the Evangelist: *I am eaten up with zeal for your house.*[14] And that is precisely what the Church has always done.

However, the reactions that have taken place within the Church, due to the recent events already described, have raised doubts and have left several points in need of clarification.

It is evident that, concerning the grave reprimands and severe sanctions now being imposed, it would have been more reasonable to enforce them at the very moment that these crimes began to sprout. This was not done, despite the fact that they were soon made known to the Vatican itself, as the abundance of existing documents on this topic undoubtedly proves; see, for example, Philip F. Lawler's book.[15] He and his book enjoy great prestige in the United States. Lately, these same kinds of serious accusations have been raised against the Cardinal Primate of Argentina.

The fact that the Hierarchy did not proceed in this way could give rise to twisted interpretations, as anyone can understand. It will always be possible to think, for example, that the Church only decided to act once the Campaign against Her was unleashed; suggesting that she did so more with the intention of defending Herself and of removing doubts than with the intention of procuring the good of the faithful and the honorable conduct of her Priests. If she

---

[14] Jn 2:17.

[15] *The Faithful Departed*, Encounter Books, New York, 2008.

had acted accordingly at the right time, the Box of Thunder would not have been unleashed against the hapless culprits precisely at the very moment when all of society was accusing them; after having done nothing, or perhaps very little, to solve the problem in the first place.

Of course, it would be unjust to charge the Hierarchy with ill–will concerning this matter. We might always call upon circumstances that, although they may not be of use in justifying her failure to act, would explain however, in some way and for those who have no prejudice, the lack of an energetic and swift line of conduct that might perhaps have prevented things from getting any worse. Such circumstances might have included, for example, the desire to avoid the greater evil of a scandal among the faithful, the hope of a swift and discreet solution to the problem, etc.

However, it is not easy to completely do away with the idea that the Church behaved, first and foremost, with an inexplicable reluctance to act. Later, She allowed Herself to be carried away, once again, by Her inferiority complex and by feelings of dread in the face of the unleashed Campaign —something which seems to have become proverbial since long ago. If this is true, it would be logical to conclude that She herself had fallen into the trap and that She was aiding, though not purposely and surely without realizing it, the strategy of her enemies.

Such a belief would be confirmed by the undeniable fact that the Church, since the death of Pope Pius XII, has often been motivated in Her actions by fear as well as by an inferiority complex with respect to Modernity. Once more the *kneeling before the World*, of which Maritain spoke, was becoming reality. One can deny this, of course, if he so wishes; but the facts and the Documents remain and are too evident. We can cite, as examples of this attitude, the concessions made to Communism, even before the Second Vatican Council; the surrender made under pressure to German Progressive Theology during the celebration of said Council;[16] or the removal of the condemnation of Freemasonry, etc.

Nevertheless, and since the situation is far too serious, it is necessary to delve even further until some explanation which makes heads or tails of these events is found, as we will try to do in what follows.

In connection with this, the reflections we are going to expound could be useful to delve into the causes at the origin of such a deplorable situation —and mainly, and above all, *to distribute responsibility fairly.* For it does not seem in accordance with Justice to lay the entire burden of punishment on the shoulders of the weakest and most helpless (and, in some way, not only on the shoulders of the guilty, but on those of the entire Priestly State), while those in power try to elude the portion of guilt that, given their actions as well as their omissions concerning the crimes described, perhaps belongs to them.

We have said that one of the fronts in the present Campaign against the Priesthood, by reason of certain crimes of a sexual nature committed by some priests, has been opened within the Church herself by many of her members who have acted inadvertently and followed a conduct which cannot be branded as ill will. However, other members, some of whom even hold positions of great respon-

---

[16]See the famous book by Ralph M. Wiltgen, S.V.D., *The Rhine flows into the Tiber: A History of Vatican II*, Tan Books, Rockford, Illinois, 1985. The surrender to Progressive German —and also French— Theology was not merely the consequence of yielding to pressure. The liberal spirit of Popes John XXIII and Paul VI were decisive in this issue. This latter explanation could provide much more determinant reasons than those which resort to an existing inferiority complex.

sibility, have not acted similarly. To properly demonstrate this, and to achieve a better understanding of the problem, it may be worthwhile to establish some previous criteria.

Firstly, we must take into account that social events, especially when they have almost universal proportions as in the present case, neither rise by spontaneous generation nor are they abruptly produced. They need, in general, a certain breeding ground which in turn creates the environment where these actions take place. To which we must add certain preceding causes, more or less remote, which are the ones that, slowly but surely, make way for those actions to appear.

Secondly, it is noteworthy that, given the social and collective character of the actions we are referring to here, not to mention the considerable magnitude they have reached, in duration of time as well as in the variety of places in which these acts have been carried out (often in countries very distant from each other), it is logically impossible *to lay the burden of responsibility exclusively on the shoulders of those who committed these criminal acts.* The direct authors of such crimes generally represent, as in this case, a tiny minority within the whole of the Class that is being accused. This does not justify those who are truly guilty, inasmuch as they really are.

We must also take into account the possibility that some of those Responsible, those in Authority, may have contributed to the creation of an environment favorable to the proliferation of such crimes. If this is the case, we would have to consider, in all justice, their culpability with respect to certain actions or omissions that, directly or indirectly, would have paved the way for the commission of these criminal acts. Consequently, these Responsible people *would also be guilty, at least in some way, of the actions that now are being condemned.*

Therefore, and logically, in accord with what we have just said, the fact that they did not personally commit such crimes, or even that they did not shelter or hide those who did, *is not enough to clear them of responsibility.*

The alleged culpability will be more or less serious depending on the respective importance of the powers derived from the position that the officials hold. And one cannot consider, as an extenuating circumstance, the fact that these officials occupy High Positions — rather the opposite— in the case that some are found liable. Doing otherwise would mean laying the blame on the weakest; not to mention flaunting a behavior that could well be branded as hypocrisy.

Thirdly, we must never forget that it is the solemn duty and responsibility of parents, and, in general, of those entrusted with the care of others, to form, educate, and lovingly guard all those who, in one way or another, happen to be dependent on them or under their authority.

Parents, in the broad sense of the word, must resort to punishment, whenever necessary, as an instrument of correction and formation and also as a duty derived from Love. As the Book of Ecclesiasticus points out, *Whoever loves his son will beat him frequently;*[17] and this is further commended in the Letter to the Hebrews when, citing the Book of Proverbs, it says that *whom the Lord loves he chastises, and he scourges every son whom he receives.*[18] From this it follows, therefore —something worth taking into account, though forgotten by some Shepherds of the Church—, that punishment, aside from its punitive character, is above all an act

---

[17]Sir 30:1.

[18]Heb 12:6.

of healing motivated by Love. Dante himself understood this as he placed, on the doorway to Hell, the well–known inscription: *Primal Love made me.*[19]

As for the Church, she is a Society organized as a Monarchy, utterly different from a democracy, in which everything is perfectly hierarchical. The Mystical Body of Christ is constituted as a Great Family, in which the Pope is the Father on Earth, or its Visible Head, together with the rest of the Shepherds (in general and mainly the Bishops); to all of them has the *scrupulous and loving* guard of the children of Christ, the faithful, been entrusted (1 Pet 5:2).

But, just as in civil society, the parents are the primary ones *responsible* for the formation and education of their children: to their credit if they faithfully carry out their duty, or to their shame in the case that they were negligent; and so it happens in the Church. The conclusion is clear: if the children have chosen misguided paths, their parents —parents by blood or in the Faith— cannot be exempted from responsibility concerning the circumstances that motivated such a choice: *it is not in accordance with justice, in this case, to try to proclaim the complete innocence of those whose charge it was to look after the guilty ones and did not comply with it.*

These previous introductory considerations having been laid out, it behooves us to examine now, briefly and in an outline of several points, the situation with which the Low Clergy —the simple Priests— has had to cope ever since the Second Vatican Council. These priests, generally speaking, have lived in a situation of abandonment, alienation, and spiritual poverty. However, one last reflection remains to be expounded:

---

[19]It is true that punishment in Hell has a punitive character, but that punishment, given its condition of definitive and eternal state, has no medicinal purpose.

We are trying to highlight here the relevance of the fact, otherwise obvious, that the bulk of deplorable events which we have been speaking of have occurred, like a torrent, *since the Second Vatican Council.* The cases accounted for previously are so sporadic, so scarce in number, that they elude any attempt at statistical measurement. This should not be interpreted as an accusation against the Council, but as a circumstance that should be taken into account. Facts are better known when they are considered alongside the conditions under which they take place and the type of environment in which they thrive. As for the rest, the explanations which try to hide behind *random chance* and *mere coincidences* exceed the limits of the serious and deserve no credibility whatsoever.

We have said above that social acts are never caused by *spontaneous generation* or without warning. Generally speaking, they originate in a particular breeding ground where several circumstances come together. Once the required amount of time has passed, these circumstances will work in partnership to the birth and development of those social acts.

Unfortunately, however, it frequently happens that these circumstances and conditions are rarely taken into account. People depend to such an extent on the Publicity Machine of the System that they know only what is spoon–fed to them by the corresponding Propaganda Section, and nothing more.

To achieve this, the System manipulates the facts in order to present them at its own convenience. Applying itself enthusiastically in the use of the brain–washing method that it employs so well, the System carefully chooses the facts, trims them, magnifies or reduces them at its convenience, interprets them, hides them..., or simply lies about them with impudence whenever the occasion demands. In this sense, both the Press and the allied Publications, like Television and Radio Networks, have become giant laboratories of manipulation that strive, using all imaginable means —and sometimes even unimaginable ones— to suppress the effort it would take for people to think for themselves.

The procedures used for this operation are innumerable. One of them, for example, is to ensure that people will not be able to see an elephant located within the scope of their noses.

As an illustrative example of this, it is enough to call to mind the case of Ireland and the United States concerning the crimes we have been discussing.[20] A far greater number of these criminal acts —and with far more sinister characteristics— have been committed in the United States than in Ireland. Nevertheless, no one seems to have noticed the fact that the Chest of Thunder —in the shape of severe reprimands and forced resignations— was opened only on Ireland, not on the United States.

---

[20]We are referring, of course, to the wave of pederasty that arose among the clergy.

About the situation of moral and social wretchedness suffered by Priests since the Second Vatican Council.

a) The Promotion of the Laity

Another circumstance about which nothing has been said, and which seems to have gone unnoticed, is the situation of abandonment, deterioration, and social contempt that has befallen the Priests since the Second Vatican Council.

Of course, various circumstances coincided here, which we are going to enumerate and try to explain briefly. And one of them is precisely what was then called *Promotion of the Laity*.

From the first moments of the Council, progressive Theology and the majority of the *media* orchestrated by it have, time and again, persistently broadcasted the idea that this was a Council dedicated to the Bishops and to the highlighting of the importance of their role, and also to consider the condition that corresponds to the Laity in the Church.

The latter, according to said Theology, had until now been subdued, oppressed, and despised by the Clergy; therefore, it was necessary to *put them in their rightful place*, by raising their condition.

Therefore, once it was discovered that during *twenty centuries* (¡?) lay people had been overlooked, lorded over, and kept out of their place, it was urgently necessary to reestablish their dignity with respect to the Clergy.

This is, in effect, what happened. Although, unfortunately, in the only way it could have happened, namely: Socialist style. This means, in general terms, that it was not so much about raising those up who were on a lower level, but about *dragging down those who were higher up*. But, things are as they are, and no other way. In reality, it was not possible to endow the Laity with powers which the Church could not grant, unless the purpose was to destroy their very condition and charism as lay members. The Laity can in no way be part of the Hierarchy, since it would mean violating the divine constitution of the Church. Besides, the lay members, with their markedly specific function, already enjoy their own *status* and charism within the Church, acquired through the sacraments of Baptism and Confirmation.

Instead, according to new ideological currents, they were given duties and functions that, in reality, ended up by turning them into a sort of hybrid species: distributing the Eucharist; reciting the Readings in the Liturgy of the Word; preaching (as the liturgy of the Neo–catechumenal Way has it established); being Ministers for a multitude of more or less odd ecclesiastical jobs...; and the most important of all those functions: they were given the authority and the capacity to decide on the organization of the parishes.

What happened then, in short, was that, setting aside their duties as mothers and fathers of a family and forgetting their important mission of sanctifying their jobs and professional tasks in the midst of the world, lay members were essentially turned into *sacristans*; they ended up being neither priests nor laity.

Since, whether we like it or not, the state of *being a sacristan* meant neither an elevation in rank nor a place of honor for the mere faithful (with the exception of the Charismatic Groups and, especially, the Neo–catechumenal Communities where the lay people have reached a rank higher than that of the Priests), the only thing strengthened was their position as administrators of the parishes. Other contributing factors were the winds of *democracy* and the crisis of authority, already rampant throughout the Church. Thus, countless Parish Committees came to life: Liturgy Committee, Pastoral Committee, Youth Committee, Committee for the Outcast,

Parish Finance Committee, etc., etc., all of them run and directed by the Laity. The Priest was reduced to a mere *official*, with a fixed salary (the amount of which being determined by the Finance Committee), and often a low one.

Meanwhile, and as a consequence of all this, Priests were seeing themselves locked away in the attic, as their role became less and less necessary. Today, as it occurs, for example, in the United States, if a *Pastor* wants to change the tiles in his bathroom or modify the Mass schedule, he cannot do so without the authorization of the Finance Committee or of the Pastoral and Liturgy Committees respectively.

The recitation of instances could continue if we had space for it. Some people might argue, with reason, in reference to Finance, the case of *some* priests who misused the Parish funds. Here we arrive at the same problem as always: Is it right to develop, from isolated cases, a general rule that will affect the entire State? Anyway, since money–related topics are not the most important thing (except when it means a loss of authority for the *Pastor)*, there is still a leading question to be asked: Might not these circumstances, as well as others of similar nature (and which no one has lifted a finger to correct), have contributed to a decrease in the esteem that Priests must have of themselves and in their enthusiasm for their own vocation? Notice how we are not talking here about *justifying*, but about circumstances that may have *influenced* the stirring of a general contempt toward the Priesthood as such. Perhaps that is why the Priest has seen himself abandoned, despised, and doomed by a sad situation that has, truth be told, ended up hurting the entire Church. In such circumstances, a more caring and paternal intervention on behalf of the Hierarchy would have been undoubtedly more desirable.

b) The Identity Crisis

It is evident that the Priests who have committed the crimes we have been discussing are *directly* responsible for such actions. But it is equally obvious that those upon whom some of the burden of responsibility may fall because of their contribution to the creation of a situation that could give rise to these actions are also a guilty party, at least *indirectly*.

On the other hand, few things can happen to a person worse than *losing his own identity*. When someone finds himself in a situation in which he is no longer capable of knowing who he is or what his role in society is (since here even the mere possibility of having any role is called into question); and if, on top of this, that person is subject to general contempt, the level of despair and discouragement to which such a person may descend can perhaps be *understood*, although never *justified*.

The *Priestly Identity Crisis* had already begun before the Second Vatican Council, though it was during its occurrence, and more still in the times that followed, that it reached its highest point. The phenomenon was an intelligent and very well–executed product of Progressive Theology, but completely lacking in solid arguments and with the clear purpose of eliminating the Priesthood. All this happened despite the fact that, during the twenty centuries since its institution by Jesus Christ, the Priesthood had enjoyed both content and a meaning as clear as they were glorious. Never, in all this time, had there been the slightest hint of doubt or hesitation, in this regard, from anyone.

However, the operation was well devised and wisely planned. The idea was to fire a large–calibre torpedo on the Boat of Peter; this torpedo was accurately designed to hit the waterline, bombarding in its blast each and every tier of the Hierarchy of the Church: the Pope, the Bishops, and the humble Priests.

As for the Bishops, the proclamations about the Second Vatican Council enhancing their roles within the Church have been reduced, apparently at least, to wishful thinking; they became effective only to the extent that they supported *conciliarism*, with the clear intention of undermining the authority of the Pope. The *Conferences of Bishops*, among other institutions begotten by this Council, frequently became magnificent instruments for controlling the activities of the successors of the Apostles, once the ease with which they could be manipulated by clever Pressure Groups was proven. Progressive Theology did not seem to care much about the fact that the Bishops' Authority is based, ultimately, on the very divine constitution of the Church.

The aforementioned Theology did not conceal its intentions regarding the Pope. Inspired by the postulates of the heresy of *conciliarism*, and well endorsed by the spirit of *democracy* that now rules the world, Progressive Theology has always sought to undermine Papal Authority and destroy its prerogatives. Also with respect to this topic, its influence has not been small, as is proven by the fact that the Supreme Pontiff himself, Benedict XVI, announced his intention of never making important decisions which will affect the Church without first consulting the Synod of Bishops. As if this were not enough, practically no one has noticed the blanket of silence that someone has taken care to spread over the First Vatican Council. This Council had solemnly reaffirmed the basic functions of the Pope concerning the Church; however, in our present times, it has passed on to History... and into the canyon of oblivion.

The figure of the Pope, at least since John XXIII, has not posed much of a problem. In our day, Benedict XVI, well known as the kind Pope, with a spirit open to all and determined to follow in the footsteps of his predecessor, John Paul II, has never appeared as a supporter of sharp and repressive decisions against liturgical abuses or doctrinal deviations. His liberal attitude and his *outstretched-hand* policy towards everyone, as well as his willingness to respectfully accept whatever measure of value all religions contain, have always appeased the System and have definitively disavowed him as an enemy to be feared.

As for the Bishops, the very fact that they belong, almost entirely, to any of the multiple Committees within the Conference of Bishops, with the consequent need to assist the corresponding reunions, assemblies, conferences, etc., not to mention their recurrent trips to Rome, frequently keeps all of them out of their Diocese and a bit removed from the problems of the faithful.[21] Also, the winds of *moderation and reconciliation* that at this moment are raging throughout the Church seem to have induced them to adopt an attitude of prudent silence, while modern Society, as well as its Governments, has decided to take a plunge into the abyss. Because of all this, they pose no threat to the System.

There remained, however, one last line of defense, surely the most perilous for the Anti–Church Operation: the State of Priests. Always in direct contact with the people and forming a single body with them, the Priests would be precisely the field where the key battle was to be fought. Thus it was understood, very artfully, by the enemies of the Church.

That is why the System, once it had studied its strategy well, began launching its fierce offensive against the Priesthood, taking advantage of a series of favorable circumstances. One of these, for

---

[21]Someone once said that God decided to punish those Bishops and Priests who lack interior life with abundant *meetings*.

example, has been precisely the feeble formation of the Low Clergy (in reality, not much inferior to that of the High Clergy), which is what has knocked priests down and left them with little space to maneuver and defend themselves. Since, as we have been saying, the attack has come simultaneously from two fronts (from without and from within the Church herself, by way of the collaboration given by some insiders), the detailed description of the fight (which began by provoking an artificial identity crisis with the objective of instilling despair) has become a complicated task in need of prolix explanations.

Neo–Modernism's Great Assault upon the Priestly State began with a direct hit to one of its more neuralgic points: This Campaign openly locked on to its target by denying, and not merely questioning, the extraordinary condition of the Priest, *the unique character of his Priestly identity.*

In the midst of an ocean of phraseologies and verbosity, both pseudo–cultured and pseudo–theological, a hurricane of innumerable essays, theological texts and books, newspaper articles, and various publications —in turn echoed by the teachings imparted by almost all of the Faculties and Schools of Catholic Theology— was unleashed upon the entire Church. Every single one of them coincided on the same topic: Does the Priest still mean anything in the Church and the World of today? And the answer to this, often hidden among preambles, digressions, and red tape, though sometimes declared in a shameless fashion, was always the same: practically, *No, nothing at all.*

Murmuring and calumny are among the more abominable activities in which we humans take part, though perhaps they are not as bad as *denying someone his own identity or deliberately refusing to acknowledge his existence.*

Whatever the case, the most important step in the process of discrediting the Clergy had already been taken —though it was only the first in a long series which made up a group of schemes that have lately waxed in strength and influence.

The *Promotion of the Laity* was a powerful weapon used to disavow the Priestly State. The Second Vatican Council, as it was proclaimed from the rooftops, was responsible for the *discovery* of the important role that the Laity had to perform within the Church. These were the very members, as everyone ascertained, that had until then been overshadowed and dominated by the Clergy. The role granted to the Laity has since grown to heights the likes of which it had never before seen, but which implied, too often, disdain for a Priesthood that has now been reduced to the condition of a practically useless object.

One must admit that it is difficult to learn whether the stupidity of human nature has the ability to surpass its capacity for malice.

Clerical bookstores —and also a not–so–small number of commercial bookstores— began to find themselves stuffed with books like *Laity on the Go, The Hour of the Laity, The Lay Member in the Church,* etc., and the list goes on and on. Everything led to the belief that the Church had lived for twenty centuries ignoring the laity, and perhaps even without knowing it...; but the time had finally come in which they were discovered. The result of this, as a logical consequence of the produced environment, materialized in the fact that many Priests felt ashamed of their condition. They started by trying to not differentiate themselves from the laity in terms of their forms of behavior and by replacing their clerical garment with fashionable attire, reaching the level of the ridiculous in many cases (the image of the seventy–year–old priest dressed like a fifteen–year–old became a trend).

In this way, like a snake biting its own tail, the discrediting of the Priestly State contributed to increasing the sense of discouragement, disillusionment, and frustration in many Priests. These feelings, reciprocally in their turn, augmented the lack of prestige for the Priestly State.

Meanwhile the System, ultimately using Progressive Theology as its instrument, fortified its positions and secured its victory. At the same time, the Clergy was feeling more and more abandoned and even less esteemed by the whole of the faithful.

Another factor, this time unexpected, also contributed to the success of the Great Offensive. The restoration of the *Permanent Deaconate* and the excessive proliferation of such Ministers (many of them married men) were responsible for making the people feel less affected by the need for Priests, thus undermining their functions. Meanwhile, Permanent Deacons were slowly pushing aside the Priests to the point of making them seem more and more superfluous. In some countries, like the United States for instance, Permanent Deacons have practically taken over almost complete control of the preaching duties.

Things being as they were, two important factors arose in the midst of the crisis which profoundly influenced the development of events and which even today are difficult to explain.

The first of these refers to the fact that a large number of Priests did actually fall into the trap so cleverly laid for them by the System. Aside from the discouragement to which they succumbed, they eventually came to doubt their own identity, as well as their fundamental importance within the Church. The explanation of this circumstance would be too complex for our purposes and would require a thick volume.

The second factor turned out to be more decisive. In the face of such an arduous and appalling situation, *a categorical and clear intervention from the Magisterium of the Church, which no doubt would have brought the crisis to its end, was lacking.* As for our present times, in which the Great Offensive rages with incredible intensity, it would be desirable that the Hierarchy (which is supposed to procure defense and protection for the Priestly State) break its silence on this issue.[22]

After contemplating such things, can anyone be surprised that such breeding grounds have aided in the growth and development of germs that, in such a forceful and effective way, strive by any means possible to attack the Priestly State, leaving it unarmed and abandoned to the onslaughts (to which the *media* of the Western World have cruelly joined themselves) of the many dangers that engulf it?

It still remains for us to expose the most serious and delicate point of this deplorable situation: The doctrinal and disciplinary chaos that, within the ecclesiastical sphere, is resolutely contributing to the festering of this problem.

c) Doctrinal Confusion and Disciplinary Chaos

The first thing that an Army needs to be confident in victory is high Morale. This, in turn, must be founded on the existence of solid principles that can be firmly believed and on the trust in the Chain of Command. An Army lacking these elements would be a *de–moralized* Army, and its defeat would be secured beforehand.

However, since the times of the occurrence of the Second Vatican Council, the humble clergy *foot soldiers* have been deprived of such

---

[22]The reader must always take into account the date this book was published.

principles. Or to say it in more direct terms, such principles were stripped from them. No one can wonder, therefore, at the great desertion that has taken place since then, nor at the hardships and sufferings that the Priestly Estate is being forced to bear at these very moments: mainly, the basis of the problems that have arisen and their exploitation at the hands of the enemies of the Church to fight its Hierarchy, most particularly the humble Priests.

It is evident that *doctrinal confusion* has been a very influential factor in the appearance of this crisis.

Nobody can deny that the Second Vatican Council was a genuine revolution —and even, according to some, an *involution*— within the life of the Church, affecting the Clergy above all. The set of factors that came together was the cause of a general discouragement which, more often than not, ended in disappointment and bitterness. These social facts *are there*, for all to see and, therefore, impossible to deny. The key player was, without doubt, the *revolution of ideas*, which seemed to give rise to a *New Church*, quite different from the previous one.

Here we can make but a brief and summarized enumeration of the facts that have caused what has happened in the Church. Therefore, the following list is far from exhaustive; it is merely descriptive and serves as a support for what we are discussing here. The list is not in form a justification of certain crimes either, as we have said so insistently. It only attempts to draw attention to the environment, deliberately created by some, which, in the end, both advanced and fostered the appearance of these acts that all of us regret today.

We must also remember that the Clergy is being accused globally of acts committed by a tiny minority that has hardly any weight with respect to the whole; and that all of this is happening, besides, in the midst of a grotesque display of hypocrisy flaunted by a World that not only commits these crimes, as well as others far worse and with far greater profusion, but which is also the very one that promotes and encourages them. We have spoken about this before.

One of the most delicate problems on this short list that we will enumerate —probably the most important of all of them— is that which refers to the deep chasm that was opened between the Magisterium and Church Doctrine before the Second Vatican Council, on one side, and the Magisterium and *New Theology* that now try to impose themselves, on the other.

This schism even engulfs Dogmatic Doctrine, as well as other teachings obviously also important. Some of these, for example, are the doctrines referring to Salvation and Justification, to the Church and Her Marks (Unity, Evangelizing Mission, etc.), to the significance of the Eucharist and the meaning of the Real Presence, to Religious Freedom, to the importance of the Magisterium, to Papal Authority, to the role and value of the Catholic Priesthood, etc. All of these *now received meanings which were at variance, and very often even contrary, to the ones they had always had.*

This transcendental issue has been, and continues to be, a cause of great confusion for many people, above all in terms of Faith and trust in the Church as well as in the Teachings of the Magisterium. *Apropos* of this, it is necessary to clarify that, in reality, there is no reason for anyone to feel confused. We have very clear criteria for discernment on our side, more than enough, in any case, that dissipate any trace of uncertainty when they are applied. Though, it would also be fair to add that not many people are aware of them.

The Sacrificial value of the Mass was deeply distorted, while its significance as a *fraternal meal* or as a *merely commemorative act* was disproportionately stressed. The distribution and the handling of the Eucharist turned into a task that could be carried out by anyone —a veritable *self–service* or *house delivery*, always in the hands of lay members—, thereby weakening, to the extreme, Faith in so sublime a Sacrament; a logical consequence totally explicable to anybody who knows human nature.

The recognition of the validity of all religions in terms of salvation, which annihilated the concept of the Church as *One*, as well as the age–old axiom that *outside the Church there is no salvation*, killed the Faith of a great number of Catholics and weakened that of many others. This gave rise to the celebration of the famous *Assisi Gatherings*, in which all religions were endowed with a character of equality and in which idols were enthroned even upon the Altar of the *Poverello of Assisi*. All this caused a faltering of Faith in the weaker souls.

For the clergy especially, this last blow was just too much. If all religions had to be considered as having the same validity in the order of salvation, the consequence was obvious: The Catholic Priest, at best, was no different from the *ministers* of Protestantism, Judaism, Islam, Buddhism, Brahmanism... or even the Shamans and Voodoo Witch–doctors.

Undoubtedly, he would be right who thinks that this is no reason for Priests to falter in their Faith or to renounce their own Priesthood; but that person must understand, at least, that this is a low blow received by the Priestly Estate. Besides, one must not forget the always admitted benefit of, at least once in a while, putting ourselves in the shoes of the ones we are judging.

Among the theological novelties introduced by Pope John Paul II, some of them materialized, after passing through the Second Vatican Council, in the New Code of Canon Law, which gave way to, among other things, a change of consideration about the primary end of marriage. This end would no longer be the procreation and education of children, as it was established from the beginning and has always been recognized by the Church since Christ elevated marriage to the rank of Sacrament; the primary end now ranked equally with the mutual expression of love between the conjugates. Consequently, the door was opened to sequester the duty of procreation to a secondary place.

The result, however, was that such a small detail, apparently of little importance, led to something so fundamental as the *admittance, de facto, of divorce by the Church.* For obvious reasons, of course, it would not be called divorce, but simply an *annulment of the bond*; mainly because the indissolubility of Christian marriage is of Divine Law, just as the Church has always proclaimed it.

Whoever ponders these facts —which, on the other hand, are no more than a quick outline of events— with serenity and without prejudice will realize that they created within the Church an atmosphere of *instability*, profound weakness, and even a loss of Faith or a loss of trust in Her on the part of many faithful: an atmosphere certainly favorable to the disappearance of many good things and to the sprouting of many other bad things. And though it is true that there is no cause that can justify the loss of Faith —which is always apostasy—, or the crushing underfoot of the Priesthood, we must also take into account the normal weakness of human nature. Understanding is not justification.

Moreover, would it be unjust to think that those who, by their actions or omissions to a greater or lesser degree, provided the occasion for such an environment to thrive are also in some way responsible for the evils that the Church is suffering at this time?

We still have to examine, though briefly, some of the consequences derived from the disciplinary chaos that currently ravages the Church.

As we have said previously, in connection with the problem upon which the enemies of the Church lean to feed their campaign against Her and especially against the Clergy as Her most sensitive and important element, the creation of an atmosphere of chaos has been allowed, even within the Church herself, which, although it does not justify the above–mentioned behaviors, certainly has to be recognized as a medium that has contributed to their occurrence. The truth is that the simple Clergy, besieged by the World and by many who are part of the Church herself, has been in a state of wretchedness and neglect which is truly disheartening.

Of course, to better understand the situation that has been created within the Church and that is causing so much suffering to the real Faithful, we should now make a summary of the tremendous *chaos of discipline* that, although being originated in the times of the Council, lives on in our time and is now reaching its highest point.

The list of details about this subject, even summarized —and omitting, out of prudence, the most serious issues—, would undoubtedly be chilling.

However, would it be worth it to describe them...? Perhaps we would be contributing to further weakening the Faith of the hesitant and increasing, in contrast, the bitterness of the faithful Catholics. It seems better, therefore, to launch a strong call to Hope and to stress the need —now more urgent than ever— for Holiness.

Surely, nothing better to do so than to return to the words of the Apostle Saint Peter, with which we started this dissertation and which we can now transcribe more amply. The Prince of the Apostles begins by recognizing the seriousness of the situation and finishes by exhorting Christians with words highly comforting and full of hope. It is worthwhile to read them slowly and carefully, for they explain in an immensely better way what we have tried to expound:

Dearly beloved, do not be startled at the trial by fire that is taking place among you to prove you, as if something strange were happening to you; but rejoice, in so far as you are partakers of the sufferings of Christ, that you may also rejoice with exultation in the revelation of his glory. If you are upbraided for the name of Christ, blessed will you be, because the honor, the glory and the power of God and his Spirit rests upon you. Let none of you suffer as a murderer, or a thief, or a slanderer, or as one coveting what belongs to others. But if he suffer as a Christian, let him not be ashamed, but let him glorify God under this name. For the time has come for the judgment to begin with the household of God; but if it begin first with us, what will be the end of those who do not believe the gospel of God?[23]

His words are quite expressive and his message is worthy of all our attention. Yet what he writes in another place of the same *Letter* is still more eloquent; it even seems to have been written precisely for the current situation and thinking of the times that we are experiencing:

And who is there to harm you, if you are zealous for what is good? But even if you suffer anything for justice' sake, blessed are you. So have no dread of them and do not be troubled. But hallow the Lord Christ in your hearts. Be ready always with an answer to everyone who asks a reason for the hope that is in you. Yet do so with gentleness and fear, having a good conscience, so that wherein they speak in disparagement of you they who revile your good behavior

---

[23] 1 Pet 4: 12–17.

in Christ may be put to shame. For it is better, if the will of God should so will, that you suffer for doing good than for doing evil.[24]

Precisely because the Church is going through the greatest crisis in Her History, there is an urgent need for true Catholics to live on Hope in God, Who is caring for His Church and will not allow the Gates of Hell to prevail (Mt 16:18). And since it has been the Saints —and only they— who have always brought the Church out of her difficult situations, we can expect with all certainty *that their hour has come again*; and we are not referring here to the saints *on sale*, but to the traditional Saints, the true ones. Moreover, now that the World denigrates the Priesthood, God is taking good pleasure in promoting Priests who are indeed *other Christs*, in numbers greater than ever. In addition, at this present time of disobedience and dispersal, it is absolutely necessary that Catholics remain *faithful and united to the hierarchy*; which, although not always so zealous in its mission, it is, however, the real Hierarchy and the only one that God has instituted. And finally, since it seems that the hour of disbelief has come, it is therefore necessary to recall the promising and encouraging cry of the Apostle Saint John: *This is the victory that overcomes the World: our Faith.*[25]

---

[24] 1 Pet 3: 13–17.

[25] 1 Jn 5:4.

THREE POSITIONS FACING THE CRISIS

Members of the Catholic Church can take one of three Positions in response to the crisis afflicting Her today, a crisis which may be the most profound in all Her history. Two of these postures are very easily adopted, but the third entails a host of difficulties and not a few problems for those who dare to assume it. We will refer to these here, for simplicity's sake, as *Positions A*, *B*, and *C*.

Position A is easy to understand and relatively simple to take up. Proponents of this position are Catholics who think that there are a number of Christian principles and Magisterial teachings which are immutable and untouchable. They believe that the present Hierarchy of the Church has forgotten, hidden, or falsified those principles and teachings and that, by doing so, it has chosen to act directly against the Faith. These premises established, and confronted with the impossibility of ever reaching an accord, supporters of Position A have chosen to sever the ties that once united them to the Hierarchy. Although rooted in a desire to maintain Christian principles, this behavior is schismatic according to Canon Law.

In all honesty, we must acknowledge the earnestness of this Position, for it seems that most of what it defends is true. Surely, one also ought to praise the sincerity and integrity of those who follow it, assuming, of course, their best intentions.

However, this Position, to my understanding, has an important shortcoming which directly concerns one of the principles that it allegedly defends: the need to maintain one's fidelity and submission to the legitimate Hierarchy, no matter how inoperative or mundane that Hierarchy may seem, at best, or even how corrupt it is, at worst. The truth is that a faithful Catholic can never abandon this fundamental principle: *nothing without the bishop, nothing without the Church.* Besides, corruption in the Hierarchy, even at its Highest Levels, is not foreign to the difficult history of the Church; but, even then, the true faithful have never before felt justified in breaking away from her: *Where Peter is, there the Church is present.*

The problem is profound and delicate, befitting the difficult times in which we live. Submitting to a mundane Hierarchy with questionable faithfulness to the sound Tradition and principles of the true Faith seems to be one of the trials which the Lord will permit His disciples to suffer and which will only worsen as the final times approach (cf. Mt 24:21). Since participation in the sufferings of the Lord has always been a characteristic of the truly faithful, it will surely become more so at the time of the final confrontation. True disciples do not forget that participation in the Cross of Our Lord, because it has to be carried on tired shoulders and contemplated by tearful eyes, is truly glorious and a foretaste of the final Crown.

Position B is easy to understand and easier still to follow. Its proponents firmly maintain fidelity to the Hierarchy, even at times when such a determination seems to be a bit unwarranted. Widespread ignorance among the faithful as to the true degree of submission due to the Magisterium and the Hierarchy permits certain ideologues and pressure groups to take advantage of the situation.

The defenders of this Position adamantly support whatever the Pope says, speaks of, thinks, or does, while momentarily or indefinitely putting into brackets (but never denying) fidelity to the intangible principles, including dogmas. This is done without paying much attention to the true content, significance, and limitations of obedience to the Magisterium. Even less do they feel the need to differentiate among Ordinary Magisterium, Solemn Magisterium, and speeches or opinions given here and there, formally or informally, by various members of the Hierarchy. Moreover, the necessity of integrating everything that is said currently with what has been said by the preceding Magisterium never crosses their minds, for they usually do not realize that the Magisterium cannot contradict itself. Summing it all up, as strange as it may seem: for the proponents of *Position B*, everything the Pope says, regardless of its content, is a *dogma of Faith*; and any disagreement whatsoever is considered as infidelity to the Church.

One must acknowledge that *Position B* is the most circumspect of the three Positions. It implies leaving both the principles and their interpretation solely in the hands of the Hierarchy (but can one be certain that it is the legitimate Hierarchy?) and following the Hierarchy faithfully and blindly; thus fidelity is guaranteed and all problems are solved. On another note, adhesion to this Position is absolutely necessary for those who aspire to any position within the Church which would otherwise be unattainable: *If a man desire the office of bishop, he desires a noble task;*[1] and they will most likely achieve their goals —which would have been unthinkable had they not subscribed to this Position.

The most difficult Position to understand and the hardest to put into practice is *Position C*. And since this position is a sort of Cinderella figure in this somewhat unique contest (although without a Prince in love or a happy ending), some may think that it is not even worth talking about, and they may not be wrong. What can be assured in advance is that this attitude is doomed to be despised and even abhorred by all. *Positions A* and *B* agree to condemn

---

[1] 1 Tim 3:1.

it (as Herod and Pilate did); therefore, its followers will always be few, yet worthy of the title of Hero, whether acknowledged as such or not.

The followers of *Position C* are convinced that they cannot ignore the unalterable evangelical principles or abandon their steadfast stance of submission to the legitimate Hierarchy of the Church; which, given the existing circumstances in the Church, places them in an extremely unstable and quite delicate balance. On the one hand, the followers of *Position A* usually single them out as miserable traitors sold to the System; on the other hand, their great effort to maintain their fidelity to the true Faith will never be acknowledged by those who adhere to *Position B*, who will unceasingly accuse the former of being rebellious and ultra traditional, notwithstanding their constant and heroic obedience.

Those who subscribe to *Position C* know well that they have been doomed *a priori* to be ignored by the Church; they are sure that no responsibility or prebend will be conferred upon them... not that they ever wanted them; perhaps because they think that the authentic and merited conferral of ranks and distribution of rewards will not take place until He Who shall give to each one according to his works comes again (Rev 22:12).

Despised and abandoned by all as they are, the followers of *Position C* feel that their own madness, which they regard as divine, leads them to consider their situation as a crest of glory, even as a guarantee of their participation in the sufferings of Our Lord. Because they know that they are destined to be scorned and to remain in total anonymity, they hope in all certitude to find in that scorn and anonymity a veritable foretaste of the happiness of Heaven; after all, they are convinced that the well–known saying will always be true: *One can apply to men what is said about nations: happy are those which have no history behind them.*

Curiously enough, however, there is a rather peculiar and unique Fourth Position: that of the *Chinese Patriotic Catholic Association* (CPCA) which is entirely submissive to the Chinese Communist State and completely separated from communion with Rome. In this sense, as one can easily notice, this Position participates simultaneously in both above–mentioned *Positions A* and *B*. Nevertheless, as strange as it may seem, this group enjoys the understanding and kindness of high–ranking Vatican Officials —in contrast to what happens with the *underground* Catholic Church in that same country, which has not received comparable gestures of understanding and encouragement from the Vatican, in spite of having remained faithful to Rome in the face of the persecutions she has undergone at the hands of the Communist Authorities. Similarly, while a whole hoard of anathemas has been emptied out upon the unfortunate supporters of the late Archbishop Lefebvre, it has not been so, by any measure, with the *Chinese Patriotic Catholic Association*. As for the reasons that may have justified such difference in treatment, they remain, so far, unknown to the common faithful.

THE DEVIL PRAYS MATINS

It was early morning in the convent when the shrill and persistent peal of a bell was heard, resounding through the hallways and piercing the doors of the cells. In religious houses where all live in community, bells almost always toll to remind people to fulfill some obligation: when it is time to wake and begin the day, or to gather in the choir loft to pray, or to keep silence, or to signal the end of recreational activities...; seldom does it ring for more pleasant things, like gathering in the refectory, for instance. The friars had often complained to Brother Agapito, the bell ringer, alleging that his ringing of bells was too strong and long–lasting; due, some friars claimed, to his excessive zeal, or, most probably, according to others, to take a sort of tiny and harmless attitude of revenge on his brethren: after all, he had to be the first one to get out of bed each morning. Some of his brethren even said, with a light touch of sly humor, that Father Abbot had chosen Brother Agapito[1] for this office of cymbal clanging because of his name. Indeed, there is no reason for convents to be devoid of humor, not even those where talking is not allowed.

The friars began to rise from their beds and, shortly after, they left their cells. They walked along the corridor leading to the chapel, treading with slow and still insecure steps that betrayed a lingering sleep reluctant to disappear. Finally, after a few minutes, with their

---

[1]In Spanish, "Agapito" literally could mean "the one who uses the whistle." (N. of T.).

usual order and identical, everyday routine, they began to occupy their seats and open their books. The singing of Matins was about to begin. Some half–stifled yawns and one or two coughs could be heard lost in the crowd.

That was when, suddenly, Brother Peter felt overcome by a shiver. Peter was a lay brother, and the reforms introduced by the Second Vatican Council did not succeed in advancing his position. According to some of his brethren, this was because he was too humble and had persistently asked to be left in the same condition in which he had decided to live at the beginning of his vocation. According to others, it was because he belonged to the extinct species of those who were not convinced of the opportunity of some of the conciliar doctrines; particularly by those which dealt with the suppression of rank in the convents or by those which tried to avoid placing too much emphasis on the role of authority. Be that as it may, this problem did not seem to deprive our good Brother of his sleep; for indeed —as was easy to see— he had not yet been able to get rid of it. Therefore, he hurried, with some unsteady steps, to occupy his seat, as usual, at the back of the chapel, very close to the rear of the choir loft. And here is where our story begins.

Brother Peter heard a squeak and quickly realized that the back door, which was hardly ever used, was beginning to open slowly. At that moment, a strange jolt ran down his spine, even before his eyes could perceive anything. Finally, not without some fear, he decided to turn his head and look behind him.

In effect..., for, at that moment, an individual entered through the small door —but, was he really an individual?— whom he had never seen or even imagined before. It would be useless to try to describe either his looks or the sensation which his appearance caused in our unfortunate Brother. Given the unmistakable aspect of the creature, Brother Peter immediately thought that he could be the Devil. Yet he was wearing the same habit as the friars, as if he were one of them, but underneath the hood a face could be distinguished which could give rise to distressing feelings and could have caused the flight of our friar had his legs allowed him to move. As for trying to describe what little was perceived under that hooded face, undoubtedly the best thing to do was to give up the attempt. But his fear was not enough to prevent Brother Peter from feeling sure of what he saw, for *that* which he had before his eyes undoubtedly was Satan.

Our unfortunate Brother Peter tried to stifle a cry which he could hardly hold back:

—But you...? Are you... Satan...?

—Do not be afraid. I have no intention of harming you —the Devil assured him trying to calm him down.

And Brother Peter:

—But, what about the other friars...?

—Don't you worry, dwarf —answered Satan, in whose resounding voice, despite everything, one could make out an attempt to calm him.

—No one can see me. And even if they did, they would sooner think me to be a ghost rather than believe that it is me. Remember that in the *New Church* neither Hell nor I exist. It is astonishing what imbeciles you humans are...! Imagine, even I am surprised at the incredible stories and nonsense you are able to admit as if they were the most normal things in the world. And that happens when you turn your back on truth and stop believing in the reality of things. For example, and to clear up your obtuse mind just a bit: when you claim to believe —or so you say, for sometimes even I do not understand you— in human dignity and human rights while you do without the One On High; or that you believe in a new unsubstantial *Universal Religion* once that even more unsubstantial *New Age* of which you speak is implemented; or that you believe in a universal peace and solidarity that have been attained by your own means; or that you believe in *Ecumenical Dialogue*... What wonderful concoctions you are able to imagine, my puny friar! Inventions which, as far as I am concerned, are bringing a lot of clients to me. Or that you believe in a new theology with a *wider and less narrow vision* —that is the term used, isn't it?—, which also is providing me with an abundant harvest. But the best yet is your belief in that mysterious *spirit of the Council,* which no one knows what it is but which grants a legal *carte blanche* to do anything; not even I, with all my skills, would be able to find an adequate reward for its intelligent inventor...

—Well, you know... —the Devil went on, showing abundant signs of complacency.

—Now, you say, the One On High condemns no one, for He wants only the salvation of everyone: Completely free and with no effort involved! What a bargain, my boy...! Fortunately, it is a lie, my sinister friar; it seems as if those who believe this were intent on leaving me no other option but an early retirement. Happily for me, all the idiots of this world came to believe it, or perhaps they only pretend that they do, for not even I myself am able to understand such a dim–witted credulity —to the point that I even sometimes think that they are deceiving me. Me! The Father of Lies and of all liars...! You cannot imagine, my puny friar, how twisted the brains of some people are out there. It does worry me; I almost believe that, before I know it, they will surpass me!

The Devil paused for a moment and soon went on:

—Well, to be honest —damn it! How much I hate to have to tell the truth, even once!— I know very well that those fools do not believe this story of universal salvation. They do not believe it for the simple reason that they *do not believe in anything*; except in themselves, of course, and in that thing, that *Universal Religion* of all Mankind, which they so foolishly claim to be their own creation when, in reality, it is simply another invention of mine. Indeed they have exceeded my expectations about how far human stupidity could go; they even think that everything will work perfectly when their golden age appears. And they are quite right there because, in due time, they will have ample opportunities to see how well the installations I have prepared for them work.

And here the Devil uttered a hoarse laugh, which seemed a jolt to Brother Peter, before stopping a bit to take a breath and to continue immediately.

—You, on the other hand, could not bring yourself to believe their nonsense. Perhaps because of the very fact that you are stupid; or, more likely —I hate to admit it—, because you never thought yourself to be a smart person. Ah, how much I would love —If only I could love, which is why I actually hate them more— those who think themselves to be clever...! They tend to increase my clients in numbers that you would not believe. Besides, you are afraid of me; and for that I respect you. As you can imagine, I do not bother to dialogue with fools who deny my existence; although I must admit that they please me and flatter me, for it is always wonderful to see the hordes of disciples who follow me, very excited about listening to lies which are also so much to their liking. That is why they count only on my mug, which is the only thing I can show them, for I am not able to experience any friendliness.

Brother Peter started to regain his breath.

—But then, why have you come here...

The Devil answered almost immediately, not without repressing a grimace that perhaps was meant to be something like a smile.

—Peter, you too ask foolish questions...? Well, let us see, why does one come to the choir...? To pray, of course, you idiot.

Brother Peter was feeling more and more amazed by the moment:

—but, do devils ever, by any chance, pray...?

The Devil immediately took advantage of the friar's pause for breath:

—Well, of course they do, you foolish bastard. And why should we not pray? Indeed, praying is one of our most lucrative businesses, you son of a [*censured*]...! I shall explain it to you, and you will soon understand. It so happens that, not so long ago, I organized a *prayer session.* It was an event with a touch of great class, at which I was accompanied by those wretched individuals whom you call your rulers but who, in reality, are my main collaborators in your world. You cannot even begin to imagine the fruits that I obtain with these theatrical farces. I must grant it to you, my insignificant insect: I have always felt passion for theater; that is, for the show business which tries to impersonate reality. I only wish you could realize how fashionable the stage is and what a transcendental role it plays in your modern world...! Although the great deal of fun I have is the most important fruit I get from all this.

The Devil paused here, as if he doubted whether to insist on this issue. Finally, he went on.

—Moreover, you could never imagine, repellent insect, the *immense pleasure* that I could get out of your current prayers, if I only were allowed something more than merely an increase of my hatred and contempt; mainly when you transform your main act of worship —I do not want to name that damn *aberration*— into an obscene desecration. You must know, miserable one, that all Hell howls and applauds in a wild orgasm of *pleasure* —try to read here "desperation"— when this happens.

By now, Brother Peter had already achieved some control of himself:

—But I have always heard people say that the Devil does not like to waste his time. If you pray, even when you are faking it, wouldn't all that be a waste of energy? Wouldn't it also contribute to increasing, to some extent, the practice of prayer?

Once again, Satan started.

—You humans are always thinking with your [*censured*]. You are hopeless. In the first place, it is true that I never waste my time —among other reasons, because I do not have any. My disgusting existence takes place in eternity, where there is no time, because that was where that Accursed you call..., you know, put me. Besides —and this is the most important thing about this issue— you cannot imagine how fruitful it is to ridicule a form of worship as unfortunately important as prayer. When your foolish fellow humans see my followers praying (?) —it is easily said— they will be more reassured in their belief that prayer is a hoax. In this sense, I must admit —with my fullest approval, for I cannot say to my total liking— that ever since the last Council things have been made very easy for us. In this world of yours, many of my human henchmen — always so foolish, not to say [*censured*]— think that they are doing me a favor by spreading filth by way of the *media*, by multiplying the atheist propaganda starting with the schools, or by making the naïve of this world believe that the worst aberrations, which are not proper even for animals, are achievements of progress. No, my hated Peter, no. While I admit that all of that is great, nevertheless, our best means of acquiring clientele are precisely those acts of your new

worship, as well as those things that you continue to call *liturgical*
functions.

And here the Devil widened his eyes and looked around. He let
out a roar that seemed as if it were trying to resemble joy. Evidently,
Satan felt satisfied with this. He gave himself a brief pause and
immediately continued:

—Of course, you do not believe in those things you call *liturgical*
functions which you have paired with derision and charade. I, on
the contrary, do believe in them; if nothing else, because of the
first–rate business they mean for me. Nevertheless, I must admit
that what most contributes to filling up my grounds is preaching.
Ah, your preaching...! I have succeeded in making you all, friars,
priests, Bishops, and Cardinals, preach *in the way I command you to
preach*...! The ease with which you bore people is impressive! How
do you do it? That is surely the one thing that I admire about you
and which I have never been able to attain: I am quite capable of
inspiring fear, even of giving rise to the mockery of those who persist
in maintaining that they do not believe that I exist; but boredom...?
Let me tell you, imbecile, that I do not know how to generate it; as
you can imagine, if there is anything we ignore in Hell it is boredom.
Moreover, it is fantastic: you never proclaim the true doctrine; you
never point out the true problems that affect the flock entrusted
to you; nay, you don't even warn them about the dangers that I
bring about to make them stumble and fall... Boy! It looks as if
we had made an agreement to combine efforts! Your big bosses are
more worried about what people might say about them and about
keeping their posts than they are about your needs. It is fantastic!
Let me tell you, Peter, if I could, I would heartily laugh and double
up with satisfaction. It has been twenty centuries since my great
Enemy appeared —damned be my existence!—, and throughout all

this time it would never have occurred to me that you were going to receive the most awful harm from those within your own House.

Brother Peter almost let out a cry:

—What do you mean by that?

The Devil seemed to become more furious:

—You ask me what I am trying to say? Let me explain it to you... Just a moment, please.

Brother Peter thought he had found a moment to interrupt the Devil.

—You are talking to me —he pointed out timidly— and I just realized that I cannot believe anything you are telling me. I have always heard that you are the Great Liar, indeed, the Father of all Liars.

The Devil winced, let out a kind of snort, and stared at the friar.

—What you have just said would flatter me were it not for the fact that it is true. Try to comprehend once and for all that anything even remotely associated with truth bothers me. In any case, you humans will always be the same fools. Certainly, I always lie... except, of course, when it is convenient for me to tell the truth. And let me tell you that you are so immersed in and so pleased with the Lie that even when I say the truth I deceive you; for you also believe it as a Lie, which, after all, *is what you have accepted as your own.*

—Look here, you wretched, —went on the Devil. It so happens that during these last years I have come up with a better method that goes like this. You are going to be amazed if you listen to me, insignificant friar; for you should not forget that I am a Master —at whatever you want, but a Master. Therefore, I have taught a truly magical trick to the great crowd of brainless people that follow and admire me. Doubtless, it is a marvelous invention. It consists of using words that sound good and refer to things that, generally speaking, arouse admiration and belief in many people; but, be amazed! They are somewhat ambiguous and consequently can be understood in a double or even a triple sense. This procedure is totally safe to pass *doctrine*, especially in Documents and high standing Exhortations. And I don't need to tell you that today there is another thing that favors my cause: the fact that almost no one exercises his faculty of thinking. All you have to do, my puny wretched friar, is discreetly change the meanings of words to make it possible —and it is always possible— to sneak in their erroneous meaning.

—Listen to this, because is one of my greatest achievements, and you will quickly understand it —the Devil continued.

—I have achieved marvelous things with words like *progressivism* and *culture*. Thanks to my own and my experts' investigations within our laboratories —I will not say "infernal" laboratories because you will misunderstand me—, you cannot imagine how greatly the number of idiots deceived by me has grown. Thanks to me — and only to me!—, forms of behavior, which are really despicable and which constitute a step farther backward than humanity has ever been before, are now classified as *progress*; indeed, those who practice them truly do *progress*... toward my delightful dwellings, where I *lovingly* wait for them and prepare a welcome for them. As for *culture* —this time you can believe me when I tell you that even I, with all my knowledge, am amazed when I see how far human stupidity is able go—, you cannot imagine the things you pompously refer to with that noun.

The Devil cleared his throat and seemed to take a breath before he went on.

—As I was telling you, my loathed Peter, sometimes I tell the truth; but only when it is convenient for me, of course, or whenever I think that I will gain some advantage. Remember, for instance, when I told your Chief that I would give Him all the glory of this world, since it had been given to me, if He worshipped me. At that time I told the truth; and He Himself proved me right when He called me *the prince of this world*; which, on the one hand, flatters me, but, on the other, it [*censured*] me that both of us agree on something, even if it is only one thing.

Satan's enthusiasm seemed to go into crescendo. Brother Peter could not tell whether it was passionate fury or furious passion. He could not restrain himself:

—Be careful, the friars are going to hear us!

—Shut up, you silly, I am getting exited!— And the Devil continued:

—To keep the words and to change their meaning...! But, what the heck! This has been my greatest success achieved in several centuries...! Can you imagine how much I have accomplished, thanks to this trick, since you had the idea of calling up the last Council? What do you think is the reason behind all this confusion and chaos caused in that freakish thing you call your *Church*? Oh, boy! That is which I call profiting from something!

Satan jumped, elated, and again let out a noise which Brother Peter could not recognize; or perhaps he felt ashamed of thinking what that growl could mean. Nevertheless, he took advantage of the brief pause and asked:

—But, Satan —may I call you that?—, you told me before that sometimes you organize with your most important collaborators a day of prayer. I do not understand; I still think that such an event would somehow contribute to fostering the faith of the people.

The Devil simulated what, for the first time, seemed to resemble a smile; then he burst into a guffaw.

—The faith of the people, you say?— He let out a new roaring laughter which this time came accompanied by a number of cutting remarks that —censure being always present— are not possible to transcribe.

—In *that thing*, of course, —he continued— they'll be speaking of God, of world peace, of understanding among men, of a valid–for–everyone *Universal Religion*... My boy, all of this is food for the disbelief of the people! Can you imagine, for example, what it means to make people believe that the only existing God is so easy–going as to accept everyone; that He does not care whether men are good or evil, whether or not they answer the call of what you call His *Love*; that He is willing to overlook any misbehavior; for Whom all religions are the same; that He considers whatever you humans do, good or bad, as something wonderful. If we can get people to believe this —and we are getting it, because I have well–trained collaborators—, congratulations and [*censured*]...! Then and there we will have made the world believe in an idiotic God!

Brother Peter was startled by the blasphemy:

—For all the saints, Satan! Don't say crazy things!

The Devil felt a shiver which, in another individual, would have been caused by joy:

—The saints? Did you say saints, you fool...? But that has been one of my best moves ever...! How I wish I could jump for joy! Yes, I know I can jump, but not for joy. You see...

Brother Peter interrupted again, this time nervous. Finally he decided to speak:

—Ok, ok! But I think the friars may have already finished their prayers.

—Calm down, my poor unfortunate friar... —continued Satan—
I have foreseen this and have opened up a parenthesis in time to stop
it. They have not finished their prayers. I should really say that
they have not even begun, for they are praying with that marvelous
routine they have gotten used to; besides, they hardly believe what
they are saying. This is another of the great achievements my agents
and I have accomplished in the convents and monasteries of the
golden post–Council era. I don't even want to talk to you about the
nuns, my candid and detestable friar; the things I could tell you...!
By the way: haven't you seen your Abbot? It was difficult at first,
but I finally got him to learn to be shortsighted when viewing the
world.

Brother Peter opened his mouth in amazement; finally, he could
continue:

—Shortsighted, you say...?

—Of course! This individual, like any of you who give yourselves the disgusting name of Christians, but even more so an Abbot,
should have opened his heart to the things that are Above... What
did that cursed Saul say, who got away from me...? "Search for the
things that are above," or something like that; but enough of this,
just remembering it makes me sick. Or that other wretched little
African Bishop —was it Augustine?— that also decided to betray
me and change sides (I think that the Clergy in general are a lot like
the politicians when it comes to this). What did he say? Oh yeah,
"You made us, Lord, for you," etc.

Here the Devil spat and almost hit Brother Peter.

—Well, you see, —continued Satan—, instead of doing that, your
Abbot forgot his vocation and decided it was better to dedicate his
time to politics. Bravo, my friend! You can't even imagine how
many priests and Bishops I have directed upon this marvelous way.

Some countries are full of Abbot politicians, Bishop politicians, and Priest politicians. Although I must admit that the best *politics* they know is to flatter those in power and to keep their posts; in this area, kid, the Church is paradise...! —Darn it, I said that cursed word again—. Can you imagine...? Religion turned into politics; in some countries, even into nationalistic and secessionist (or Marxist liberation) politics. The Gospel substituted by the *Communist Manifesto!* Who could offer more? Aren't they being shortsighted when they look at religion and the world?

Here was when Brother Peter started to feel an onset of anger. Some of the things the Abbot had done that seemed to fit what the Devil was saying came to mind. But then, Mary Mother of God! Could it be true that Satan tells the truth sometimes...?

—Ok, ok. But you said something about saints.

The Devil looked slowly to Brother Peter, but he soon seemed sort of flattered and pleased. His gesture could not go further than snorting, undoubtedly a diabolical snorting.

—Oh, the saints...! Kid, I am more than convinced that I am an *awesome* Devil. What a success, what a great success! For, you see, I don't know if you have realized that those you call *saints* have always been pretty bothersome people; well, surely you have noticed it. You also know that, throughout the centuries, they have taken many people from my Mansions and have turned them away from my side definitively. Since I was robbed of so many, I realized that I had to eliminate them (the saints, I mean); or at least end people's devotion to them, which is something that I haven't been able to achieve in twenty centuries. But at last, kid, the marvelous post–Council era arrived. Finally...! Of course, man...! They call it the era of the *New Advent* or the *Ecclesiastical Springtime*; I would called it the *Era of blessing*, but I hate that word! Therefore, I have simplified things and reduced the expression to *Time of rejoicing and good harvests*; true, a string of words, but at least it has the advantage of meaning something to abide by. For you must know, my little indecent friar, that in the world of priests and friars you have an amazing aptitude for creating pompous phrases, whose meaning nobody cares about: *Ecclesiastical Springtime*, eh...? *Church of the New Advent*...? I ask myself how you do it. As for me, I recognize that, although I am able to come up with a barrage of lies, I am incapable of inventing such collections of meaningless flattery.

Brother Peter, who had been intrigued by this issue about the saints, was becoming impatient about finding out the trick the Father of Lies had used in this particular case.

—But, what about the technique you were talking about being used for the saints?

Again snorting, this time almost of astonishment.

—Haven't you guessed? Economics, boy, pure economics. To achieve what I wanted, I only had to apply the *market saturation law*. It is infallible. You should know that Economics is an important Science that you must study. Economics and Finances, ignorant friar, are a wonderful resort that shelters those preachers who wish to look good and not say anything about what really is their own responsibility. Not to mention that a Highly Important Document about these issues suggests taking precautions —which seems quite funny to me; you are cretinous enough to have always believed that it is necessary that the world knows it can count on you; thus, there were [before] so many *social* dealings and [now] so much effort in collaborating with it to foster *social welfare technical advances*. Consequently, since the One Above not only recognized me as the *prince of this world* but also awarded me the title —which I must parade around with for all eternity— of *the biggest Clown in all Creation,* you are worshiping me to the extent that you make fools of yourselves along with me. Indeed, you are so stupid as to forget that the Church does not belong to this World and will never get the World to recognize her as its own; and you are lucky here, for if the World would ever accept her then the hour has come for her to cease to be the Church. If you did not have so many vanguard theologians —by the way, if I could love anyone I would embrace them with so much love... how repugnant!— who have convinced you that the Holy Scriptures are not reliable, you would keep well in mind that your Chief already said that His Kingdom was not of this world. But let us leave this and let me explain to you the *market saturation* law. You will be surprised at its brilliance.

Brother Peter began to regard the Devil with an air of distrust; at the same time he asked himself if, in fact, there were another way to regard such a character. Undoubtedly, at that very moment the Liar was plotting one of his old tricks; but, thought our friar, it would be worth it to listen to him. Thus, Brother Peter cleared his throat and shyly said:

—You are saying that the *market saturation* is a law of Economics; but what does Economics have to do with the saints?

—A lot, you idiot, a lot. You do not know, among many other things, that the essence of Marxism has its foundations in Economics? Frankly, I do not know what my friend Marx would have done without it. I myself could never thank him enough for the number of people he has brought to my Mansion. Yes, the very Mansion which, according to your experts, is empty. Sometimes I think that they mistake my dwelling place with their empty heads, although I'd rather say with their souls. And there is more: High Finances, the powerful Banks... If I could rejoice, I would, whenever I think about it...! With such instruments and with the great power of control that they wield, I have infiltrated myself even up to their [*censured*]. I am sorry, kid, it is just that the substitute of joy that these things bring to me, in spite of everything, amuses me...! At any rate, let us get back to your saints.

Brother Peter would not have been able to get over his astonishment, if the very fact that he was speaking with the Devil were not already astonishing enough. He was startled when the Devil jolted and shouted at him:

—Wipe that stupid look off your face! I do not understand your astonishment at talking with me. If you only knew the number of people I hobnob with constantly, as if it were the most natural thing in the world... relax; you will be happy to know that those [*censured*] On High, Who have allowed me to speak with you, have set as a condition that I tell you the truth at all times. Nasty, isn't it! Could they have picked a worse way to insult me?

—Look —went on Satan— the law of the *saturated market* is quite simple and foolproof; when you apply it to the saints, it has spectacular results. Erasing, once and for all, the devotion that fools and simpletons always professed to them...? A piece of cake! Let me give you an example that even your batrachians brain will understand. Diamonds are a rare, precious, and very scarce thing, hence their high price. But imagine that, all of a sudden, we flood the market with them, making them as easily obtained as potatoes are. Do you understand what that would mean? They would automatically lose their worth, and people would cease to value them and to look for them.

—*Do you get it*, as you say nowadays? —continued the Devil— Look at me and listen, you worthless insect of a lumber room! It's all about boosting the number of saints indefinitely and continuously. It's awesome. Until recently, you, the simple folk, thought that the saints were extraordinary beings. They were the champions of your Faith, your role models to imitate, and intercessors to whom you could pray; but that was before the arrival of modern times. Now, the abundance of saints means that everyone has a saint at hand nearby: your brother–in–law, your distant cousin, or your upstairs neighbor could very well be saints. Can you guess what happens? Saints no longer seem champions of great deeds, nor do they appear extraordinary because of their scarcity. Therefore, their role as special intercessors you can turn to asking for help is becoming increasingly difficult. For who has never met his upstairs neighbor, or known of a distant cousin, or argued with his brother–in–law...? This profusion of saints was unimaginable when the canonization process used to take many years and, in some cases, several centuries.

—Aren't you exaggerating? —put in Brother Peter.

This time, the Devil did not seem to take much notice of the friar:

—Maybe; but consider that exaggeration is just the truth with some emphasis.

—I am getting the impression that you like the canonization of new saints —Brother Peter insisted.

At this, Satan's eyes flared up with special intensity. He continued:

—I certainly do, when they are abundant. You would be surprised to know that I even promote them sometimes. At some other times, there is a vested interest in certain Circles because they need to exalt someone in particular. There is much at stake, you know, and all this hanky–panky is to my own advantage; although things are not always so easy. This business in particular, crappy friar, constitutes a great triumph for my side. In times past, the saints were my most feared enemies, but now we have managed to elevate to sainthood shady characters who, therefore, give rise to discussions and doubts on both sides of the spectrum; and everything open to dispute is a wonderful source of division. Besides —not to mention the camouflaged divorce that you have invented and now grant to everybody—, with these things you drive a wedge into what in former times were accredited and prestigious Institutions of your so–called *Church* because they too are now proved to be vulnerable to the *winks* of the World.

   —On the other hand, you must understand my meritorious efforts in favor of the *market economy* —the Devil went on after a sort of deep breath.

   —I have devalued sainthood, Peter...! You must admit with me that it used to be most expensive and difficult. Heroic deeds, terrible mortifications, taking the love of God and the Gospel seriously...; especially this last one, Peter, is something I could never bear. *Taking the Gospel seriously!* What nonsense...! Tell me, then, what is the use of the Documents which are constantly being published by the Conferences of Bishops (they don't seem to care that nobody reads those Documents); of the abundant and countless number of references to Social Doctrine; of the sickly–sweet and corny Writings of founders and she–founders; of the Speeches and Exhortations of many Bishops, who are gifted with the talent of never hitting the nail on the head; of the writings and doctrines of the *avant–garde* theologians; of the exciting and sharp articles —gosh, I almost forgot, "journalism"— of the *L'Observatore Romano*...? Should not Christians express to me their gratitude because now anyone can be a saint, thanks to my campaign for the devaluation of religious life...? Think, Brother Peter, even though that function by the brain is not often cultivated by you friars: it would be enough, for example, to write some absurdity, say, *Democracy and the Rise of Spirituality in the Twentieth Century*, and bam! There you go...! At any rate, I do not want to frighten you. Let us drop this subject of the saints and pass on to another theme.

Brother Peter did not know what to think or what he could say.

—What do you think about all this, silly friar? —the Devil was getting more worked up by the moment —I have made cheap not only holiness but also salvation...! Pay attention: Now, salvation is free and for everyone...!

—Are you saying that salvation is for nothing and for everyone? That this has been your doing? But then... —Brother Peter felt bewildered and confused.

—Yes, of course...! It has been a masterpiece! Let me explain it to you. Gosh! You humans and your puny brains...! Listen:

—Your Chief has always made the ticket to that place you call *Heaven* very expensive. One has to lose his own life, renounce his very self: the path to Heaven is too narrow and steep, and few walk upon it; on the contrary, broad and easy is the other path, and most humans walk along it... Let me tell you, Peter, that, among so many statistics and opinion polls you are so proud of nowadays, your Chief's data are the only true ones I know of.

To the increasing astonishment of Brother Peter, Satan continued after a brief respite.

—Cheap salvation —or better yet, *salvation for nothing*—, which means that man has nothing to do on this issue, is based on the wonderful doctrines of *Anonymous Christianity* and the *Union of Christ with all men merely because of the fact that they are men and that your Chief also became a man...*, and you know the rest of this setup. Presently, the recently discovered infinite dignity of man suffices for salvation because of its union to your Chief through what you call *Incarnation*. Gosh, Brother Peter, if I were not Satan I would give you a huge hug...! Not even I could have dreamed of a better thing! Consider that nothing else is needed: neither Redemption, nor Faith, nor Baptism, nor conversion; and as for that accursed Cross, there it goes, to the lumber room. All of you are saved, Peter, because you are all Christians; whether you know it or not, whether you like it or not. We are in the times of automation and *self–service*! Unbelievable! A Love that claims to be infinite but which is indifferent to whether or not it is requited... or whether it is sent to..., well, to wherever...! Almost without intending it, Brother Peter, I have succeeded in passing this kind of God off as a good God who, otherwise, would have been considered a stupid person by anyone who is able to think.

—And now I want to tell you about one of my latest victories. Truly, it is another great invention in modern times. It is the so–called law of *compatibilities*.

Brother Peter almost sprang.

—Another one of your laws of Economics, I suppose; or perhaps a law for civil servants or for people in high positions?

—Bah...! —Satan seemed to become furious. —You are even more useless than a lay pastoral agent. You mean those laws regulating the holding of multiple posts; my law works the other way around —truly speaking, everything that concerns me works backward— because it makes two most opposite and outlandish things become compatible with each other. Let me explain:

—The first compatibility occurred when I accommodated Marxism to the Gospel. Well, to tell the truth —only because the Ones Above compel me to—, I accommodated the Gospel to Marxism. You cannot imagine the amount of fresh meat that this, what you call *Liberation Theology*, has provided us with.

—Then, the *New Catholics* came. And here we have a wonderful list, kid: Traditional Catholics; *progressive* Catholics; Catholics for Socialism; Socialist Catholics; pro–abortion Catholics; feminist Catholics; divorced Catholics; non–practicing Catholics; Catholics who do not accept the Pope; Catholics of autonomous conscience; liberal Catholics; pro–dialogue, pro–*spirit–of–the Council*, pro–revision–of–the dogma Catholics...Ugh! I don't need to go on. Who was the imbecile that wanted to establish an antithesis between *black and white* when actually both colors can coexist simultaneously? No, nothing about a middle–ground–centered grey; please, do not be more stupid than you normally are, Brother Peter; we'd better leave half measures for your well–known *spirit of Dialogue*. What I have accomplished is the only true thing: black and white at the same time...! Why could that thing you call *eucharist* not be given to somebody who defends and promotes abortion; or does not believe in the eucharist? Ah, my hated Brother Peter! It is so wonderful to see that it is precisely in this area where I have found my best collaborators: Bishops, Cardinals...! On the other hand, there always are the simpletons, the paladins and defenders of the Faith; they are convinced that those high ranking officials who allow these things —they always think well of others; pig–headed people— behave like that because they suffer from weak Faith. Weak Faith...? Totally the opposite, slow friar; these fools do firmly believe: they believe in the position they hold and the life they live; they believe in me, in me, Peter, in me! That is why they have become my most faithful servants; they believe in that stupid *universal solidarity* which I was so pleased to invent and later to introduce into their empty brains and into their even emptier hearts...

Satan jumped again and let out a snort before he continued.

—Listen to me, you trashy friar. One of the best *devilish* creations I have come up with is taking advantage of *democracy*, that invention of yours. Your Chief founded a Monarchical Church, there is no question about it, even though now many of you try hard to conceal this fact or, at least, to make others forget it. From the start, there was the Pope, for the whole Church; the Bishops, each one was the supreme head and Shepherd in his own diocese; in turn, all the Bishops were subject to the Pope; and then, if you want, there were the humble parish pastors, who were working in their parishes, governing their parishioners according to their good consciences and understanding.

Here the Devil paused and looked at the friar with seemingly triumphant eyes.

—But I have succeeded, Brother Peter, in introducing into your Church the idea that democracy was necessary...! I resorted to three tricks that work like a dream for me. They are *Collegiality, Convenience of Dialogue*, and, finally, the apex of my work and the best of the three: what the experts know as *Promotion of the laity*. They sound good, don't they? Now the Pope has to take into account the Synods; the Bishops, in their turn, are under the control of the Conferences of Bishops —and I take good care to introduce into their midst pressure Groups which are in direct contact with me. And what should I say about the wretched parish priests? Fantastic! I have laid them off, Peter...! Pay close attention: permanent deacons are in charge of preaching; lay people are responsible for the readings and half of the liturgical functions; the finances of the parish are exclusively in the hands of the laity; the organization of the pastoral activities in the parish has to be under the tutelage of the lay Pastoral Counsel; parish Liturgy is closely monitored by the Parish Committee for Liturgy which is made up of lay people; not to mention the priestly duty of taking into account the inter–confessional celebrations and anything else that appropriate coexistence with the separated brothers may demand; add to this..., but you do not want me to continue, do you? Perhaps you are wondering whether there is any activity left to the exclusive domain of the Pastor; but of course: signing the checks to pay the bills... but only if he has previously obtained permission from the Parish Financial Committee...

—...made up of lay experts, too —said Brother Peter, finishing the sentence.

—Jolly good! I see that you understand me. Not even I, the Devil —continued Satan— could ever have imagined, since I was expelled from... well, you know from where!... that an honest worker and head of a family would ever think that his job, as a mere lay person, would be to take part in the readings of the mass, distributing that which you call *eucharist*, planning the liturgy and the organization of the parish; to sum it up, acting as a perfect sacristan but with the airs of a general, that is, with commanding authority. That tops it all, Brother Peter. Let me tell you that, until now, Hell has been filled with evil–doers; after the Council, mainly fools are the ones who occupy the greatest spaces there.

—My sweetest and most productive achievement, Brother Peter, is that the democratic Church, once she has changed her internal constitution, is no longer the Church founded by your Chief. In this area, my hated friend, my triumph has been complete and clear; my achievement has been to have sophism turned into a fantastic dogma; imagine that nowadays there are no longer dogmas! This current lie is one of the best among the infinite lies I have been able to concoct throughout my accursed existence; I even made it pass as a splendid achievement in the New Times. Which sophism? It cannot be clumsier, but here it is: *Any exercise of authority is an abuse of authority.* What do you think? Why do you suppose that nowadays the members of the Hierarchy seem to be afraid to exercise their role in the Magisterium with authority, to the extent that they completely refuse to implement it there? The best of all, Peter, is that once they have swallowed this lie, the next step is the possibility of their mistaking vain ostentation for humility. The day that Paul VI renounced to wear the tiara and got rid of it was a wonderful day for me. Finally, Peter, finally...! I have always hated damnable Authority ever since I was not allowed to enjoy it the way I liked. And let us not forget, my apprentice to a cockroach, that there is an open window for misconstrued humility to end up in ridicule; a ridicule which, as one would expect, would also be cloaked under the form of virtue and pastoral originality. Perhaps you do not recall that, once the tiara disappeared, John Paul II wore upon his head hats from all kinds of professions: firefighters, policemen, clowns..., except his own, which he never wore.

Brother Peter began to feel uncomfortable and tired. What about his brethren? Unpleasant things —the more unpleasant the more they seemed to be true— presented by loads and in a short span of time causing anguish to any person. Besides, what had happened, in the meantime, with his brother friars? Shouldn't they have finished their prayers by now? He did not mind showing signs of fatigue in front of the Devil.

The Devil did not fail to notice his pupil's feelings.

—Wait a bit, Peter, for I have left the best for last: the zenith of my success. I have introduced another source of division within the Church! And to think that She calls Herself the *One* —and I don't know how many other names too— *Church*! Have you ever given any thoughts as to how much I have gained by spreading among the faithful the firm idea that now there are two different and even conflicting Magisterium: Pre–Conciliar and Post–Conciliar? The extremely naïve and so–called watchmen of order do not realize that the more they stress, time and again, that there is no rupture between now and before, the more they convince people that *where there is smoke there is fire.*

Our friar, despite everything, found some strength to show his anger and to answer:

—No matter how much of a Satan you are, you are well aware that what you say is impossible. There is only one Magisterium. We also have the Pope, his infallibility, and all that.

The great Liar let go a rabid roar.

—What are you saying, you miserable...?

The Devil wanted to go on, but suddenly everything seemed blurred to Brother Peter. He felt that a deep darkness had shrouded him; then, light again; finally, he heard something like a distant sound.

The ringing of a bell dispelled his state of confusion, causing him a great shock. Brother Peter felt paralyzed as he desperately tried to move. Finally, little by little he came to his senses until he found himself lying on his bed inside his own cell; he was sweating, distressed, and panting. What...? Everything then had been a horrible nightmare...! The poor friar tried to take a deep breath as he felt like a castaway who, having spent several days lost at sea, was finally rescued just when he was about to die.

He donned his habit as quickly as he could, for he was not totally recovered from the tough time he had just had, and headed for the chapel of the convent. He could hear the friars already intoning the first verses of Matins: *Deus, in adjutorium meum intende...* Brother Peter went to occupy his usual seat at the back of the choir loft, and got ready to open his breviary. He had barely started the Sign of the Cross when he heard a noise behind him that made him turn his head. When he looked back he could not repress a shudder running down his spine which filled him with dread.

The back door of the choir loft was turning on its hinges at the same time that, carefully and silently, it began very slowly to open; enough to instill deep fear before the unknown and tremendous... before something foreboding which Brother Peter knew with certainty was going to appear.

DE GLORIA OLIVÆ
***
(CONCERNING THE GLORY OF THE OLIVE TREE)

The Prophecy of Saint Malachi is said to have been revealed to Saint Malachi, Archbishop of Ireland, upon his finishing a pilgrimage to Rome around 1140 A.D., even though its content was unknown until many years later. It consists of two parts, of which the second and most famous corresponding to the Popes (the first part refers to Ireland) was first published around 1595. According to some, it lay in the Vatican Secret Archives for over four hundred years. This is the part which we are going to discuss.

The Prophecy, short and concise in form, contains a series of epithets or maxims in the form of short phrases, both ambiguous and esoteric in nature, and refers to 112 Popes. It begins with Celestine II (1143–1144) and ends with the Pope who supposedly marks the end of History. According to what is said there, the present moment would be the penultimate of the series: Benedict XVI, who has as his maxim *De Gloria Olivæ* (Concerning the Glory of the Olive Tree). The maxim of *Petrus Romanus* (Peter the Roman) relates to the last Pope on the list, who will mark the end of Time — that is, the moment at which the Supreme Judge will appear and will preside over the Final Judgment of all men who have lived throughout History.

Needless to say, since this *Prophecy* is of the class of private revelations, it has no official status. The Church has never approved it; neither has it been condemned. As such, anyone may consider himself free to believe it or not without it seeming honest to label a person, because of his position regarding its content, as being naïve for accepting it or as incredulous for rejecting it.

The text in which the maxims or appellations appear is obscure. This should not seem odd since prophetic language is always mysterious and ambiguous by nature. Sometimes it is easy to discover the meaning of the mottos of a certain Pope or Popes, to the extent that frequently the conformity of the text to the subject (or to the circumstances that surround his Pontificate) is frankly quite astonishing. On the other hand, other mottos either make it difficult to find an application to the Pope alluded to, or the task seems impossible and the meaning remains indecipherable.

Of course, the mottos may be interpreted in different ways without any of the interpretations being absolutely certain. Yet some may come closer to the truth than other possible ones, in that they seem more plausible or fit closer to the historical data. However, none can be considered definitive.

Either way, we must take into account that prophetic language was not given for everyone to understand. It may even be true that this language is designed to be understood by very few persons or *even nobody*, this being the norm when dealing with the charisma of prophecy. And, notwithstanding, that at times it is *present* and very clear: *To you it is granted to understand the secrets of the kingdom of God; for the rest it remains in parables so that they may look but not perceive, listen but not understand.*[1] The prophecies of Jesus Christ about the end of the world are clear and entirely understandable; the signs of which they speak have little mystery to them while, at the same time, they are very tragic and powerful.

---

[1]Lk 8:10.

And yet they will be accepted by practically no one, something which also was foretold.

Sometimes, Jesus Christ spoke prophetically with the express intention that he who is able would understand what He said, as if, using a common expression: *let him who can, get it*. Therefore, it is here understood that *there may be* someone who understands Jesus' meaning, although it is also possible that nobody comprehends it: *When you see the abomination of desolation, of which the Prophet Daniel spoke, erected in the holy place —let the reader understand—...*[2] The prophecy *is there*, if by chance anyone can understand it; although it so happens that, until now, no one has managed to know for sure what *the abomination of desolation set up in the holy place* really means. Yet, the prophecy has been uttered so that the disciples may *know* that, when such a circumstance is present, the time for the Final Moment of the History of Humanity has come.

In view of this, it seems reasonable to think that the prophet does not speak just for the sake of talking, as if in the knowledge that his announcement would be meaningless because it would not be understood by anyone. Since the prophet is dealing with important things, such a consideration is not admissible; and it is even less admissible when the prophet is Jesus Christ. Therefore, it must be assumed that in his mind the prophet considers that his words will always be understood by some people; who, without a doubt, are likely to be a small minority —perhaps the *elect*, or some of them. They, in turn, will certainly not be believed by anyone.

The Prophecy of Saint Malachi —let us not forget its character of private revelation— possesses all the appearances of belonging to the latter genre. Everything seems to indicate that the maxims that relate to the person and the work of each one of the Popes —or

---

[2]Mt 24:15.

to the events or their environment and to their era— *are there* to provide a key for whoever is able to unravel their meaning.

Here we are not going to favor them, nor are we going to reject them. We do recognize, at any rate, their disturbing and mysterious character. For in quite a few of them, once they have been thoroughly examined, one is able to establish a clear concordance between the motto and its corresponding character.

Keeping in mind all that we have said, we will study the motto referring to the present Pope, Benedict XVI: *De Gloria Olivæ* in Latin; *Concerning the Glory of the Olive Tree* in English.

And the first thing one has to ask himself is this: Is it really reasonable to believe that this motto contains a more or less obvious meaning which may seem to *go well with* the present Pontiff? For our part, we feel inclined to believe that the answer is in the affirmative. There are a number of historical circumstances which *seem* to fit the prophetic motto.

Let us try to examine this issue in greater detail, although briefly.

Is it possible to find any relationship between Pope Benedict XVI —or his Pontificate and historic moment— and the motto, *Concerning the Glory of the Olive Tree*, which the Prophecy attributes to him?

The answer, as anyone can see, does not seem easy. There will even be some people who will feel compelled to think that no such relationship exists.

It should be taken into account, however, that the prophetical genre is ambiguous and arcane by nature. Therefore, even an affirmative answer —if there is one— cannot be regarded as absolutely certain. Should someone believe that he has actually found the said relationship, that person could never impose his discovery as definitive and final.

It is also important to point out that any prophecy, when it is authentic, belongs by nature to the supernatural order. Therefore, it would be futile to attempt to unravel it *through purely natural means*. But this is not a deterrent to using some of them, namely study and serious historical investigation, which can be not only useful but also necessary, although never totally sufficient —not even the most important ones, based on the reasons given above, for the study that we will try to initiate.

And given the fact that we are moving within the supernatural realm, we must add that prayer is also needed, which restricts even more not so much the field and the possibilities of this investigation but its potential outcome, for not everybody practices prayer nor do people generally have faith in its effectiveness.

And since this Prophecy —let us begin with the hypothesis of granting it a prophetical character— refers *indirectly* to Jesus Christ and more directly to the *outpost* of His Kingdom on Earth, the Church, it seems most appropriate and logical to go to the Gospels in the hope of finding in them some key which could provide clues to our investigation.

If one examines the motto carefully, he will notice that there are two nouns which, since they are in the same sentence, must be closely related.

One of them —O*live Tree*— seems to play the leading role in the declaration, for our attention is immediately drawn to it; the second —*Glory*— rather performs the role of qualifying the former. In other words, it is as if the motto would be saying: *the Olive Tree that shines in its Glory.*

The only place in the Gospels where mention of the olive tree is made is the transcendental passage of the Agony of Jesus in the Garden of the Olive Trees (Mt 26; Mk 14; Lk 22). Some people speak of the Garden or of Gethsemane, located at the base of the Mount of Olives. At any rate, there is no doubt that the historic event we are referring to, which was crucial to the History of Mankind, took place at the Mount of Olives.

The events that happened there, right after the Celebration of the Last Supper of Our Lord with His Disciples on the Night before His Passion, are well known; although they have never been sufficiently studied in depth. We will try here to outline a summary of them, to draw on their consequences later.

The Garden of Olives represents the zenith, or climax, of the *human failure* of Jesus Christ. The place in which the countless miseries of all Mankind concentrated on His Person, causing in Him a paroxysm impossible to be grasped by human understanding and which led Him into such a deep anguish that it resulted in His spontaneous shedding of blood through the pores of His Body; as the Gospels clearly testify.

The place that witnessed distress and suffering such as are impossible to be described by human language or understood by the human intellect, that place is the same one which witnessed the — apparent?— definitive triumph of Evil over God. The initial scene of Mel Gibson's film, *The Passion of the Christ*, reflects —to the extent that it is possible— this reality with acceptable seriousness. On that historic Night, the Olive Trees of the Garden witnessed what seemed to signify the Final Victory of Satan over the Son of God made Man. In this sense, talking about the *Glory of the Olive Tree* cannot be taken as anything but *respectful and serious.*

Was it the Supreme Triumph of Evil over Goodness and the loving Plan of God for Men? The victory of Disbelief over Faith? In that Night at least, everything seemed to indicate an answer in the affirmative. That is why what we are going to say now about the historic milieu of this Pontificate is not going to be pleasant for many people and will indeed be disturbing for all.

With regards to the tremendous events that took place during the Night of the Garden of Olives, we have hinted at the fact, without assuring it, that the Triumph of Satan over Jesus Christ in those crucial moments was merely *apparent*. Truly, that was simply a figure of speech used in order to introduce the theme: the Victory of the Great Enemy over the Son of God made Man was, then, absolutely *real*.

It is not less true, however, that it was a *transitory* Triumph; although Satan, wrapped as he was in the nets of his own *Lie*, was convinced that it had been *definitive*. He did not discover his mistake —a decisive and unspeakable error— until the moment when Jesus breathed His last breath on the Cross. It was there, and when any going back was no longer possible, that Satan finally realized the unfathomable depth of his mistake (1 Cor 2:8). It is very interesting to see how liars end up believing their own lies, following a rule which finds its greatest degree of fulfillment in the Father of all lies; hence he became the Father of all the Deceived (Jn 8:44).

The Triumph of the Great Enemy over Jesus Christ that terrible Night was not at all simply apparent; quite the contrary, it was entirely *real*. It was a Victory which had already had its origin in very remote times when, disguised as a Serpent, the Enemy of God and man was able to *deceive* the First Parents of Mankind; although now, at last, after thousands of years, the Enemy achieved its consummation. The Night of the Garden of Olives was, therefore, the moment of the *Glory* of Satan (*the Glory of the Olive Tree*, that is, the one that took place in the so–named Garden of Olives) as opposed to what appeared, at that same moment, to be the total *failure* —and so it was— of the Mission that the Son of Man came to this world to accomplish.

The *horror* of what that Night meant for Jesus Christ will never be understood in its total depth by men because it truly was a horror saturated with *reality.*

And His Anguish was also real, *to the point of death,* according to His own words. And the same may be said about His sweating of blood; or about the unfathomable abyss that the Temptations to which He was subjected meant; or about the indescribable Darkness of the Night of His Soul in which He —the Innocent above all other innocents— was loaded with *the miseries and sins* of all Mankind; or about the infinite anguish of feeling Himself abandoned by His Father, *even as if He had been found guilty...*

In that terrible Night, had the *Glory* to which Satan was elevated been *merely apparent...,* then the horrors that destroyed the Soul of Jesus Christ would have been also *merely apparent.* It is impossible to ignore the relationship of one with the other.

This doctrine is true as it is equally true that Jesus Christ — true Man, after all— would have been willing to reject such Anguish: *Father, if it is possible, remove this chalice from me...*

In the life of every man, and more so if he is a Christian, there occur moments of terrible darkness, in which he feels abandoned and everything seems to be lost —the *Nights of the Spirit,* of which the mystics speak. In such situations, the intensity of the Faith cannot dispel the feeling of having been abandoned by God; of the darkening, to the point of paroxysm, of the very idea of God; of the futility of one's own existence; of the lack of meaning of all things...; in a few words, of *total failure.*

Jesus Christ —true Man and true God, let us not forget this— lived in that Night all those feelings to a degree that exceeds all human knowledge. It is an interesting point that the Christian People, and even the very Doctrine, have always suffered the trend of placing greater emphasis on the Divine Nature of Jesus Christ than on His Human Nature. Although it may seem incredible, it seems easier to believe in His miracles than in His sufferings. And yet, it is precisely not through such wonders and spectacular actions but through His pain and blood that Jesus Christ is going to look like and become *one of us*. The Letter to the Hebrews said that *without shedding of blood there is no remission*.[3]

And how does all this relate to the motto *Concerning the Glory of the Olive Tree* which the prophecy of Saint Malachi applied to the historical moment of the Pontificate of Benedict XVI?

For those who want to see it, such a relationship is not difficult to discern: there is an absolute parallelism that exceeds the limits of what is disturbing for anyone who possesses good will and is able to understand.

For the Church has never suffered, throughout her entire History, a crisis as deep and dangerous as the current one. Despite all the deceivers and liars of the Propaganda of the System, she seems at this time about to disappear.[4] Even the great crisis brought about by Arianism (in the fourth century) had nothing to do in any way with the totality of the Faith; in any case, the heresy was concerned with only certain aspects affecting the right doctrine (dogma, heresy). Not so the current crisis, in which it is not this or that aspect of the Faith that is at stake, but *the very existence and meaning of the Faith Itself.* In this terrible Night to which the Church is being subjected, she would have reasons for doubting her own subsistence

---

[3]Heb 9:22.

[4]The Propaganda apparatus concerning the Church that the Powers launched after the Second Vatican Council (usually to harm her and to influence her deliberations) has been impressive and unique so far in History.

—there are many people, even within Her, who already consider her defunct—, for she is living through moments of such Anguish as she has never experienced before: another Night of the Garden of Olives which is becoming another Night of *Glory* for Satan.

Within the realm of hypotheses in which we are moving, if we consider the prophecy of Saint Malachi to be true, and if we take into account the motto *Concerning the Glory of the Olive Tree* as applied to the current Pontificate of Benedict XVI, and if, on the other hand, we also accept the reality of the unspeakable horrors that Jesus Christ suffered in the Night of the Garden of Olives... horrors that became an authentic triumph for Satan, who contemplated them with an assumed Glory through the trees of the Garden —the Night of the *Glory* of the Devil before the Olive Trees of Gethsemane —if we can realistically consider all of these events, then it seems completely plausible to draw on them as a parallel to the present time in the Church.

Throughout her history, the Church has never suffered a crisis as serious as the current one. It is so widespread and so profound that we may say, without any exaggeration —though the pusillanimous and the liars may disagree— that it seems capable of actually making her disappear. Nevertheless, for many Catholics of good will who suffer and are confused, there will always be the marvelous consolation of the unshakable words of our Lord referring to the Church: A*nd the Gates of Hell will not prevail against her.*

For a long time, immediately after the Second Vatican Council, a triumphant moment of the Church —which evidently was in all respects exaggerated if not false— was proclaimed from the roof tops: the famous *Springtime of the Church* or the *New Pentecost,* announced everywhere by Pope John Paul II, etc., etc. Afterwards, with the passing of the years, when the *debacle* became too evident, members of the Hierarchy chose to be *silent*, never acknowledging that the crisis had originated, above all, from the twisted interpretations of the Council by interest Groups. And neither did they admit that the Documents of the Council had been previously manipulated to this effect, making them liable to being understood in multiple ways. And Pressure Groups —Neo–Modernism— took advantage of that ambiguity and wisely turned things to their own benefit; and nobody dared to put a stop to their actions.

The silence about the reality of the crisis went on for too many years; indeed, for as many years as the lack of remedies to fix it lasted. Desertions multiplied at a frightful rate, and an immeasurable number of Catholics was allowed to remain buried in doubts about the Faith; the Hierarchy was debased; the Priesthood was degraded; the Sacraments were slowly suppressed; faith in the Real Presence of Jesus Christ in the Eucharist was *blurred* so as to be on the same level as the Protestants'; the Concepts of the Church and Justification were altered; Papal Authority was lost in favor of conciliarism; the revelations of Fatima were manipulated and falsified; ...and a very long *etcetera*.

Throughout this long period, there was an attempt to *entertain* the Catholic faithful with a multitude of external goings–on and an abundance of *shows,* which served well two clear purposes: on the one hand, to distract people's attention from the real problems, and, on the other hand, to make them believe, due to the enormous din, that *something* was there, when deep down there was really *nothing.* The Hierarchy multiplied its trips; large Youth Gatherings proliferated; spectacular and abundant canonizations —almost every Sunday— were celebrated outdoors or indoors; vulgar *closer relationships* of the Pope with the People...; while, at the same time, people of dubious faith and even more dubious conduct were be-

ing appointed to influential positions within the Government of the
Church at an alarming rate; etc., etc.

Meanwhile, the poor Christian People languished in their Faith...
and began deserting the Church. The splendor of the Liturgy with
which we had worshiped God for hundreds of years was, gradually and without pause, being substituted by the noise of guitars,
rock music, Festivals held inside the temple, the commotion of the
charisms that the Spirit inspired everywhere —among the charismatic and non–charismatic alike, but the Spirit blew everywhere:
everyone possessed the Spirit. Until the Church finally began to
realize that the worship of God had been replaced by the worship
of man.

Finally, the facts won the day and became realities; they were
too obvious. And now, at the present time, important members of
the Hierarchy of the Church are beginning to admit, though timidly
and while playing down its importance, the reality of the crisis. Unfortunately, they have not put forward any remedies. Meanwhile
they go on preaching. A lot of preaching but without content, and
without confronting the real problems: *Faith must form the life
of Christians... Laymen must be conscious of their vocation as laymen... The ministerial Priesthood is of paramount importance... The
prominence of women in the life of the Church...* But they do not
specify how to fulfill that ministry, or what that prominence consists of; and they do not show the dangerous errors in Faith and
Morals that are proclaimed even by Cardinals... A comedian once
said, either laughing or crying, that the current Church has made
preaching about *Birds and Flowers* a trend, alluding, undoubtedly,
to the lack of presenting authentic doctrine. And so on.

Of course, we have not addressed the root of the crisis in which
the Church is submerged. The crisis —and the ensuing danger— is

much deeper and more horrible than it seems to the naked eye. It is the moment of the true *Glory* of Satan, which had its beginning and foretaste in the Garden of Olives.

A deep and serious study pertinent to the intensity and profound significance of the horrors suffered by Jesus Christ in the Night of the Garden of Olives is something sorely missed throughout the History of Christian Spirituality. The ancient Prayer Books dedicated to the Passion of the Lord used to begin their considerations from the moment of the Arrest and the beginning of the interrogations. In the movie *The Passion of the Christ* (nowadays forgotten and, it seems, willfully vanished), Mel Gibson has the Virgin, who, accompanied by the other Holy Women, contemplates how Jesus Christ was taken to Caiaphas, say the following words: *It has begun, Lord. So be it...*

Christianity, it is true, has become used to perceiving the events of the Night of the Garden as a merely *painful occurrence* that signaled the *Prologue* to the Passion of the Lord. The reality, however, was not exactly thus. But this perception is not surprising if one takes into account that human beings are more prone to consider the sufferings of the body as something more obvious and tangible (and even more painful) than those of the soul. The truth, though, —and even more so in this Story— is very different.

The true *zenith* of the Passion of the Lord; the moments of His *most deadly anguish* and His feelings of supreme failure in His Mission; His horrible shame because He felt Himself burdened with the sins and miseries of the whole of Humanity; to which it should be added His sensation of finding Himself wrapped up in the most terrifying of solitudes...; all these moments which the Man Jesus Christ suffered had already taken place in the Garden of Olives. What followed was but the visible, physical development of what was already first contained *in potency* and then accomplished, with a dreadful intensity, as an act in the Garden. The *physical* tortures suffered by Jesus Christ in the following hours (flagellation, crowning of thorns, the very torments of the crucifixion...), carefully considered, in no way differ from the same sufferings that an infinite number of martyrs who gave their lives for the Faith would suffer. Later on, we must consider that it is not there where the deepest core of the *Mystery of the agonizing Suffering to the point of death* undergone by Our Lord lay.

Such Agony of Death, with its ensuing sensation of Failure and Defeat, together with the feeling of *guilt* before His Father, was suffered, in turn, before Satan's very countenance. The very one who, with his horrible grimace of Victory and satisfaction, looked on, convinced of the reality of his Triumph. It was the moment of his *Glory*, to which, in the darkness and silence of that horrible Night, the Olive Trees of the Garden became witnesses. All of which must have brought about in Jesus Christ an *Affront* of truly lethal pain and intensity, impossible to be fathomed by any human being.

His *loneliness* was total in spite of His having looked, in vain, for consolation. His most intimate friends had abandoned Him and surrendered themselves to sleep (*You could not stay awake with me even for an hour...*).

Should we admit the hypothesis with which we have been working —that *Concerning the Glory of the Olive Tree* is a motto applied to the current Pontificate—, such premise would authorize us to transpose the events that occurred in the Garden to the current moments of the Church (the Church being the Body of Christ and He being her Head). Then we are facing a horrible and disturbing reality: *Never before has the Church found Herself more discredited vis a vis the World, less reputable, and in greater loneliness than in these current moments.* The influence that for so many centuries the Church had exercised in the World has almost completely disappeared. To top it all, her discredit has reached heights that would have been unthinkable fifty years ago. Of course, these statements will create a scandal for many and evoke denial from not a few; which, of itself, is not enough to demonstrate that these statements *are not based in reality.* The Word of the Pope no longer means anything (although, according to some, it is worthwhile to take into account that, almost continually, all seems to point to the fact that the Pontiff himself avoids facing real problems). Never before has his Person been so accused, slandered, despised, and persecuted in the way and manner in which it is happening in the present time. Even the United States Supreme Court dares to accuse and condemn the Vatican (an independent State ruled by a religious Pontiff who is also Sovereign in the civil sphere). The most prominent theologians, Archbishops with prestige, and even Cardinals do not find any inconvenience in confronting the Pope and criticizing him openly and even opposing his decisions (the Austrian Church, for instance, has rejected Episcopal appointments emanating from the Holy Father; and nobody has raised the slightest objection to such action). The Catholic Church, formerly the Supreme Teacher defining behavior and human relationships throughout the World, has practically been reduced nowadays to simply one more NGO.

In the Night of the Garden, Jesus Christ felt Himself a complete failure before His Father. And He felt the same before Satan's countenance, the latter being completely convinced of his definitive Victory. The defeat of the Son of Man was also, from that moment, the defeat of His Church that would take place some day: according to the prophecy of Saint Malachi, precisely in our own time.

One should notice, nevertheless, an important point that implies a decisive difference: Jesus Christ, through His Humanity along with

His Divinity with which it forms a whole (although without inter-mingling) in His one Divine Person through the Hypostatic Union, was, at all moments and in spite of everything, the Innocent among the Innocent. The sins and crimes that He willed to carry and make His own *never were, truly, committed by Him*; which is not an obstacle in defining His Failure as entirely *real*; otherwise, his absolute Victory and definitive Triumph would never have been *real* either. The Church, nevertheless, which is His *Mystical* Body (He is the Head) is formed by men who truly are sinners —and absolutely guilty. They have not carried somebody else's crimes, no; they have really committed them. That is why it is fittingly stated that the Church is both *Holy and Sinful*. Already since time immemorial, the Church was known as *Casta Meretrix*, an expression that the early Church Fathers made their own.

Hence it may be stated in all truth that the current crisis is entirely imputable to the men who constitute the Church. Now it is not an *Assumed* Failure, but a *Personal and Guilty* Failure. The Desertion (one may also say Apostasy) of the Catholic World has reached such a depth and seriousness that merely alluding to it gives one the chills. In fact, we have been outlining the depth of the crisis, at least in its most visible and graspable aspects, for the average Catholic faithful. There exist, nevertheless, in such a crisis, two issues of extreme seriousness and profound iniquity which current Catholicism has fallen into. Both suppose the highest, most serious and detonating point of the current crisis; so much so, that one may legitimately think that it is impossible that God will refrain from intervening with the strength of His Justice.

We are compelled, against our wishes, to introduce a parenthesis in this extraordinary story —more fantastic than a Dantesque narrative and more difficult to grasp in all its profound significance than any concoction of the human imagination. This interruption is necessary for the sake of clarification and for a better comprehension of the issue at hand and in order to provide some details that may facilitate a better understanding for the reader of what is being said here.

We have repeatedly stated, in this explanation of the Prophecy of Saint Malachi which we are providing, that the corresponding motto for the Pontificate during which the Church is living in these moments, the Pontificate of Benedict XVI, is *Concerning the Glory of the Olive Tree.* Such motto occupies the next–to–last place on the list of all Pontiffs; the Prophecy points to a certain *Petrus Romanus* (Peter the Roman) as the last one, whose Pontificate will take place in the last moments of History. He is a mysterious character about whom commentators have given much lucubration throughout the centuries. According to the Prophecy, though, it is very clear that the Pope about whom the *last* motto is concerned will coincide with the final moments of the History of the Church and of the entire Humankind; the very moment when Humanity will be judged by the Supreme Judge at His Second and Final Coming.

The name *Petrus Romanus* appears surrounded by the most profound of mysteries within the context of a Prophecy which, in the hypothesis that one may want to admit as certain, is, in itself, sufficiently enigmatic. It is curious to note that, throughout the History of the Church, no Pope wished to attribute to himself the name of Peter, doubtless out of respect and devotion to Saint Peter, Prince of the Apostles and First Pope of the Institution of Salvation founded by Jesus Christ. This is a historical fact that eludes any type of speculation. Such name —Peter— has been virtually reserved, according to the Prophecy, to the Pope that will close History, coinciding with the Second and Final Coming of the Supreme Judge.

Now, such as always occurs in any prophecy —and even more so regarding this one—, no one knows either what the name *Peter* signifies or answers to exactly or to what such presumed *Romanness* refers. According to some commentators, such appellation is purely generic in this case, they may even add that the lapse of time between the Pope pointed to as next to last —*Concerning the Glory of the Olive Tree*— and the one established as the last of all —*Petrus Romanus*— is indefinite; which might entail that between one and the other there could reign other Popes not explicitly mentioned in the Prophecy of Saint Malachi. This is a hypothesis, nevertheless, that the Prophecy itself seems to belie, according to what we will see immediately.

And if this were not enough, an important concern remains to be added, as something able to increase the mystery. In reality, the Prophecy does not definitively end with the enumeration of the 112 mottos; at the end of all of these, the text incorporates a sort of *postscript*, as disturbing as it is enigmatic, which reads exactly thus:

> *In prosecutione extrema S.R.E. (Sanctæ Romanæ Eclessiæ) sedebit Petrus Romanus,*
> *qui pascet oves in multis tribulationibus,*
> *quibus transactis, civitas septicollis diruetur.*
> *Et Judex tremendus iudicabit populum suum. Finis.*

Which translated from the Latin means the following: *During the final persecution that the Holy Roman Church will suffer, Petrus Romanus shall reign, who will tend the sheep among a multitude of tribulations; after which, the City of the Seven Hills* (Rome) *shall be destroyed. And the terrible Judge shall judge His people. The end.*

And we have not yet reached the end of the series of question marks which the allegedly prophetic text presents. For no one can agree on whether the *Shepherd,* who will tend what still remains of the Flock of Jesus Christ during those terrible moments, refers to the Pope marked as Peter the Roman or to the one to whom the motto *Concerning the Glory of the Olive Tree* (Benedict XVI) belongs. According to which, it is necessary to recognize that the Prophecy is also quite ambiguous on this topic too.

As far as we are concerned —and we still remain within the realm of commentaries and hypotheses—, we are inclined to think that the aforementioned *Shepherd* is undoubtedly Peter the Roman. There are arguments which support this affirmation which will certainly appear as shocking to some. We will endeavour to say something in this regard, but we must first make an important observation.

As anybody may suppose, this whole problem has given rise to a multitude of speculations regarding both the moment of the End of the World and what is known in Theology by the name of *Parousia*, or the Second Coming of Our Lord. We do not pronounce ourselves in either way regarding this theme, nor do we lean either in favour of its proximity or remoteness in time. The main reason for our position being that God has reserved to Himself the exact moment of such a transcendental Event, according to the Words of Jesus Christ Himself; and in no way has God willed to reveal it (Mt 24:36; Acts 1:7). On the other hand, this Essay does not refer to that moment concretely; therefore, I will make no attempt to expand on it. The present work merely endeavours to develop a commentary on the prophetic motto *Concerning the Glory of the Olive Tree*, which anybody may feel free to either accept or reject.

We have stated above that the prophetic text that points to the Shepherd who will lead the decimated Flock of Jesus Christ during the last Great Persecution refers to Peter the Roman, not to Benedict XVI. The main reason at the base of our statement is that the current reigning Pope does not seem to possess the sufficient qualities to attribute to him such a laudatory title. To expound this statement would require a historical–theological essay, not this article which by nature is, after all, predominantly pious.

Regarding *the decimated Flock of Jesus Christ* —those who will remain in those terrible moments—, let us remember the words of Saint Paul in which he speaks of the Great Apostasy that will take place during the Final Times (2 Thess 2:3); as well as those words of Jesus Christ Himself: *But when the Son of Man comes, will He perchance find Faith on Earth?*[5]

Returning to our theme: we said that the Church nowadays is the Great Defeated One before God. The Big Culprit of an Apostasy of which it will have to render account before the Justice of the Terrible Judge. In this regard, we alluded to two especially serious faults, which seem to have been the main ones that have brought the ruin of the present crisis down upon the Church. Regarding this ruin, there remains only the promise of Jesus Christ which grants us the certainty of overcoming it: *And the Gates of Hell shall not prevail...*

Before we continue, we must state that we were compelled to reflect upon the expediency of continuing and culminating an Essay which, after all, is based on mere speculation (which does not cancel the absolute truth of the foundations upon which the Essay lies). In what we have written above, the corresponding *motto* from Saint Malachi has been interpreted as an allusion, in prophetic form, to the actual crisis the Church is suffering —something which has been done succinctly and without resorting expressly to the support of bibliographic references because we did not want to turn this Essay into a prolix composition. There exists, however, a most abundant

---

[5]Lk 18:8.

and entirely reliable Documentation which may serve as proof of what is being affirmed here and which is easily accessible to anyone who wants to asseverate the veracity of the opinions contained in this Essay.

We have insistently repeated here that, in our modest opinion, the crisis to which we are alluding is the gravest and most dangerous the Church has suffered during her entire History.

We have also endeavoured to show that the current terrible situation the Church is undergoing is but the consequence of the sins of Christians (although here we are referring mainly to Catholics, who constitute the Only and True Church) and, more specifically, a tremendous and general Apostasy which the Ecclesiastical Hierarchy itself is not alien to.

Apostasy, which presupposes a conscious and wilful abandonment of the Faith, is perhaps the gravest treason members of the Church can commit. The different forms under which this Apostasy has manifested itself have been briefly and superficially enumerated here, along with the ensuing grievous faults that Catholics have borne upon their backs. But the two most important forms (at least according to our opinion) have been deliberately reserved for this final exposition.

The situation is so serious that it has given rise to two factors whose extraordinary sensitiveness and transcendental repercussions are undeniable. Hence, the idea has crossed the mind of the author to abandon this theme. It is always necessary to think about the possible scandal one could cause in those of weak Faith, given that the vast majority of the Faithful ignore the seriousness of the moment in which they live —although that is not enough grounds for them to escape its consequences: many have freely opted to abandon their Catholicism; meanwhile others, even more numerous, have ceased being Catholic without knowing it.

The problem should be posed in the following terms. Can one consider it right to remain silent when Evil wreaks havoc and expands freely, finding hardly any opposition, thus causing the deception of multitudes, consequently placing the salvation of their souls at stake; when the Great Enemy of the Faith is succeeding in changing the concept and configuration of the Church which have remained safe and sound during twenty centuries; when this Enemy has deprived the Redemption effected by Jesus Christ from any meaning, blurred the sphere of the supernatural, transformed the cult of God which is substituted with the cult of man —provoking the desertion of Catholics by the hundreds of thousands... Can one remain silent when all that is happening —and we have made but a brief enumeration of events—, without pointing out the danger, so that one can alert whoever still wishes to be free from the power of Deceit and not to risk his own salvation? Is it not perhaps even a duty to denounce it?

Having reached this point, it is already time to expose the first of these two situations, reserving the most serious and frightening one for the final part of this Essay. One must keep in mind, however, that we will have to proceed succinctly and concisely.

As any Catholic knows, the sources of Revelation are only two: Sacred Scripture and Apostolic Tradition. The Church has never recognized the *subjective individual interpretation* of such sources (which is exactly the heresy of Luther, who professed the free and personal interpretation of the Bible and completely rejected Tradition). It is the Church as such, and only She through the Hierarchy, who enjoys the assistance of the Holy Spirit with the purpose of interpreting with total guarantee the data of Revelation. Written Revelation (Sacred Scripture) became definitely closed with the death of the last Apostle. Apostolic Tradition stems from the Apostles and transmits what they received of the teachings and example of Jesus Christ and what they learned from the Holy Spirit.

Given that, as we have said, the possibility of subjective interpretation of Revelation within the Church does not exist, the Church is the only one called to guarantee the security and veracity of the revealed data and to keep them intact. In this sense, her infallibility is guaranteed by the assistance of the Holy Spirit *through the authentic and legitimate Magisterium.* Throughout the centuries, this Magisterium has studied in depth the revealed data, *although maintaining always its immutability* —for man cannot add or subtract anything from the words revealed by God. But delving deeper into the study of revealed data does not mean adding to or subtracting from or changing anything in it.

Hence the fundamental and transcendental importance of the Ecclesiastical Magisterium, which, assisted by the Holy Spirit, has remained safe and sound and immutable throughout twenty centuries, constituting *the only guarantee Christians possess that whatever is taught by the Church is exactly the content of authentic Revelation.*

The consequence is self–evident: should the Magisterium waver or become discredited (through changes, additions or subtractions, or being challenged partially or in its entirety) there could exist no certainty whatsoever that the Church continues to teach the authentic Doctrine of Jesus Christ. Thus, the whole edifice of the Church would collapse and the entire content of the Faith would no longer possess the characteristic of certainty.

It is the case that, during twenty centuries, the Magisterium remained intact and immutable; it could not have been otherwise.

Catholics have remained in perfect unity, enjoying unanimity and security regarding the content of their Faith (except for heresies, which, precisely because of what they are, remained separate from the Church).

We have said *during twenty centuries.* Nevertheless, from the commencement of the Second Vatican Council, a powerful Movement within the Church *has endeavoured to torpedo the Magisterium* —and very successfully too, apparently. Hence the dreadfulness of the current situation: Numerous masses of Catholics no longer know where to go for shelter or what exactly is the content of their Faith.

The neo–Modernist Theology at the time of the Council and subsequent to it has questioned the value of the Magisterium prior to the Council. And even some high ranking officials of the Ecclesiastical Hierarchy, relying on the same Council, have attacked the Magisterium of the Popes that preceded it. On the other hand, the ambiguity of some conciliar texts has given rise to doubts regarding fundamental truths of the Faith and has offered grounds for their being interpreted as changes regarding the prior Magisterium.

The doubts introduced by the neo–Modernist Theology regarding the Magisterium prior to the Council, by apparently attacking that Magisterium through the subsequent Magisterium —and consequently stripping both of their credibility—, are the cause for the current moment of confusion and obscurity within the bosom of the Church, which are precisely the weapons that the *New Religion* of the *New Age* needed to destroy her.

The attacks of neo–Modernist Theology against the Magisterium prior to the Second Vatican Council were frequently, though not exclusively, aimed against the Council of Trent; they tried to support themselves, as it could be expected, on the Second Vatican Council itself. But perhaps that Theology did not realize that the consequences of those attacks could be devastating for the Church.

If a previous Council can be attacked by another which follows it, then for that very same reason and according to the rules of Logic, the *latter may also be rebutted by the former.* Once it is admitted that a Council is capable of calling into question the Doctrines proclaimed by another, then it is evident that the value and credibility *of all Councils* self destruct and fall apart.

If one adduces, as the neo–Modernist Theology has been doing —especially aiming at the Council of Trent—, that the Doctrines promulgated in a Council are valid only for its time and according to the thought parameters proper to that time, it is then evident, following that line of reasoning, that *the exact same thing could be said of any Council.* Who would be able to guarantee that the Documents of the Second Vatican Council will not be rejected by a subsequent Theology, arguing that those Documents are only valid for the time when they were written down and that they will have to be interpreted according to the trends of current modern thought?[6]

If, on top of that, the attack would have been carried out *purposely,* then undoubtedly one could affirm, with all certainty, that the object deliberately pursued in this attack was the destruction of the Magisterium. Assuming for a moment that this attempt were successful —which is something unthinkable, given the promise of Jesus Christ regarding which the Gates of Hell shall not prevail against the Church— then, once the Magisterium disappeared or

---

[6]This is the foundation of the *historicist* doctrines which have permeated Catholic Theology ever since the Second Vatican Council, resulting in out–and–out Modernism (which was thought to have disappeared). For these immanent ideologies, it is not Revelation that determines man but man of *each historical moment* who judges and interprets Revelation. The equation is clear: subjectivism equals Modernism.

became completely discredited, *Catholics would lack of all firm basis for their Faith.* The moment that any given truth of the Faith could be questioned, without anything or anyone guaranteeing and assuring it, then it would all be tantamount to the impossibility of believing in anything transcendental and supernatural. To say it more simply: We would be facing pure atheism.

The Church *appears* to find herself in that moment —or perhaps on the brink of entering it. Never before has Satan envisioned, as he does now, the moment of his Victory to be so near and complete. And never before has the Church seen Herself so severed and torn asunder as She is in this current moment; just as it happened to Jesus Christ on that Night among the Olives Trees in the Garden.

In spite of their attempt at concealing this fact —so that it does not look like an *attack* but rather a *deepening* or a better way to adapt revealed truth to the language of modern man—, the disparity and even contradiction among Magisterial statements, before and after the Council, even in reference to *fundamental truths* are such obvious facts that nobody can deny them.

Cardinal Ratzinger (now Benedict XVI), when he was *peritus* in the Council, brought to notice during this Council that a fracture had taken place in the Doctrine of the Church regarding the consistent teaching of the primitive Church, the Church of the Fathers, *apropos* the collegiality of the Bishops. According to the Cardinal, the one responsible for such fracture had been Saint Thomas of Aquinas (and all the Scholastic or Medieval Theology along with him). The Second Vatican Council, according to the Cardinal, came to repair that breach which had remained opened in the Church for *seven centuries.*

Now as Pope, Benedict XVI has denied that the Second Vatican Council has caused any kind of rupture regarding Tradition or the

Primitive Church; an asseveration which, in relation to the previous one, deserves to be accompanied by a clarification on the part of the Holy Father. Indeed, it would be important to know whether such *connection*, never broken between Tradition and the Primitive Church —carried out by the Second Vatican Council and confirmed by the Pope— comprehends and includes those seven centuries of Medieval Theology as well, or, on the contrary, should one rather accept that enormous *hole* or void in time and just jump over it.

It is also difficult to explain that the Magisterium of the Church may have erred —and in fundamental questions too— during so many centuries, without the assistance, consequently, of the Holy Spirit.

It is equally well known that Cardinal Ratzinger (never refuted by Benedict XVI) publicly maintained that the Constitution *Gaudium et Spes* of the Second Vatican Council, is an *authentic Counter–Syllabus Document* (the *Syllabus*, by Pius IX, was published at the same time as his Encyclical *Quanta Cura*).

If one takes into account that the *Syllabus*, together with the Encyclical *Pascendi* of Saint Pius X, are the Documents that solemnly condemned Modernism and attempted to nip such heresy in the bud, undoubtedly the problem of the apparent *discrepancy* between Magisterial documents and declarations is clearly posed.

And the problem still worsens if one takes into account that some declarations contained in the Documents of the Second Vatican Council which refer to fundamental truths of the Catholic Faith are in evident disagreement with the previous Magisterium, which causes an obvious concern; as it happens with the concept of Church, for instance.

During twenty centuries, the Church has upheld, without the least vacillation, that Jesus Christ founded only *one* Church, which is precisely the Catholic Church: *Credo... in Unam Sanctam Catholicam et Apostolicam Ecclesiam.* The last Magisterial Document regarding this issue, prior to the Second Vatican Council, is the Encyclical of Pius XII *Mystici Corporis* (1943), in which the Pope expressly states —after insisting on the fact that the Church is one Body and that there is only One— that *the Church of Christ 'is' the Church of Rome.*

Nevertheless, the Second Vatican Council (*Lumen Gentium*, Chapter 8, n. 8, b) introduces the important change of substituting the expression 'is' with the phrase '*subsists on.*' According to which *the Church of Christ subsists on the Catholic Church.* Something which unquestionably removes its condition of Oneness, giving way then to other religions which are also repeatedly given recognition as legitimate instruments of salvation.

That this is not an arbitrary interpretation on our part is proved by the *Gatherings of Assisi,* where parity among all *religions* was granted, including those which do not profess a cult to any God. On the altars of the Homeland of the Seraphim of Assisi were enthroned, on equal terms, Christian, Jewish, Muslim, Brahman, and Hindu cults... even the practices of African witches and black magic of the voodoos.

Any doubt disappears when considering that in the Encyclicals of Pope John Paul II (especially the first three, which he named *Trinitarian*), a legitimate salvific value is recognized for all religions. A Magisterium which, when all is said and done, completely ended the missionary activity of the Church, given that the Encyclicals of John Paul II also defend the theory of anonymous Christianity and the universal salvation of all men without exception.

On his turn, Pope Pius XII (in his Encyclical *Humani Generis,* 1950) expressly condemned the theory of Henri de Lubac (according to which grace is owed to human nature) as well as the doctrines of creative evolution by Teilhard de Chardin. Both characters were later rehabilitated by Popes John XXIII and John Paul II (de Lubac was elevated to the rank of Cardinal).

The nature of this Writing advises against adding here more testimonies regarding this theme. A task whose complete exposition would require several extensive volumes and whose bibliography exists. We have provided a few, by means of example, which nevertheless offer sufficient elements of judgment for considering the possibility of a rupture, referring in this case to the Magisterium both prior and subsequent to the Second Vatican Council.

Once virtually every tenet of the Faith has been called into question and the value of the Magisterium has been weakened, then it is not too surprising that while many Catholics have deserted their Religion, others have abandoned all religious practice.

Furthermore, despondency and confusion reign even among many Catholics who have remained faithful. The *unity and the firmness* of the Faith of the Catholic people which had remained intact for centuries seem to have vanished. Ours are times of desolation, well suited to recalling the words with which the Gospel of Saint Matthew describes certain sentiments of Jesus Christ: *Seeing the crowds, He was moved with compassion for them, because they were battered and dejected, like sheep without a shepherd.*[7]

All men have to endure a lifetime of work in this *valley of tears*. But we Christians in particular face suffering in a special way because we are called to share Jesus Christ's death. Therefore, our sorrows and anxieties are finally transformed into joy, for they are always wrapped in the Hope and in the certainty that we are going to gather with Jesus in the Father's House.

---

[7]Mt 9:36.

Consequently, it would be something very sad if, in one way or another, we were to be deprived of the consolation provided by the *eternal life* in the manner and form promised us and for which we have always been longing.

In one of his recent homilies, His Holiness Pope Benedict XVI stated that when we speak of *heaven* we are not alluding to one particular place: *we are not referring to any given place in the universe, a star or something like it.* The Pope goes on to say that when we use that term we want to affirm that *God has a place for us;* which he explains by comparing it to the loving memory of a deceased person that his loved ones preserve in their hearts: *We can say that a part of that person is still living in them; although that part is like a 'shadow' because that survival in the heart of the loved ones is also destined to end.* And he immediately adds that *because God never passes... we all exist in the thoughts and love of God. We exist in all our reality, not only in our 'shadow.'* The Pope clarifies his explanation by saying that *in God, in His thoughts and in His love, not a mere 'shadow' of ourselves survives, but we are introduced and kept in Him, in His creative love, for all eternity with all our lives, with our whole being.*[8]

In short, according to the Holy Father, eternal life consists of our living *in God*; in His heart and in His love.

---

[8]Homily delivered by the Pope at Castelgandolfo on the Feast of the Assumption of the Virgin Mary, August 15, 2010. The thought of the Holy Father seems to indicate that although the memory of a dear person remains in the memory and the heart of his relatives and friends, even if that *shadow* or memory also tends to vanish because they have to disappear too..., it is not so in God; He being Eternal, we will remain in His thought and Love forever. This is an ambiguous statement which seems to contradict the permanence in the eternal life of the *person as a real being.* Besides, the statement also runs the risk of inducing Pantheism. One may think, nevertheless, that precision of the written text cannot be demanded from the oral language.

Although, in truth and strictly speaking, we are in fact already *living in God*, in His thinking and Love, as Saint Paul proclaimed in his Speech before the Areopagus in Athens (Acts 17:28). And we might even say that we *were* in the mind of God from all eternity; which in no way authorizes us to consider the awful falsehood that we have always *existed*.

Perhaps the Pope's words can be understood in an entirely correct sense. In that case, it may have been desirable to exclude some ambiguities, as well as to add some clarifications.

It seems more accurate to say that in eternal life we will live *with God* rather than *in God*. For it is in eternity where, at last, the plenitude of the loving relationship between God and man, or the perfect Love our hearts always longed for, will take place. A Love, however, that can only exist in a complete and total distinction of persons, which is an essential property to every Love; for Love always demands absolute *reciprocity* and total *distinction* between the two lovers (be they divine or human). Otherwise somebody would be induced to think that there is a possibility of falling into Pantheism.

Other than that, it is absolutely true that the term *place* cannot be understood, when referring to eternal life, in the same sense in which it is used in this life. Nevertheless, it has to have a *real* meaning. Otherwise, where are the *human bodies* of Jesus Christ and the Virgin Mary now? Moreover, the resurrection of the bodies is a dogma of Faith, and their location in eternal life cannot be reduced to the condition of a mere remaining as a memory in someone's mind (even if that someone is God). In this regard, maybe it is worth remembering what the XVI Council of Toledo (693) said in Article 35:

[Jesus Christ] Giving us example with His resurrection that He vivifies us, after two days He resurrected on the third, alive from the

dead; in the same way we believe that we also, at the end of this world, are to resurrect in all places; not with an aerial figure or like among the shadows of a fantastic vision, as the damnable opinion of some people stated, but in the substance of real meat, in which we are now and live, and appearing in the hour of judgment before Christ and His holy angels, where each will render account of what belongs to his body.[9]

Neither can we forget Jesus Christ's very words: *In my Father's house there are many mansions. Were it not so, I should have told you, because I go to prepare a place for you; ...that where I am, there you also may be.*[10] What would the Master mean by these words...?

It is natural, therefore, that we Catholics, who have been called to live in an age of so many vicissitudes and contradictions, want to live in peace according to the Doctrine in which we were baptized and according to the Gospel that the Church has taught us ever since, without further changes or novelties. For indeed, *not that there is another gospel, but there are some who trouble you and want to pervert the Gospel of Christ. But even if we or an angel from heaven should preach to you a Gospel different to that which we preached to you, let him be anathema!*[11]

The revealed Word of God is not the same as the Magisterium of the Church, which depends on the former. But in the Church there is no individual and subjective interpretation of this Revelation; the interpretation depends on all of the Magisterium, which is the only one that, assisted by the Holy Spirit, can guarantee the truth and the correct understanding of the Word of God. From this it follows

---

[9]Denzinger–Hünermann, n. 574. The Councils of Toledo always enjoyed great respect and acceptance within the Church, being considered almost equal to the Ecumenical Councils.

[10]Jn 14: 2–3.

[11]The Apostle Paul, in his letter to the Galatians, 1: 7–8.

that if the Magisterium of the Church would disappear, then any kind of certainty as to the intelligibility of what has been revealed by God to man would collapse. Any changes or modification in the content of the Magisterium —which has been a closed and granite Body for over twenty centuries— would affect, no doubt, the correct understanding of the content of Revelation; which would then be subjected to all sorts of manipulations, either regarding the admission of apocryphal or false texts, or under the form of changes, additions, or subtractions to it. So we end here with a text contained at the end of the Sacred Book of the Apocalypse:

For I testify to everyone that hears the words of the prophecy of this book: If any man shall add to these things, God shall add unto him the plagues written in this book. And if any man shall take away from the words of the book of this prophecy, God shall take away his part out of the book of life, and out of the holy city, and from these things that are written in this book.[12]

It only remains to allude to the last and more serious determination carried out by modern Catholicism: the *practical* suppression of the notion of Redemptive Sacrifice effected by the will of Jesus Christ in the Holy Mass. Therefore, we fear that the wrath of Heaven will descend upon the Church Herself, as indeed it seems is already happening.

To understand this, and as a historical note, it is good to recall that the New Mass, enacted in 1969 as the *Ordinary Rite* of the Catholic Church by Pope Paul VI, was prepared by a special Commission appointed for this purpose, which was composed of six Protestant experts and three Catholics. Out of these three, Archbishop Bugnini was the President of the Commission. When his

---

[12]Rev 22: 18–19.

affiliation to Freemasonry was discovered beyond any shadow of a doubt, he was banished from Rome by the Pope —Bugnini was sent as Nuncio to Iran. But his work, which was carried out with the collaboration and to the satisfaction of the Protestant experts, *was not modified at all.* Hence, the hitherto perennial and revered Latin Mass of the Church was virtually eliminated, and a great number of centuries were left behind and submerged into oblivion.

Among the olive trees in the Garden, during that terrible Night and before the imminence of the Passion and the Cross, the Devil was convinced of his all–encompassing Victory. Only when Jesus exhaled His last breath did the Angel of Evil realize his blunder. It was then and there when it clearly appeared that the Death on the Cross of the Son of God was the great asset that God had kept to Himself; the very one by which the Evil One was definitively vanquished. These two moments, the alleged Victory of Satan and the real Defeat by Jesus, are clearly portrayed at the beginning and at the end of the film by Mel Gibson, *The Passion of the Christ.*

But from that moment, the Devil already knew what to anticipate. If the Sacrifice of the Cross was the key, then it was precisely this Sacrifice which had to be eliminated at all costs. Thus, he took upon himself the difficult task of eliminating the Mystery of the Redemption —the ideal of the Sacrificial Death of Christ on the Cross— from the minds and hearts of Christians. For twenty centuries he was not successful... until Modernism, which was believed to have disappeared, came alive again under the form of Neo–Modernism in the heart of the Church from the time of Vatican Council II.

It was then that what seemed impossible, as well as unthinkable, actually happened. The concept of the Mass as a renewal of the Sacrifice of Christ —not a repetition, but a *becoming present*, here and now, in all its reality, the Death of the Lord— fades to almost nothing and is replaced, in turn, by the prevalent and almost single idea of the Mass as a *meal of solidarity* or fraternity.

Any idea of an atoning sacrifice was relegated to the attic of obsolete concepts, as something that belonged to past times and primitive cultures. Man no longer has to think so much about *participating in the Death of Someone* but about *living* in communion and happiness with his peers; he lives in a World that is self–sufficient and that recognizes Man himself as the only value within its reach. The worship of God gives way to the cult of Man —so much so that, from now on, the supernatural value of suffering and death, the need to atone for sins and to share the Death of the Redeemer, are replaced by modern concepts like the *New Spring* and the *New Age*, which open themselves up to a *New World* which thus becomes the final stage of human existence.

So it was that the *New Church* of Modernity consummated her Apostasy, by turning her back on the death of the Redeemer and slapping God in the face with her contempt and rejection of the most wonderful of His works; the very work by which He had given up His life and thanks to which He had accomplished, in reality, the greatest imaginable Act of Love towards man.

There are details and gestures that speak for themselves. In a great number of Catholic churches and temples, the pews and kneelers have disappeared, replaced by chairs and comfortable seats too close to each other so as to impede the Faithful from any possibility of kneeling. The Charismatic and Neo–catechumenal Communities, properly approved (it is fair to say), have seen the hour of their triumph: by denying the value of the Mass as a Sacrifice, the celebrations (always outside the temples and in total absence of altars and appropriate symbols) of those communities gave way to festive elements like guitars and rock music; almost exclusive intervention by lay people, virtually ignoring completely the Priestly element; and meals of solidarity and brotherhood.

It is not worthwhile to add more examples, which, on the other hand, all Catholics have seen and experienced. And this is how the new Night of the Garden of the Olive Tree has been updated. Satan is again confident of his Victory, and this time there is no one to prevent it. At long last, the Church, having received this deadly and definitive Blow, has been destroyed and defeated.

There is no one to prevent it... until the Supreme Judge comes and what was prophesied becomes a reality: *And the Devil, who had deceived them, was thrown into the lake of fire and brimstone where the beast and the false prophet were, and they will be tormented day and night for ever and ever* (Rev 20: 9–10).

And they will see the longings of their heart finally fulfilled who have remained faithful to the Lord and lived on Hope, in spite of everything, trusting in the Promise of Him Who had said that He would come again: *Then I saw a new heaven and a new earth; for the first heaven and the first earth had passed away, and the sea was no more. And I saw the holy city, the new Jerusalem, coming down out of heaven from God, prepared as a bride adorned for her husband* (Rev 21: 1–2); ...*and the gates of Hell shall not prevail against Her* (Mt 16:18).

THE ABOMINATION OF DESOLATION

The prophecies of Jesus Christ concerning what will happen at
the End of Time are contained in the Synoptic Gospels along with
those announcing the destruction of Jerusalem. It must be said,
despite the fact that they are linked, that the secular Tradition
of the Church, the testimony of the Fathers and the Magisterium,
and also the consensus of the faithful have shown no hesitation in
considering the two prophecies separately, apart from one another.

Obviously, once the historical moment of the events that destroyed the Jewish nation and confirmed the exact fulfillment of
what was predicted had passed, Christians were only interested in
the predictions about the End of History.[1] These predictions, both
because of their transcendental character for all of Humanity and
because they had been uttered by Jesus Christ Himself, have always
been regarded as being of *paramount importance*. In short, this
is one of the three major milestones in the History of the World,
namely: Creation, Redemption, and Parousia.

Among the prophesied events that must immediately precede
the arrival of the *Parousia* (the second and final Coming of our
Lord), there is one particularly important one which, along with its
strange and arcane content, has powerfully attracted the attention
of Humanity for centuries. It is well known that the prophetic text
to which we are going to devote our attention has caused a rather

---

[1]Once facts belong to the past, they no longer fall within the field of prophecy
but of History.

intriguing interest among human beings from the time it was uttered until today.

The text to which to which we are referring has to do —for him who knows how to understand it— with one of the events that mark the End Times: *the appearance of the abomination of desolation, which will be erected in the holy place.*

The prophetic text is found in the Gospels of Saint Matthew and Saint Mark —with a slight difference in hue in the latter which is almost negligible and, in fact, confirms what is said in Saint Matthew. Our study will be focused on Saint Matthew's version, for it seems to us the most appropriate for our analysis, which reads:

When therefore you shall see the 'abomination of desolation,' which was spoken of by Daniel the prophet, standing 'in the holy place' —he that reads let him understand—, then they that are in Judea, let them flee to the mountains; and he that is on the housetop, let him not come down to take anything out of his house; and he that is in the field, let him not go back to take his coat.[2]

But before we investigate the possible significance of this prophecy, we should remember some previous notions that, together with their ability to keep us within the realm of reason, will help to prevent our slipping into the realm of fantasy and vain speculations.

First, we must take into account the peculiarity of prophetic language: dark by nature, ambiguous, in need of interpretation, vague, and disconnected from concrete circumstances —of time and place—

---

[2] Mt 24: 15–18. According to the text of Saint Mark, *And when you shall see the 'abomination of desolation' standing where it ought not —he that reads let him understand—, then let them that are in Judea flee unto the mountains...* (Mk 13:14).

that could be easily recognized. This does not preclude prophetic language —if it is true Prophecy— *from being absolutely truthful and worthy of acceptance.* Its content is often difficult to interpret; hence it is so often misunderstood. It is no wonder, therefore, that it can be perceived by only a very small number of privileged persons.[3] We must insist, however, that true prophecy is not questionable, since it comes from a God Who is infinitely Truthful and uniquely knowledgeable of events as well as of future and free actions of men; therefore, it deserves full compliance from the faithful, even considering the obscurity of its meaning.

This said, we can address the first problem that prophecy presents: the reason for the use of prophetic language. Why the prophet uses an arcane and ambiguous language, difficult to interpret and likely to be misunderstood, when he —in the end God, from Whom prophecy comes and acquires its value as prophecy— could have expressed himself with sufficient clarity as to be understood by, and consequently easily useful for, everyone?

It is clear, with regard to research on such sensitive issues, that it is necessary to proceed with caution. Based on what is known with certainty, we must carefully handle the available data: eliminating prejudice, seeking to establish reasonable and logical conclusions drawn from true premises... and always without allowing oneself to be led by one's imagination or purely personal hypotheses.

---

[3]As for the veracity of the prophecies contained in Holy Scripture, most especially those uttered by Jesus Christ, they do not offer any problem. Nevertheless, there is imprecision and ambiguity when it comes to the few number of people who shall be able to penetrate their meaning, for nobody can claim to have understood them in their true and total signification.

But ultimately, and returning again to the core of the question, why use obscure language when something could be said clearly? And must not one keep in mind that the eternal destiny of many people is at stake here?

First of all, one should be clear about an issue concerning which there can be no discussion: God always acts for the sake of the good of man and never by chance or without any reasonable justification for His actions.

An approach to this issue, which may provide some clues to clarifying the problem somehow, could be found by establishing a parallelism with the parables. Somebody once asked Jesus Christ why He spoke in parables, and He clearly replied that His doctrine was intended to be understood by some, but not by all. Such *discrimination*, as reflected in His own words, seems to depend solely on the good or bad disposition of the listeners: they hear and understand who are willing and have a heart to hear the good doctrine; while they hear, but do not listen or understand, who, because of their ill–will, have closed their hearts stubbornly:

And his disciples came and said to him:

—Why do you speak to them in parables?

He answered and said to them:

—Because to you it is given to know the mysteries of the Kingdom of Heaven but to them it is not given. For he that has, to him shall be given, and he shall abound; but he that has not, from him shall be taken away that also which he has. This is why I speak to them in parables, because seeing they see not, and hearing they hear not, neither do they understand. And the prophecy of Isaiah is fulfilled in them, who says:

'By hearing you shall hear, and shall not understand;
and seeing you shall see, and shall not perceive.
For the heart of this people is grown gross,
and with their ears they have been dull of hearing,
and their eyes they have shut;
lest at any time they should see with their eyes,
and hear with their ears,
and understand with their heart, and be converted,
and I should heal them.'[4]

From this it follows that, indeed, God speaks sometimes in a deliberately obscure language; apparently, in order not to be understood *by those who did not want to hear*, but to be understood by those who have a willing and open heart: *To you it is given to know the mysteries of the Kingdom of Heaven but to them it is not given.* This approach of God, however, is far from being arbitrary or capricious. The reason some do not hear or understand is simply because they do not want to: *For the heart of this people is grown gross, and with their ears they have been dull of hearing, and their eyes they have shut.* It is clear in the Scriptures themselves that the Word of God can only be understood by those who receive it with good will; hence we can say, using notions taken from the Parable of the Sower, that His Word bears fruit only when It falls onto good ground: *And another part of the seed fell on good ground and grew, and yielded fruit a hundredfold.*[5] Conversely, when someone has decided to do without God and opted for the Lie, he becomes unable to hear and understand the divine teaching: *He who is of God hears*

---

[4] Mt 13: 10–15.

[5] Lk 8:8; cf. Mt 13:8; Mk 4:20.

the words of God; the reason why you do not hear them is that you are not of God.[6]

One might ask why God insists on talking to those who, however, will not listen. Why parables, or prophecies, expressed in an arcane language, knowing that they will not be understood by many?... and even more, because, in fact, we should say that God does not act here merely *knowingly*, but even *intentionally* —although for some it may seem outrageous. And yet, the reason for such a procedure is not difficult to understand: everything simply follows from the most stringent demands of Justice, namely, *for the record*, as the words of Jesus Christ clearly say: *If I had not come and spoken to them, they would not have sin. But now they have no excuse for their sin.*[7] God speaks and warns man with words animated by the love He professes toward him: words of life for those who want to hear, and of which man can take full advantage. But for those determined to neglect and despise them (which is tantamount to making God a liar) there remains only the impossibility of understanding what they hear, apart from that corresponding punishment that will ensue. Classical Theology, or what the Church has always taught, would point out here that the teachings to which we refer are only for the *chosen ones*; they are the only ones who, according to Jesus Christ, will overcome the difficult trials and tribulations of the End Times which will immediately precede the Parousia. But Modernist Theology would reject outright the expression *chosen ones*, since it is not willing to accept the notion of predestination because, according to its theory of universal salvation for all Humanity, all men have been saved.

---

[6] Jn 8:47.

[7] Jn 15:22.

In order to capture the rich content of God's Word a certain affinity with the Spirit is needed, because He alone is the Master able to provide discernment of the teachings of Jesus Christ and, in general, of Scripture: *These things I have spoken to you, while I am still with you. But the Counselor, the Holy Spirit, whom the Father will send in my name, he will teach you all things, and bring to your remembrance all that I have said to you.*[8] This, as can easily be understood, is of particular relevance when it comes to prophetic words, which already use an obscure and ambiguous language.[9] Keeping this in mind, we can now think about the content of our prophecy:

When therefore you shall see the 'abomination of desolation,' which was spoken of by Daniel the prophet, standing 'in the holy place' —he that reads let him understand—...

For centuries, exegetes and writers of all kinds, clergy and non-clergy, have sought to investigate and discover, with practically no results, the mysterious meaning of *the abomination of desolation*; in these issues the efforts of human imagination and fantasy are not enough. Only by carrying out a careful study of texts, on the basis of what can be extracted from them with some certainty and with the help of the light from On High, can it be possible to reach conclusions which, although small in number and always insufficient in their results, partially satisfy our desire to know. And what is

---

[8]Jn 14: 25–26.

[9]Here is the reason for the existence of so many *theologians*, well supplied with academic titles and laurels, whose lack of inner life leads them to a *total ignorance* regarding true Theology. They made the serious mistake of believing that the *science of God* is acquired only in books and libraries, as is done with the treatises of some human sciences. Moreover, this human *science*, in which they consider themselves experts, has been endorsed by prominent Universities where there are many *Masters* who do not even believe in God.

more important: those conclusions may provide us with elements that are useful on our way to salvation.[10]

If we confine ourselves to the rule that we have established —not to move forward except on safe ground—, we can already advance a first conclusion: the expression *abomination of desolation* has a meaning that, in effect, *responds to reality*; it is not, therefore, a *flatus vocis.* For it is not God's policy to contact us in a language devoid of content, and even less in the form of hieroglyphics or riddles. The mere thought that it could be possible that God spoke to us to tell us nothing is completely absurd. The fact that for so many centuries there has been practically no advance as to the meaning of this expression does not mean that God has spoken so mysteriously as not to be understood by anyone. Were that the case, He would never have decided to address Himself to us. At any rate, we can blame only our own limitations for the lack of results.

One can assume, nevertheless, that at least a few people will have succeeded in getting some intuitive knowledge, albeit confused and incomplete, about the content of this prophecy.[11] We must re-

---

[10]The Word of God was not pronounced to be sounded in a vacuum or to not be heard or understood by anyone; it was pronounced, rather, for our profit and salvation. According to Saint Peter, we have the prophetic word made surer. *You will do well to pay attention to this as to a lamp shining in a dark place, until the day dawns and the morning star rises in your hearts* (2 Pet 1:19). As for the teachings of our beloved brother Paul —also says Saint Peter (he recognizes that there are difficult issues in them, as in many places in Scripture): *There are some things in them hard to understand, which the ignorant and unstable twist to their own destruction, as they do the other Scriptures* (2 Pet 3:16). Scripture then was written for our benefit, and in It there will be difficult, or very difficult, questions; but *only the weak and ignorant* will interpret them in a twisted way.

[11]Generally, prophecies are not destined to reveal their full meaning until the moment of their fulfillment has arrived —and more so the prophecies which refer to the End of Times: *until the day dawns and the morning star rises in your hearts*, said Saint Peter, as we have seen.

member, however, that the lights that these charisms provide do not mix well with publicity, as it always happens with the extraordinary graces that God gives to certain privileged souls. At the end of the day, as far as these issues are concerned, we must always take into account the words of the Archangel Raphael to Tobias: *It is good to hide the secret of a king.*[12] It is well known that God does not reveal His best secrets, or His most intimate communications, except to His friends, those who truly love Him; as Jesus Christ Himself expressly said: *I no longer call you servants, for the servant does not know what his master is doing; but I have called you friends, because all I have heard from my Father I have made known to you.*[13]

But of course, as mentioned above, the prophetic language, dark as it may be, is meant to be understood at least by some —because not everyone has the proper disposition to receive it. Anyway, it is certain that Jesus Christ has sent a message in this prophecy, and an extremely important one too, for men who have to live through the End of Times. As the prophet Amos said: *Verily, the Lord does nothing without revealing his plan to his servants the prophets;*[14] to the prophets, of course, but also to his servants who love Him and are led by the Spirit.

That the expression *the abomination of desolation* indeed contains a communication from On High is expressly stated by Jesus Christ Himself: *When you shall see... he that reads let him understand.* If we pay close attention to the second phrase —*he that reads let him understand*—, we arrive at two conclusions: first, that the expression is capable of being understood and has, therefore, content; secondly, that only a few, probably an insignificant minority,

---

[12]Tob 12:7.

[13]Jn 15:15.

[14]Amos 3:7.

will be able to perceive something of its meaning, as derived from the obvious connotation of the phrase —*he that reads let him understand*— as used in everyday language. And of course, not everyone has a heart so willing as to achieve that perception.

Thus, *the abomination of desolation* is such a terrible reality as to cause real fear among men..., if they could believe in it. In any case, once its existence is admitted, as we do by faith, what can that expression be or mean?

In order to honor our previous intention of trying with all necessary effort not to misstep, the most convenient course of action apparently would be, first of all, to concentrate our efforts and dispense with imagination. Certainly there are many fantasies and imaginings that have been developed regarding *the abomination of desolation.* They have often been constructed by assembling extravagant and absurd figures, apparently drawn from novels and tales of terror, designed by feverish minds trying to frighten chiefly simple and credulous people: to imagine, for example, a powerful and evil Character, seated on a smoking throne from which he spreads terror and death, is something rather well suited for comics and thrillers. Unfortunately, we can be sure that *the abomination of desolation* will be something much more serious and devastating than all that.

Jesus Christ Himself clearly says, although indirectly, that *the abomination of desolation* will be something definite and extremely daunting. According to Him, once that abomination has been erected in the holy place, *let those who are in Judea flee to the mountains, and let him who is on the housetop not come down to take anything from his house; and likewise let him who is in the field not return back to take his mantle.* Although everything seems to indicate that these words are figures of speech, they actually contain a *real meaning* which, no doubt, refers to *a very serious situation* where the danger of losing bodily life will probably be the least severe peril to be feared. What we are dealing with here is something much more important and decisive, since *what is really at stake has to do with the salvation or eternal damnation* of many whose fate will depend largely on that Mysterious Power to which *the abomination of desolation* is referring.

And this is not a gratuitous assertion; far from it. Although we will discuss the issue later, we can advance that the context in which Jesus Christ speaks when He alludes to the erection of *the abomination in the holy place* certainly refers to salvation; it is not possible to assign to His words —much less so to the words pronounced on this occasion— another purpose or a different meaning.

As we continue with our intention to proceed carefully, we must rule out in our study —regarding any suggestion we may have made about *the abomination of desolation*— the idea of war and telluric or cosmic disaster, which must certainly occur at the End of Times.[15] But this warning of danger will probably be the most formidable danger that Christians will face once the mysterious *abomination* has been erected in the holy place. The Lie, as its most proper characteristic, will be the main weapon of devastation and destruction wielded by the Apocalyptic *Beast* —in turn, an instrument of Satan.[16] Besides, its incredible ability to deceive will be exercised by one whom believers would never suspect and in a way least imag-

---

[15] At any rate, given the logic of events it is very probable that *the abomination of desolation* will precede the series of universal catastrophes prophesied for the End of Times and which will certainly occur.

[16] *The abomination of desolation* is probably not identical with the apocalyptic *Beast*. It seems more logical to think that *the abomination* will be one of the events which will also carry the trademark of the Beast. Nevertheless, although all signs seem to indicate that the *Beast* will show itself clearly after the abomination (Mt 24:29), both are undoubtedly intimately connected.

inable to them. And hence the very *elect* would be vulnerable to being led to deception, if such a thing were possible. In short, *whole masses of the faithful will be seduced by 'the abomination of desolation,' while they acclaim it with enthusiasm and are willing to follow meekly its instructions.* In this connection, the Apocalypse contains truly disturbing words: *The whole world was in admiration after the beast.*[17]

What has been said, that *the abomination of desolation* —despite the awfulness of the notion evoked by such words— will be accompanied by Deception as a primary weapon of seduction, is not a gratuitous assertion. It should be noted that it will *stand in the holy place.* This latter expression does not lead precisely to situations of fearful terror or flight from imminent danger. Quite the contrary. Since *the abomination* will be enthroned in the *holy place*, this fact more likely suggests ideas of adoration, veneration, respect, and probably even worship. Far from fleeing to the mountains or staying in the countryside —as Jesus Christ advised, announcing the arrival of a devastating threat—, the faithful will feel induced to offer their fullest testimony of submission and praise. In short, the result will be countless numbers of believers *worshiping what is nothing but a blasphemous testimony of apostasy which, in turn, will become for them the unmistakable signal that their doom is at hand.*

Another important point, rarely taken into account, is that *the abomination of desolation* will particularly affect the Church; which means Catholics. The fact that *the abomination* will be erected in the *holy place* clearly indicates that this will directly and primarily

---

[17]Rev 13:3.

affect the Church, and therefore the faithful.[18] This does not mean that it will have no significance for the rest of Humanity. Certainly the events of the End of Times are universal. For if Jesus Christ endorses the prophecy of Daniel (Dan 9: 26 ff; 11:31; 12:11), it is because He understands that the exaltation of *the abomination* in the holy place transcends the New Testament to include the Old, and even the entire History of Mankind. But it will happen, however, that most men, once they have consummated their rejection of God and their full acceptance of paganism, will remain indifferent to what they will witness in the Church..., until the time comes when the cataclysm will also affect them and they will not be able to escape (1 Thess 5:3).

The conclusion of this reasoning suggests that the occurrence of *the abomination of desolation*, whatever such a mysterious expression means, will undoubtedly possess a *religious* character. And it is just by leaning on this *religiosity* that it will contribute to carrying

---

[18]Since the Catholic Church is the Only True Church founded by Jesus Christ for the salvation of men, it would not make much sense to speak here about *Christians*. As much as Ecumenism —whether it be true or false— regrets this, the term *Church* or *Christian* cannot be applied to the multitude of the so–called *Christian* Churches except in a gratuitous way and without any basis in truth. When Scripture, Tradition, the Fathers, and the centuries–old Magisterium speak about the *Church* they are exclusively referring to the only one that exists, that is, the *Catholic Church*. The sheep that do not belong to this fold must be *brought in* so that they become part of the only one that there is, according to what Jesus Christ Himself taught: *I have other sheep that are not of this fold; I must bring them also, and they will heed my voice and there shall be one flock and one shepherd* (Jn 10:16).

out the work of perdition that the Beast, in turn, will be consummating among the vast multitude of those who will be deceived.[19]

Another serious mistake of estimation, easy to make on this subject, is the widespread belief that *the abomination of desolation* will have to do with some active element of devastation, as the expression itself leads us to think. It seems, however, that in reality it will be something quite different, since the appearance of *the abomination* is intended to be more of *a signal*. When the faithful have it before their eyes —the few ones who should know how to recognize it—, then they can be certain that the time of Ruin and Desolation has arrived. Jesus Christ says it expressly, in one of those phrases that are often read superficially and that, consequently, run the risk of not being well understood: *When you see... Then, those who are...* etc.

This error of assessment to which we are referring shall have, in turn, two facets. Even though, in reality, both will go unnoticed by the perception of Christians in general. Hence, although it may seem that we are stressing this point too much, it is expedient to recall that *the abomination of desolation* will appear within the Church and it will be considered neither as an *abomination* nor as a *desolation*, far from it. Rather it will be regarded as an object of veneration and worship: and for that very reason it will be standing in the *holy place*.

Regarding the first of the two facets, we mean that the appearance of *the abomination* will indicate the definitive sign of the coming of the End of Times and *the beginning of birth pains* (Mt 24:8). This announcement, despite the clarity of meaning, will be recog-

---

[19]Deceived indeed, but guilty nonetheless. Let us not forget that we are contemplating a *Great Apostasy* which will have taken place and, at this moment, been consummated within the Church.

nized only by the small number of the elect. Meanwhile, Christians
in general will continue with their normal pace of life; they will even
mistake the signals heralding the imminent Ruin for the emergence
of a time of splendor and of joy: *As in the days of Noe, so shall
also the coming of the Son of Man be. For, as in the days before the
flood they were eating and drinking, marrying and giving in marriage, even till the day in which Noah entered into the ark. And they
knew not till the flood came and took them all away; so also shall
the coming of the Son of Man be.*[20] And because these words were
uttered by Jesus Christ Himself, they leave no room for doubt.

However, this state of affairs should not surprise anyone. The
Kingdom of Satan being the Kingdom of Lies, and since in the
Last Days his dominion and power will have reached their peak,
the smoke of Deception and delusion of Falsehood will have taken
over the minds of most Christians. This moment, which should be
one of alarm and trembling, will be marked by euphoria and the belief, on the part of Christianity, that it is living in the best time of
its History. However, the true time of terror will come later, when it
is too late and the Prince of Lies has already achieved his purpose.

The second facet of the error that we are analyzing refers to the
appearance of *the abomination of desolation* as being the apex of
the Great Apostasy predicted by Saint Paul for the end of times
(2 Thess 2:3) and, in an even more terrifying and clear way, by
Jesus Christ Himself (Lk 18:8). At that point, the Church will
have already reached the highest state of decay in her entire history
(Lk 18:8; cf. Mt 24:24), although, because of the promise of permanence received from her Divine Founder, she will not disappear
completely (Mt 16:18). As for the *apostasy* of which the Apostle
speaks, it will spread throughout almost the entire Church; it even

---

[20]Mt 24: 37–39.

seems most reasonable to think that the apostasy will also include the Hierarchy.[21] Thus, the standing of *the abomination* in the holy place will be marked by the culmination of a process of decomposition within the Church that will result, in turn, in the deepest crisis of her entire History: the widespread loss of Faith, the abandonment of the Hierarchy and a multitude of the faithful, the calling into question of all the dogmas, and the *defenestration* of the Papacy. This does not necessarily imply the disappearance of the latter, but the practical impossibility for the Roman Pontiff to exercise his high office as Vicar of Christ and his Authority over the whole Church. Regarding this last point, it is not even possible to rule out *a priori* the possibility that this event may occur through a voluntary resignation sponsored by the Authority itself —given the trend observed in the Popes particularly since Paul VI. And these are only some of the occurrences that will coincide with the appearance of *the abomination of desolation.*

We have been talking, within the limitations that characterize any investigation into the mysteries of prophecy, about the possible consequences to occur in the Church because of the arising of *the abomination of desolation.* But it is obviously important to gain a more concrete knowledge, if possible, of the nature of such a mysterious reality. And hence we must formulate the question that

---

[21]The important fact that Saint Paul speaks simply of apostasy without any further qualification —ἡ ἀποστασία—, as a noun with the article, probably refers to a situation that will comprise the universality of Christians. In regard to the Hierarchy, it is true that nowhere in Scripture is it explicitly named in connection with this event. However, anyone would think that a *Great Apostasy*, which will affect the multitude of Christians, would be unimaginable without the Shepherds being one of its main causes. Sheep follow their shepherds and walk to where they lead them, for better or for worse.

deeply disturbs human curiosity: What actually is *the abomination of desolation*?

If one does not forget that this is one of the deepest mysteries in connection with the End of Times, then there is no need to warn people that any answer to this question will always be inadequate and based on conjectures. Conjecture —and this is important— which will have to be established on reasonable and serious grounds, and carefully disregarding at all times imagination and purely personal hypothesis.[22]

Although one cannot be optimistic about the possible results of any inquiry made into this mystery, we must not forget what was explained at the beginning of this study. It was already stated there that prophecy always uses arcane language whose mystery is only fully known at the time of its fulfillment. Which is not at all an obstacle, as was also stated above, to reaffirming the certainty that when God speaks, He indeed does it to say *something* which, of course, is *true*, and which also is able to be *understood* by men; an understanding which is only comprehensible to a certain extent and which also is destined only for those to whom He has decided to provide such knowledge.

Once we take this into account, a beginning of an answer may be found in the fact that *the abomination will be standing in the holy place*. Therefore, what is the meaning of that standing of *the abomination of the desolation in the "holy place"*?

If we proceed step by step, it seems most imperative to make a preliminary examination of the possible meaning of *the abomination*

---

[22]Of course, all arguments made in connection with this issue must be carried out on the basis of a serious exegesis of the revealed texts obtained through prayer and in–depth study —without forgetting the importance of keeping an eye on the teachings of Tradition, the opinions of the Fathers and ecclesiastical writers, etc., ...as well as of shrewdly observing reality and the events of history.

of desolation as such. It seems reasonable to conclude that this expression refers to the *mystery of iniquity*, which rules a world whose lord is the Prince of Darkness. *The abomination of desolation* would epitomize the enormous evil of sin and the consequences of an intelligent and constant work whose satanic origin cannot be doubted. Such a diabolical task would have finally reached its apogee and become the true essence of *Iniquity* itself. It does not seem inappropriate to think that the appearance of the *abomination* is the clear signal that it will have previously accomplished the work of perdition in many believers.

What is most extraordinary and, if you will, most mysterious, deep, and even more disturbing is that *the abomination* is now *enthroned on the place of worship*, to be revered and admired by all those who, in one way or another, more or less aware of what they do, have abandoned their membership in the true Church.[23]

What can the expression *standing in the holy place* mean?

Undoubtedly, it indicates that *the abomination of desolation* is put (set up) in a *certain place,* which is the most significant and prominent one within the Church and the most apt, at the same time, to receive the veneration and worship of its followers. It is evident that *sacredness* and *worship* go hand in hand here. Again, we must stress the fact that *iniquity* will necessarily appear in the guise of *holiness*. Therefore, it would be dangerous to forget that

---

[23]In keeping with biblical language, we should have said *by all followers and worshipers of the Beast*. They may even still believe that they are part of the Church; in fact, they will not be. For the Church of which they are now members is a false Church, while the true one has been spirited away. In any case, it is beyond doubt that those who have opted for *the abomination* will always be described as guilty regarding their abandonment of the Faith. No one is deceived, or becomes a victim of the loss of Faith, without providing some kind of cooperation on his part.

Satan's preference of disguise is precisely to appear as an *Angel of Light*. The word used here by Saint Matthew's Gospel is ἑστὸς; it means to put, place, set at the sight of all, confirm, etc. In short, it is, in the present case, a public exhibition, universal in nature, destined to receive recognition, submission, and veneration from all.[24]

And here we end our rambling about the mysterious biblical expression *the abomination of desolation*, to which Jesus Christ Himself refers in one of His prophecies as a warning sign that will appear and precede the final moment of history.

But, as the reader who has been able to complete this chapter will see, we, on our part, in sketching this composition, have merely attempted to scratch the surface of the mystery; knowing in advance the only possible outcome to be achieved: the writing of a series of speculations, probably without foundation, and which no one should feel compelled to take too seriously. The mystery will remain a mystery. And as to the time of its fulfillment, it is known by God alone. However, based on biblical texts, we have been able to deduce —with high probability in this case— that we will not know how to recognize the reality of *the abomination of desolation* when the time comes that it is standing in the holy place, despite having it before our eyes. Or maybe it is already in front of them...? It is not easy to know. Once again, we encounter the same problem when it comes to the time of the *Parousia* and the events that must precede it: God has reserved for Himself the knowledge of the precise moment at which the clock of time, destined to mark the steps of history, will stop working. Taking into account all that can be said regarding

---

[24]The corresponding verb of the word ἑστὸς appears, for instance, in Romans 3:31 meaning to confirm; also in Matthew 26:15, meaning to expose (to be seen), and, with identical or similar meaning, in other passages.

the prophecies about the End Times, one thing can be deduced as
certain: to claim that *the time has come* would be as great a folly
as to assure that *it has not yet arrived.*

Another true thing that also follows from what we have said
refers to the advisability, supported by many biblical warnings, that
the disciple of Jesus Christ be always ready and willing: *Be prepared,
because at the hour you least expect the Son of Man will come.*[25]
Anyway, and we have stressed this point so much, we have been
given signals, otherwise quite patent, to understand what is to come;
signals which, nevertheless, few will recognize. For our part, because
of our extreme limitations and lack of knowledge, we have tried
to say something about what our understanding has been able to
speculate about *the abomination of desolation.* Although, to tell the
truth, we did not intend at any moment to say everything; it is not
always good, nor possible, to speak of the totality of what we know.

Meanwhile, the Barque of Peter continues its path, suffering
hardships and facing storms, but always animated by the promise
of permanence received from Her Founder, according to which nothing or nobody, on earth or in hell, can destroy Her. And men of
good will, those who never tolerated any negotiation with error and
never chose to love the lie; the faithful disciples of Jesus Christ will
feel their hearts strengthened by the joyful order that came from
their Master's mouth: *Let not your heart be troubled, nor let it be
afraid.*[26] With full confidence that, as surely as He left one day and
seemed to leave them alone, so will He come back to take them and
bring them with Him: *I go away, and I come back unto you...*[27] *So
also you now indeed have sorrow, but I will see you again and your*

---

[25]Lk 12:40.

[26]Jn 14:27.

[27]Jn 14:28.

heart shall rejoice. And your joy no man shall take from you...[28]
*And if I shall go and prepare a place for you, I will come again and
will take you to myself, that where I am, you also may be.*[29]

---

[28] Jn 16:22.
[29] Jn 14:3.

THE "NEW AGE" AND EASIER LIFE

THE ELIMINATION OF "SACRIFICE"

The sacred Book of the *Song of Songs* narrates the affectionate plea that the enamored bride addresses to her Bridegroom:

> *Come, my beloved, let us go forth into the field;*
> *Let us abide in the villages.*
> *Let us go up early to the vineyards,*
> *Let us see if the vineyard flourishes,*
> *If the flowers be ready to bring forth fruits,*
> *If the pomegranates flourish...*[1]

The bride, who wants to flee the City of Men, is moved by her longing to take refuge in solitude. The drive behind her wish is nothing other than her ardent need which compels her to live the deep intimacy of Love with her Bridegroom.

She urgently wishes to leave behind her own City from which Life and Truth and Beauty had been expelled to allow room for Darkness and Confusion, which have brought along their horrifying parodies: Death, whose Banner had already been hoisted and proclaimed as the triumph of Progress; Lies, widely endorsed and acknowledged as the best and most efficient instrument to subjugate people's minds;

---

[1] Sg 7: 12–13.

Ugliness, universally acclaimed as the means through which what now is considered *New Art* expresses itself.

One woe is past.   And behold there come yet two woes more hereafter.[2]

As for Love, the City of Men had already condemned it to Oblivion and reduced it to Nothingness, with the open and clear intent that the flesh would freely replace the Spirit; so that animal pleasure would cast into exile —as if it were a reprobate— Perfect Joy, with the sole intention of stopping its incessant flow from the generosity of clean hearts; ultimately, so that the abyss of selfishness and the bottomless Dark Pit of the *Only–for–me* should take the place of the Perfect Bliss which used to gush like pure and fresh water from the stream of the *I–am–yours* Spring, always yearning for self–giving.

Therefore, the bride longs to flee and to be together with the Bridegroom, both of them far away from the City of Men and seeking the peace and sacred silence of the fields:

> *Let us join our hands as one,*
> *As we travel the pathways through green meadows,*
> *Apple orchards in the sun,*
> *Pomegranate trees in groves,*
> *And silver poplars on river banks in rows.*[3]

---

[2]Rev 9:12.

[3]Alfonso Gálvez, *op. cit.* n. 52. In the Spanish original:

> *Juntemos nuestras manos*
> *y vámonos a ver los verdes prados,*
> *los huertos de manzanos,*
> *los bosques de granados,*
> *las riberas de chopos plateados.*

The bride longs to meet with Him and breathe together the fresh
and pure breeze of the hilltops; there, once Men are left far behind
and forgotten, both are bathed by the cool and limpid morning air,
or caressed by the soft and warm afternoon zephyr.

> *My Beloved, let us fly*
> *To misty hillsides of craggy mountains high*
> *Where hidden dens of foxes may be close by*
> *And mountain tops with their silver caps are nigh*
> *Where sweet forgotten nights in grand silence sigh...*
>
> *We will stay there, high above,*
> *And sing together the blissful songs of love.*[4]

In the meantime, the City of Men doubled its efforts to eliminate
the very memory of God from both the minds and the hearts of
Men. Once Beauty and Truth —the eternal sisters and companions
of love— had been eradicated, the next essential step was to blur the
idea of *Sacrifice*. As everybody knows, the method of *blurring and
weakening* the reality of something —dissipating, by doing so, its
contour in the mist of ambiguity and haziness— is the scheme that
the astute Liar has always used as the initial, and perhaps most

---

[4] Alfonso Gálvez, *op. cit.* n. 83. In the Spanish original:

> *Amado, en las brumosas*
> *laderas de montañas escarpadas,*
> *con cuevas de raposas*
> *y cimas plateadas*
> *en silencio de nieves olvidadas...*
>
> *Allí nos estaremos*
> *y los cantos de amor entonaremos.*

indispensable, step before dealing the killing blow: the definitive *elimination* of that reality.

All of the following contributed to making life more bearable and comfortable for men: the establishment of the City of Men as the *only possible one...*; the rejection of any futile thinking anchored in the hope of a future City which, in reality, would never come; the acceptance of the *Absence–of–Effort* as the supreme and legitimate ambition; the condemnation of the Narrow Path; the purging of ideas like self–giving and self–surrender from the hearts of its inhabitants, along with the enthronement, at long last, of the Paths of Comfort and Ease as the only ones to be trodden. All those things would take place when the moment arrived in which, in the most radical and definitive form, any feeling of love for Neighbor —once that love had been disparaged and made obsolete— had been gobbled up by the new Reality of the great Universal Community which Humanity would become; a Humanity, which, like a huge Organism in the fashion of *One Body*, would erase for good any attempt to recognize anyone as *Neighbor*.

It has not been an easy task, however, due to Men's common tradition of living firmly rooted in their beliefs. It became necessary, therefore, as an initial practice to be implemented in the City of Men, which had already entered its phase of *New Age*, to blur the idea of *Sacrifice* to make it more feasible and within the reach of its inhabitants. For it is a well–attested reality that, when Religion becomes less willing to acknowledge itself as a transcendental reality, the idea of *Sacrifice* as self–denial and self–surrender of one's own person out of love inevitably tends to fade away. Then Religion begins to see, as something necessary which does not brook any delay, the need to make *Sacrifice* compatible with the criteria of a new World with Man at its center —Man understood as a being whose existence, when all is said and done, should be defined as a search for his own well–being and satisfaction of the Self.

Unfortunately, as is usually the case, it seems that not many people had thought of the possibility that Joy would no longer be possible for human beings once the idea of *Sacrifice* had been banished.

Nevertheless, this predicament reached unexpected consequences when Religion decided to face this problem at a crucial and decisive juncture for the History of Humanity. And since Religion Herself based Her foundations upon a worship whose high point is the centrality of a *Sacrifice* —and a Divine Sacrifice, according to some— it then became logical to consider the need for a revision —as the new circumstances of the World counseled it, which was to be accomplished with two guiding considerations in mind:

The first consideration took into account —for the sake of efficacy, they said— the need for a greater participation and cooperation by the faithful in the functions of the Sacrificial Worship.

As for the second one, it had to do with the pragmatism of carrying out a deeper and more detailed study of the Sacrificial Act, so that they for whom it was destined had a better comprehension of its meaning.

After that, the only thing left to be done was to experiment with the facts and check the results. Both facts and results then reached such transcendental proportions that they changed the course of History in the City of Men.

Nevertheless, in order to understand better the situation and its historical development, we must go back and examine, if only briefly, how the events occurred.

In those days, Religion was very intent on not appearing to be at odds with the City of Men. The City's decision, which was welcomed with practically universal applause, to adopt definitively the new vision of the Word —known as the *New Age*— had impressed Religion deeply enough as to give rise to many doubts and not a few hesitations; consequently, she did not feel strong enough to contemplate any alternative other than a possible *rapprochement* to the new ideas.

Religion was convinced that the *New Age* —which the World unanimously acclaimed as *Progress*— did not contemplate any possibility of turning back. Therefore, she thought that the moment had come for her to find *a compromise solution* as a condition *sine qua non* for her survival. Urged by sudden compulsions, Religion understood that it was urgent for her to begin a new task with as much promptitude and diligence as possible: to modernize herself and to keep up–to–date. All of which was to be accomplished, according to the imperative circumstances of the times, by following the strict criteria adopted by Modernity. The starting point should be the main Act of Worship, or Sacrificial Act; after all, it was considered to be the neuralgic point which would affect Religion as a whole.

At the same time, the modern Society of the *New Age* of Men had taken as its own two fundamental principles, incorporating them into its new lifestyle: *Easiness* —a derivative from the more general principle of *Well–Being*— as the very thing to be achieved by Men in the only life which they were to know; and *Solidarity* or participation, which had already definitively displaced the fundamental reality of *love* —that reality which some people continued to identify with the *Charity* of the Old Religion.

Thus, Religion, pressed by the environment, felt that it was necessary, or expedient, to modify the Sacrificial Act. Since the purpose was to bring it closer and make it available to the Men of the City

—at least that is what they said— Religion believed that a few changes might suffice. They would be non–essential changes, just enough to pave the road to achieving *a better comprehension of and a more intense participation in the Sacrificial Act.*

And yet, the Reality of the World does not seem to be too worried about whether it coincides with the thoughts of Men or not; neither can one say that this Reality always goes hand in hand with the feelings harbored in the hearts of Men. Consequently, the bride — probably anticipating the consequences which would soon appear— began to feel herself dismayed and saddened to the point of soon falling into despondency.

She was passionately in love with the Sacrificial Act. It was for her the culminating Moment in which she *shared the Existence, the Life, and the Death of her Bridegroom* in the highest and most intense manner. But if the Sacrificial character of the Sacrificial Act was now to be reduced, and if the mystery of one's own Immolation was to be diluted, *how could anybody convince her* —once the Sacrifice is less a Sacrifice— *that precisely now, in this manner, she was participating more in the Sacrifice?*

The bride did not wish for an *easier* Sacrifice, which, to that extent, perhaps would no longer be the Sacrifice of her Bridegroom. She had already learned from Him that the way which leads to Life is narrow (Mt 7:14); that he who dies is the only one who yields fruit (Jn 12:24). That is why she distrusted everything that avoids effort and fears sacrifice; she knows that her Bridegroom chose the way of the Cross —and no other— to suffer Death out of Love for her. From then on, she was convinced that *ease* is —always and everywhere— the polar opposite of Love.

Above all —and this is her most powerful reason— she was longing to *suffer the same Sacrifice and share the same Death of her*

Husband. Indeed, she had always thought that suffering —which of itself has no meaning at all— perhaps is not so important *as the act of undergoing it for the sake of the Bridegroom and with the Bridegroom.* In this way, and following the same trend of thought, neither Death nor even Life would hold any meaning... *if we disregard the Perfect Joy of being together with the Bridegroom, or the awareness that whether one lives or whether one dies, all belongs to Him* (Rom 14:8). Life is beautiful and lively indeed when it is lived together with the Bridegroom, like the shining of the stars in the peaceful summer nights; but Death —being, after all, the consummation of Life— is even more beautiful when it is freely accepted and assumed in Him and from Him. Thus, she does not hesitate to proclaim, deeply moved, that they belong to each other; calling to Him in anguish because she realizes that she can no longer live without Him:

> *My beloved is mine and I am his.*
> *He pastures his flock among the lilies.*
> *Before the day–breeze rises,*
> *Before the shadows flee,*
> *Return! Be, my Love,*
> *Like a gazelle, like a young stag,*
> *On the mountains of Bether.*[5]

She wants to follow Him, whatever the appointed cost may be, and to be with Him; she has finally understood, in some manner which defies description, the only way —for there is no other— in which her dream could become a reality: to climb with the Bridegroom the very mountain where the true Sacrifice dwells:

---

[5] Sg 2: 16–17.

Allow me to follow you, my companion,
My dear friend, beloved Husband, my sweet Love,
That we may walk together the paths that run
Through the valley up to the hills far above.

And in solitude we shall stay, you and I,
Leaving the World of Men behind, forgotten;
And we will contemplate the blue of the sky,
Surrounded by the breezes of the mountain.[6]

But Religion, more in tune with the City of Men, had already accepted and made its own the idea of a Sacrifice to be shared by the bride, but now with *two important specifications*: first, the New Sacrifice was to be imbued with a toned–down sense of immolation and was to always keep its eyes on the Society of the *New Age* —since this Society was an indisputable achievement; secondly, Religion should not insist too much upon ideas that had already been considered obsolete, such as denying oneself, or giving oneself up out of love, or sharing, out of Love, the Death of the beloved. Religion tried hard to make all Men and places aware —being very persistent so as to be accepted by all of them as well— that the fact

---

[6]Alfonso Gálvez, *op. cit.* n. 95–96. In the Spanish original:

Déjame que te siga, compañero,
mi dulce amigo, Esposo bienamado,
para que andemos juntos el sendero
que sube desde el valle hasta el collado.
Y luego en soledad nos quedaremos
del Mundo de los Hombres olvidados,
y del cielo el azul contemplaremos
del aura de los montes rodeados.

that the faithful share the Sacrificial Act was now sufficiently expressed by particular ordinary and simple actions that should take place precisely during the Acts of Worship: reciting readings during the celebration of the Liturgy; taking part in the distribution of the Eucharistic Bread; or encouraging the Community with stories of personal experiences which could be accompanied by cheerful playing of guitars and *effusions* of the Spirit... Thus the old immolation, which meant self–negation and which would have led to some kind of mystical —perhaps even real— death, was replaced by merely external acts that did not demand any sacrifice or effort. In the end, it was all about substituting *death* with *life*. Although some could have also said, probably with greater certainty, that *Life* was relegated to a second or third place only to be substituted by *Death.*

The second woe is past; behold the third woe is to come quickly after it.[7]

The Bride always knew, nevertheless, that sharing the Sacrifice of the Bridegroom means making *her own* the Sufferings and the Death that He endured. She was convinced that the mystical character of such an experience —destined by its very nature to reach its climax in the course of the everyday life of the bride— did not make it less real. It was obvious to the soul of the bride that sharing the Death of the Bridegroom demanded her very own death... otherwise, the whole matter would be reduced to a mere metaphor or a simple memorial; but it is well–known that true Death is usually accompanied by pain and real tears which spring from a truly and completely troubled heart. All these realities form a well–joined whole made up of feelings so personal and intimate that they cannot be assumed by just any stranger who dares to try:

---

[7]Rev 11:14.

> *A small wounded nightingale*
> *I once begged to tell me her sorrows so deep.*
> *She said —but told not her tale—*
> *That I'd be better to keep*
> *My own way of mourning for what makes me weep.*[8]

That is why she addresses her Bridegroom to tell him that she has not found his footprints anywhere, neither on the trodden nor the unknown paths, though she has searched far and wide:

> *I sought him whom my soul loves,*
> *I sought him, and found him not.*[9]

She has discovered them only after having given up her life for love; in the same place where both have shared the Sacrifice and Death. For it was there where the Bridegroom impatiently waited for her, from the very beginning, before the dawn of Time:

---

[8]Alfonso Gálvez, *op. cit.* n. 8. In the Spanish original:

> *Al ruiseñor herido*
> *pedí que su lamento me dijera,*
> *mas él me ha respondido*
> *que yo mejor hiciera*
> *en continuar llorando a mi manera.*

[9]Sg 3:1.

To the distant stars I climbed
Thinking in those lights afar
Some small vestige of your footprints I would find.
But I did not find a star
While walking towards the Sun, from the Moon stellar.[10]

In the meantime, Religion, encouraged by the new momentum, was quite willing to present the *Sacrifice* to the Men of the City... but now as something more accessible and far easier for modern mentality. Therefore, it seemed necessary to clothe it with a more *intelligible* character.

To accomplish this task, it was necessary to modify two elements whose relevance in the configuration of the Sacrificial Act was unquestionably vital. The first element had to do with the simplification of the ceremonial rites. The second was concerned with the language to be used in the liturgy. Thus, the introduction of simpler rites was aimed at achieving both brevity and simplicity. In the same way, the banishment of the archaic language which had been traditionally used for centuries would leave room for the novelty of bringing into play the modern languages used here and there by the various peoples of the Earth.

The bride was told that this new orientation would help Men to better understand the *meaning* —a term preferred to *content*— of the Sacrificial Act, which would be useful to Men, of course, once

---

[10]Alfonso Gálvez, *op. cit.* n. 10. In the Spanish original:

Subí hasta las estrellas
pensando que en alguna
iba a encontrar vestigios de tus huellas;
mas yo no hallé ninguna,
caminando hacia el Sol, desde la Luna.

they made use of their own languages. One must add here the convenience of putting into practice rites more in accord with the particular psychology, customs, and traditions of the Men of the *New Age.* For everything seemed to indicate that the old rites suffered from excessive sumptuousness and baroque complexity, more in alignment with those of ages gone by whose meaning was difficult to grasp for the modern man. Logically, the old rites had to be divested, as well, from an excessive sense of transcendence which made them appear as though shrouded in a kind of remote and unreachable character. In sum, languages and rites were now arranged and ready to be presented in their new context, undoubtedly more easily assimilated by Modern Man's mentality.

Nevertheless, sometimes it happens that feelings of sadness abruptly spring forth from the human heart without any known cause or reason which could possibly justify them; so it happened this time with the bride who, contrary to what one could have expected, suddenly felt herself terribly perplexed. She could recall the events —narrated in the Books of the Chronicles of the Bridegroom— that happened long ago, at the dawn of the History of Men. It was said in these Books that life was once peacefully lived in mutual society where everyone commonly used the same language; but a moment came when God unleashed His punishment on Men because of their iniquities. God transformed their common language into a distressing diversity of tongues which plunged Men into confusion. They realized that it was practically impossible to understand one another and that they were doomed to a division among themselves so profound that to date it has never been mended (Gen 11: 1–9).

Many a century has passed since then, and the circumstances are indeed not identical. Nevertheless, the dejected and grief–stricken bride is suffering; she is in agony because she feels that the *Sacrifice*

—the Death of the Bridegroom out of Love— runs the risk of being as differently *interpreted* as it can be differently *expressed*. For, even admitting that language is the vehicle that transports ideas, no one can deny the decisive influence that words acquire over those ideas. Much more so when the varied forms used to express *Sacrifice* are subject to the opinions and discretion of different Organisms which belong to Cultures and Countries equally different, or even to mere individuals whom the new System allowed to speak and to act according to their own particular understandings.

The bride, being aware of the possibility that those Realities so much loved by her might be distorted, felt herself overwhelmed with anguish: she feared —not without reason— that she would be robbed of the Death of the Bridegroom; that consequently there was a risk, clearly perceived by her, that she would be deprived of the maximum expression of the Love of the Bridegroom for her: the Sacrificial Act. And she foresaw, at the same time, the danger that she would be impeded from answering Him in the same manner; that is, by sharing, with Him and in union with Him, the *Sacrifice*. That is what their mutual and shared *Death out of Love*, which she had for so long and so ardently desired, would really mean for both of them. In the last analysis, what the bride really feared, were she to be deprived of the possibility of contemplating the Bridegroom, was the risk of not being able to find Him again:

> *I opened the door to my Beloved,*
> *But he had turned aside, and was gone.*
> *I sought him, and found him not.*
> *I called him, and he did not answer me.*[11]

---

[11]Sg 5:6.

Her fears were far from being exaggerated or unfounded, for there were many people who no longer believed in the *Sacrifice*, as their forms of expressing it and referring to it clearly proved. Indeed, the expressions they used no longer evoked *Sacrifice*, since that term had been replaced by words like *Memorial*, *Symbol*, or mere *Allegory*. Those who still confessed themselves as followers of the Bridegroom could not even remember the last time they used the proper name of *Sacrificial Act*. They now referred to it with expressions whose ultimate goal did not seem to be other than hiding discreetly the disappearance of Faith. They spoke now of a *Meal of Solidarity*, for instance, trying to allude to acts which —they forcefully assured the people— would foster an alleged fraternity and solidarity among Men. Others described the *Sacrifice* as a *Thanksgiving* through which they tried to express feelings of gratitude about something or to someone, but nobody knew what or who it was.

Things being so, how could it be possible that the bride should not cry...? She contemplated the Death of the Bridegroom, debased, signifying a Meal among Friends! Or an Act of Gratitude with no other intention except to express appreciation for a service whose meaning barely matters and whose purpose does not matter at all...; could she stop her lamentations and her bitter moaning?

The bride's attempts at keeping her relationship of Love with the Bridegroom alive —or at trying to prevent that true Love, Immutable and Eternal as It is, be nullified— caused her to be ridiculed and persecuted everywhere. To this end, and to no other, are always led those who maintain their fidelity to the Bridegroom; contrary to the way in which the World proceeds toward those who accept and serve it, as the Scripture says, *those who want to live piously in Christ Jesus will suffer persecution.*[12] Therefore,

---

[12]2 Tim 3:12.

> *The keepers that go about the city found me;*
> *They struck me, and wounded me;*
> *The keepers of the walls*
> *Took away my veil from me.*[13]

But the bride never contemplated an *easy* way of sharing the Life, and much less the Death, of her Bridegroom. She always knew that Love is not found along the paths that climb up to *Mount Absence-of-Effort*. Why would she want her relationship of Love with her Bridegroom to be made up of small trifles, absence of sacrifices and renunciations, while ignoring, at the same time, the meaning of self-giving out of a love which is consummated in Death...? Since the Bridegroom had chosen for Himself the Narrow Path, she did not wish to follow another. She longed only to walk with Him, to live with Him, and to die with Him. That is why she tells the Bridegroom:

> *Of all your great longings, which dream stands apart?*
> *You asked yesterday as we walked, just we two.*
> *I looked in your eyes and they captured my heart.*
> *All that I want is to die of love for you.*[14]

According to Religion, the purpose for using simplified rites and vernacular languages, as they were introduced in the new liturgy of the *Sacrifice*, was to make it more *intelligible* to Men of today.

---

[13]Sg 5:7.

[14]In the Spanish original:

> *¿Cuál de tus ansias es la más soñada?*
> *Me preguntaste ayer por el sendero.*
> *Y yo, en susurro, dije enamorada:*
> *morir de amor por ti es lo que yo quiero.*

Nevertheless, one can easily realize that *understanding* the *Sacrifice* and the Death of the Bridegroom is ultimately tantamount to understanding the Bridegroom *to the same degree.* Conversely, to consider that it is impossible, or very difficult, to perceive the meaning of the Sacrificial Act equally implies accepting as fact that true knowledge of the Bridegroom is out of the reach of human understanding.

It was here where the anguish of the bride reached its zenith.

Indeed, according to what has been said above, and adhering to the obvious meaning of the concepts and words used, making the *Sacrifice* intelligible to the Men of today evidently signified *making it more accessible to their mentality.* In other words —but meaning the same thing— it signified the intention of putting the *Sacrifice within the reach of Man's reason; that is, within the measure and according to the capacity of his intellect.*

The bride had heard about the early centuries of Christianity when Men, bewildered by the doctrines of Arianism, similarly tried to *understand* the Bridegroom —but to understand Him in a *human way,* for such was the nature of the error Men fell into.

The bride, then, felt dejected and in pain. For today, even within Religion itself and inside its own Circles, they also try to *understand* the Bridegroom according to the finite and limited measure of human understanding only. Whoever has eyes and wants to see will perceive that the *old* Arian heresy maintains its vitality and has become *modern.* Nobody can deny that now, even within the most influential Circles within Religion, they usually draw a line of separation between the Bridegroom of the Books of His Chronicles, on the one hand, and the Bridegroom as He was imagined by the first generation of His followers, on the other.[15]

Hence the cause for the grief of the bride: could there be some connection between the *better understanding* of the Sacrifice —which now had been adapted to and placed within the reach of the mentality of the Men of today— and the putting of the Bridegroom on a level with, or perhaps reducing Him to, the capacity of human reason?

Therefore, they who see her cry should not judge the bride wrongly. She loves the Bridegroom, not so much because He is God or due to the fact that He is Man, but for the simple and plain reason that He is *He*. For he who loves always looks at and contemplates a person. It is true, then, that the bride rejoices in the divine character of her Bridegroom as well as in His human condition; but above all and most particularly, she gives Him her Love because He is *He*, her Bridegroom. She knows well that if, per chance, the Bridegroom were dispossessed of His divinity or perhaps His human character, *He would no longer be He*, and, consequently, He would no longer be the Person she is in love with. We must say it again: love being eminently *personal* (in Its origin and in Its object), he who loves always tends toward the beloved person *because this person is precisely this person and no other*. That is why the bride does not love the Bridegroom mainly because He is God, or for the special circumstance that He has become Man; she loves Him because He is *He*. It goes without saying that if this Person Whom she loves were not God, or perhaps were not Man, He could no longer possibly be the Bridegroom for whom her heart yearns.

---

[15]It is an allusion to the Rationalist and Modernist doctrines according to which we must distinguish between the historical Christ, designed by the writings of the New Testament (Who never existed as such), and the Christ of the Faith, imagined and invented by the early Christian Community.

In addition to this, in the bride's eyes the Bridegroom is *Wonderful*. She uses this word because, although she is aware of its total insufficiency, she does not find another term which could better express her feelings. What words could be used to describe the Beauty and the Goodness of a Humanity which is translucent to His Divinity? Or to describe a Divinity which becomes transparent —to the extent that it is possible— through the charm and the seduction of His Humanity? How can anyone think that human language can depict the image of a God who is contemplated, at the same time, as true Man? How can one outline the features of a Man in Whom one perceives Ineffable Divinity? And the bride could go on talking, time and again, of the Beauty, the Goodness, the Tenderness, the Affection and Love, the Intimacy and Loving Self–Giving, the Integrity, the Purity, the Truth, the Grace, the Honesty, the Courage, the Light, the Joy... and of anything else that could somehow show Goodness and Beauty together in the highest degree of Infinity. But the bride would end up realizing that, after all, she is still very far from being able to express what she perceives in the Bridegroom.

How could anybody have thought that it would be possible for merely human reason to describe the Bridegroom, so as to be *understood* by everyone? Has Man believed himself to be so big and, at the same time, has Man imagined the Bridegroom to be so ridiculously small? Indeed, what seemed incredible has happened: somebody has accepted the possibility of reducing and minimizing the Bridegroom... to the extent of making Him able to be *apprehended* by the capacity of this wretched creature that is Man. How did it become possible to imagine that one could explain in a *better and more intelligible manner*, without resorting to help from Above, what it means that such a Person assumed, freely and out of Love for Men, His Death on the Cross?

That is why the enamored bride believes herself unable to describe her Bridegroom when people ask her about Him. Therefore, she resorts to the last resources available to her: the metaphor, for example, and the whole colorful variety of figures of speech which Poetry makes use of; thus she wants to say it all... while realizing that she can barely express anything:

> *What makes your lover better than other lovers,*
> *O loveliest of women?*
>
> *My love is fresh and ruddy,*
> *To be known among ten thousand.*
> *His head is golden, purest gold,*
> *His locks are palm fronds*
> *And black as the raven.*
> *His eyes are like doves*
> *Beside the water–courses...*[16]

Only those who look at the horizon can *somehow* reach the whereabouts and the ends of the ways and the thoughts of God; somehow indeed, because one can never state that those whereabouts and aims are entirely able to be seen; like the Sky, which only on the far horizon, the very place where the Sky becomes Land or Sea, seems to unite Himself with Them; although in a special manner, and at a spot that has never been found by Man (Is 55: 8–9).

One cannot *bring down* from the Peak —to make it equal to the human mind— that which, being so *high*, is, therefore and at the same time, so far above the human intellect.

Nevertheless, the Sacrificial Act, after having been simplified in Its rites, was finally rendered into the languages nowadays spoken

---

[16]Sg 5: 9–12.

by Men. The intention was to make it easier to be *understood* —and
better used— by the inhabitants of the Age of Modernity; an Age,
by the way, not very willing to accept any form of thought different
from its own.

For simple–minded people —who tend to be naïve and are not
especially afraid of being deceived— this attempt merely manifested
the desire of *bringing Men closer* to the meaning and the content of
the Sacrificial Act without diminishing any of Its essential elements
but providing It with a presentation more in keeping with the ways
of the thinking of the *New Age*.

And yet, all this could not appease the anxiety of the bride.
She foresaw what was really going to happen in the world of Men
—which was exactly what did occur, thus proving her right.

For, the Sacrificial Act, through which the Bridegroom rescued
Men from their wretched condition and showed them the degree of
His love for them, *was the Highest Manifestation of Love known
throughout all Ages*. Therefore, Love being the Greatest of all Mysteries —in Its Infiniteness as well as in Its Ineffability— and having
sprung directly from Being with Whom It is One Thing and the
Only Motor of all Life..., that Love Man cannot attempt to *diminish*, much less order It within the reach of his reason, which is always
so limited, or of his sentiments, which ordinarily have such tiny and
short–sighted scopes. For Love undoubtedly is the Most Sublime,
Non–Created Mystery... and the greatest of all created ones.

> *For love is strong as death,*
> *Passion as hard as Sheol.*
> *The flash of it is a flash of fire,*
> *A flame of Yahweh himself.*[17]

---

[17]Sg 8:6.

According to this text, Love is made equal to the irresistible Strength proper to Death; for Love is provided with an impetus similar to the impetus of the Reaper who, with his unwavering and unstoppable will, always puts an end to the earthly existence of Men. Because Love cannot tolerate being overcome or replaced by anything, Its passion is put on the same level as the stony hardness of Sheol.

Apparently —but only apparently—, we are again facing a metaphorical language, and again in a human fashion, for no other way of expression could be found in the Book of the Bridegroom.

The fact is that the Sacrificial Act, or the Death of the Bridegroom for the sake of the bride, is the greatest demonstration of Love she has ever received or anyone has ever imagined; a demonstration carried out in such a way that no equal has been ever known throughout all the Centuries. Finally, Love and Death are thus mysteriously united, as if they were walking hand in hand. For Man has not been granted any greater way of showing Love than by giving up his Life, freely offered to Death and for the beloved person: *Greater love than this no man has, that he lay down his life for his friends.*[18]

Death, like Life, only has meaning and makes sense in Love and together with Love:

> *For whether we live, we live unto the Lord;*
> *Or whether we die, we die unto the Lord.*[19]

And since Death —the Bridegroom's Death, which happened out of Love— only finds any meaning in Love, why should one wonder at the fact that the Sacrificial Act —where the Bridegroom gives

---

[18] Jn 15:13.

[19] Rom 14:8.

up His Life out of Love— is just that and nothing else: *The Act and Demonstration of Love never before offered to Man.* Thus, only Death out of Love —that is, only when Death has turned its old character of Punishment into Victory (1 Cor 15:55)— allows the light of Joy to permeate her [Death], so that she finally becomes, in Joy's blissful arms, a lovely Death. That is why, ever since the very moment that the Bridegroom made Death His own, only Death out of Love matters. As the bride says:

> His eyes fixed on my eyes; his gaze pierced me through
> Before the rose–colored dawn awoke early
> And I was wounded so deeply that I knew
> If he took his sweet gaze from me, then surely
> Death caused from love would quickly overtake me.
>
> His loving eyes looked at me
> Before white Apollo appeared in the sky,
> And they wounded me gravely
> With such sweet love that if I
> Could not see them again, I would surely die.[20]

---

[20]Alfonso Gálvez, *op. cit.* n. 36–37. In the Spanish original:

> Sus ojos en los míos se posaron
> antes de que la aurora despertara,
> y en tal manera herida me dejaron
> que si el dulce mirar de mí apartara
> pronto en muerte de amor yo me encontrara.
>
> Sus ojos me miraron
> antes de que la aurora apareciera,
> y herido me dejaron
> de amor, en tal manera,
> que sin verlos de nuevo yo muriera.

The Book of the Bridegroom goes on speaking of Love and of Death out of Love; and it does so in such a sublime way that it seems a human way and, simultaneously, in such a lofty way that it makes us believe it is divine. According to the Sacred Book, Love cannot be purchased and does not brook being sold. What price would suffice to acquire It? What amount of money could possibly be asked by the vendor? There is no money, nor anything in this Universe, capable of buying it. Only Love can be equaled to Love and only by Love be acquired. Love can only be reached by Love, and only by Love can be given. Love is so *Unique* as to seem to be lost in a supreme and infinite solitude... except that Love always gives Itself to the beloved person, and it is the beloved person which Love always receives. Love never makes any demands when giving Itself; Love is never requited in the hope of receiving, in even the smallest way, an equivalent reward:

> *Many waters cannot quench love,*
> *Neither can the floods drown it.*
> *Were a man to offer all his family wealth to buy love,*
> *Contempt is all that he would gain.*[21]

But then Men...? Can they —who have been able to confuse and equate Love with *sex*; who have only trusted their reason and the possibilities— always so limited —of their own language— are they now able to understand what the Sacrifice of Love is...?

Thus, for all who want to hear it, this is the Message of the stars, which has been translated into a twinkling, sparkling language and sent from the lost immensities of the astral space, to be picked up, finally, by those who look at the Sky in the tranquil, transparent nights.

---

[21]Sg 8:7.

"Because Love can only be *understood* by Love, they who do not love are destined to never know It" (1 Jn 4:8). For the same reason, the Death that the Bridegroom assumed freely and out of love for the bride, will never be *understood*, much less *shared*, if It is not assumed in Him and together with Him.

Therefore, the Sacrificial Act cannot be classified, nor made to fit by any means, *into* the possibilities of understanding of any created intellect..., unless that intellect has been previously flooded by the light which illuminated the Mystery of Death out of Love; the very light which cannot find room in the thoughts —narrow and unfit as they naturally are— of those who have never surrendered themselves to the Mystery of Love. Someone already apprised us, from Ancient Times, about what Men are capable of thinking, when they prefer to act on their own, about Dying out of Love: foolishness, according to some people; a stumbling block, according to others (1 Cor 1:23).

Love being the most *solid* and even the greatest of all the realities that fill the Universe —to the extent that Love's highest degree of Infiniteness is identical to Being— then Death out of Love is an equally *hard* reality, which cannot be reduced or confined to the fields of allegory, nor perchance of the symbol, nor even of tender and loving memories; for all of them —allegory, symbol, and memories— are but mere products of the human imagination, and only that imagination walks on those fields.

> *For love is strong as death,*
> *Passion as hard as Sheol.*
> *The flash of it is a flash of fire,*
> *A flame of Yahweh himself.*[22]

And because Death can only be *shared* in the mode of Death, he will be taken for a fool who claims to have *shared* It...; for all of his

---

[22]Sg 8:6.

claimed sharing would have been made through merely superficial
forms and manners, futile in themselves as well as empty, as distant
from the reality of Death as they were strange to the immolation
which opens the doors that lead to the mysterious Abyss of Love.
For Love being the most sublime and the greatest of all realities, it
would be foolishness, even deserving of punishment, to claim that
one has *shared* in Death out of Love because he has managed an
insignificant human action. A human action which, far from being
the sharp reality of either a self–giving as donation or a total self–
renunciation, has not even experienced the palpitation of a minute
sacrifice or the softest sigh of the tiniest of efforts:

> *Were a man to offer all his family wealth to buy love,*
> *Contempt is all that he would gain.*[23]

Whoever declares that he has made Dying out of Love *understandable*; whoever tries to make *easy* the hard destiny of sharing
in Death, all that he is really after, once he has turned the hearts
of Men into dry wells —or bleak wastelands—, is the destruction of
Love. For, from that moment on, Men will not be able to love... because they will also have been deprived of suffering for the beloved
Person: Him, and no other, Who wanted to choose the Cross as the
supreme demonstration of His Love. For Men would no longer be
able to walk near the Bridegroom along the same path, or to share
the same destiny; the very destiny which would have led both of
them to the Perfect Joy of final consummation, that is, to the sweet,
amorous, total, and reciprocal self–surrender of their own lives.

Men have abandoned the path of sacrifice to search for the path-
way of an effortless life. They have deserted the anguish of the
narrow path —which is now left to the personal choice of a few

---

[23]Sg 8:7.

people— to choose instead the easiness offered by the wider path that is trodden by many (Mt 7: 13–14). In the last analysis, Men have refused to open their hearts to Love..., whose only guilt —as if Love were a criminal— in the eyes of Men was that He wanted to share the suffering and death of the beloved person.

Consequently, Men no longer know Love. For Love is a reality that flows from one person to another, so that, at once, It flows back from the latter to the former, making the two lovers one sole entity; therefore, now Men have become isolated: there is no one to talk to, no one to listen to; each person is wrapped in the dreadful loneliness of those who will no longer be able to love or to be loved.

Meanwhile, the World has been flooded with darkness; at the same time, weeping has supplanted the joy of feeling oneself in love and of knowing that one's love is reciprocated. And the pain of despair has taken over the place of sweet nostalgia; the same nostalgia that fed on Hope in the loving waiting for the Bridegroom and whose soft voice, at the same time, sang the sweet Songs of the dying dusk:

> *Before the day–breeze rises,*
> *Before the shadows lengthen...*[24]

> *In the peaceful calm of night*
> *Of the silent, wooded valley without gloom,*
> *With soft, sweet pain, now so right,*
> *The waiting for the Bridegroom*
> *Fills the soul with ardent, impatient delight.*[25]

---

[24]Sg 2:17.

[25]Alfonso Gálvez, *op. cit.* n. 11. In the Spanish original:

> *En la noche serena*
> *del silencioso valle nemoroso,*
> *en honda y dulce pena,*
> *la espera del Esposo*
> *de ardorosa impaciencia mi alma llena.*

Now, *Sacrifice* is finally accessible to all, for It has been made easy and does not demand any immolation; although now, at the same time It appears to be closer to the World, that *Sacrifice* shows the soft grief caused by the nostalgia of divine realities. In addition to no longer taking pleasure in Joy, Men even seem to have forgotten how to listen, in the peaceful deep valleys, to the melodious echoes of the Ancient Songs:

> *The lights of an afternoon already spent*
> *Spread long shadows throughout the entire valley;*
> *And one can hear, at times, the far and distant*
> *Strumming that combines soft rhythmic melody*
> *Like quaint guitars and rebecs*
> *And droning murmurs of cicada insects.*[26]

---

[26] Alfonso Gálvez, *op. cit.* n. 35. In the Spanish original:

> *Las luces que la aurora derramaba*
> *las sombras de los valles deshacían;*
> *y a lo lejos, a ratos, se escuchaba*
> *el melodioso son que al par hacían*
> *rabeles y guitarras*
> *y el áspero runrún de las cigarras.*

As an Epilogue

The human Word —written or spoken— could never express, even by far, what is Love. Nor was Poetry able to do so. But the latter, taking the path where Prose, despondent in the end, had finally abandoned it, directed its steps again toward a Goal which, even though Poetry knew that it was unattainable, promised, in the end, the reward of the effort, not so vain nor perhaps so useless as not to capture at least a remnant of What it is searching for.

Song of the bride in search of her Bridegroom

If only in my walking through the valley
Near the wood of acacia trees I found you,
And could contemplate you quietly anew,
We would share death out of love then finally…![27]

---

[27] Alfonso Gálvez, *op. cit.* n. 31. In the Spanish original:

¡Si al recorrer el valle yo pudiera
junto al bosque de acacias encontrarte,
hasta que al fin, de nuevo al contemplarte,
muerte de amor contigo compartiera…!

SAINT FRANCIS AND MODERNITY

We can say, without fear of error, that Saint Francis of Assisi was not a Saint whose greatness could be compared to the value of a product placed *on sale* or offered with a *rebate* in Large Stores. Saint Francis unquestionably shines with his own light among the Lives of the Saints of the Church.

We have always been suspicious of products that are *special offers* or *on sale*. Whatever they say, a price reduction always runs parallel with a cut in quality. Trade worldwide does not give anything away.

The law of supply and demand is perhaps the first lesson to be learned in the Science of Economics; the price of the product inexorably depends on it. A supply of goods offered in bulk quantity is usually consistent with poor quality or is due to an overabundance of the product, which makes it easily acquired and, therefore, of little importance. If, however, the offer is very scarce and the demand is high, the price rises; and the more the price rises, the more the offer decreases and the demand increases. If diamonds were to become as abundant as potatoes or tomatoes, they would undoubtedly cease to be so highly valued and so eagerly sought.

Not even the History of Christian Spirituality can escape the law of supply and demand. It is not surprising, therefore, that as the number of Saints in the Church, ever since Vatican Council II, has increased exponentially (and maybe more), the appreciation and devotion of the Faithful for them have declined and almost disappeared. John Paul II alone canonized and beatified more Saints than all the other Popes throughout the History of the Church put together. In this way, devotion to the Saints, like so many things in Catholicism, *is history* —a common and current expression by which we mean that something is defunct. In this regard, it may be said that the Council has become the great archivist of obsolete things (now considered a waste) in the attic of useless junk.

Devotion to the Saints was always something very peculiar to and hopeful for the Christian People. Saints were admired as heroes and true titans, both because of their love for Jesus Christ and because of their valuable testimony before the world. The Faithful invoked them as intercessors before God and saw them as role models. In one way or another, the Saints have always been the subject of fervent admiration. Cities, towns, villages, and even the most humble hamlets have their Patron Saints, whom the people frequently resorted to in all their needs. The feasts and the commemorations of the Saints were also causes for joy and fun among the locals, all of whom took great pride in being named after one of them.

Things changed, however, from the time when winter seemed to loom upon the Church. Now almost everyone has a brother, or a cousin, or a relative, or at least an acquaintance who has been beatified or canonized; or perhaps a neighbor who lived two floors up, with whom one often held brief elevator–conversations. Someone will say that we are exaggerating, we know; and it is true. But that person must at least concede that there is a lot of truth in all that we have said.

For, indeed, even here, the gold coin, precious and rare, has been replaced by common currency circulating in the hands of everyone. The proof that an overabundance of the product has decreased its quality is also evident: the draconian suppression of the requirements to be followed in the process of canonization. We could compare the process in place before the Council with the current one; the result would be most impressive for anyone who would bother to find out. There is very clear and easily obtained official information to validate this.

As for the required miracles, the process no longer looks so much for the overwhelming clarity of their reality as for the importance attributed to other elements. We can make mention here, for example, of practical and political criteria of convenience, pastoral and ecumenical usefulness, etc., etc.

In this regard, the figure of the Seraphim of Assisi is something clearly exceptional. Like all great Saints, the story of his life is filled with such brilliant and, by the same token, sometimes *strange* insights... as only the great men that Humanity has known may provide.

It is for this reason that Saint Francis was considered in his time slightly less (or slightly more) than a madman. And even in our own time, after eight centuries, he is still misunderstood, *albeit* admired. He had the brilliant idea of writing a Constitution —the *Regula* (Rule)— for the members of his own Order which followed the Gospel *to the letter*, without further commentaries; that is, without subtractions or additions. Does the Gospel by any chance —so reasoned Saint Francis— need any modifications that can improve the teachings of Our Lord?

Of course the Church —*Mater et Magistra*— has always mistrusted radicalism. And surely she has a reason for it. A human being who firmly believes in the Gospel and who, on top of that, is determined to practice it *as it is*, becomes a dangerous element. Poverty, for example, as embodied in the evangelical text, is considered impracticable when taken at face value. And this is how it began, the long story, distressing for the Saint, of the various *Rules* and successive *Mitigations*. Pope Innocent III, for example, went so far as to tell Saint Francis: *This kind of life that you want to embrace seems to me too difficult.* When the Church, in the person of Pope Honorius III, appointed Cardinal Hugolino as *Cardinal Protector* of the Order, it was due, no doubt, to the fact that the ecclesiastical world did not trust Saint Francis. Everybody knew that the *Protector* was, in reality, a watchman whose responsibility it was to keep at bay the *eccentricities* of the Saint. But we will talk more extensively on this subject later.

The contradictions that Saint Francis had to suffer, as so often happens with great men, came to be summarized in the trick that History played on him. Determined as he was to live the Gospel to the letter, he was forced to allow many *Mitigations* for his *Rule*.

His misfortune was, precisely, that the theory of *hermeneutics of continuity* had not yet been discovered. Our Modern Catholicism would not have had any quandary in admitting the claims of the Saint. After all, thanks to this theory, it does not matter how literally one may take the Revealed Word or the Teachings of the Magisterium; one must always take into account that upon which everything depends, namely the concrete man and individual who lives in a particular place and during a specific time in History; it is he who interprets them, therefore, according to his own subjective criteria and the *historical* conditions of the moment, applicable only *here and now*. The Revealed Word or the Magisterium can say what they want, no problem, for they are subjected to being *interpreted and adapted* to the mentality of the moment. If the Popes of the thirteenth century had known *historicism*, they would not have had any trouble with some of the claims of Saint Francis.

Saint Francis was at all times faithful to the Church, with an obedience like that of his Master Jesus Christ, that is, *even to death* (Phil 2:8). He accepted that his ideal of living the Gospel seriously —literally— was not understood or accepted; and he did not mind being taken as an eccentric and extremist. That is why he was treated by the Church with complete fairness and great reverence —to the point of being considered by her, even today, as one of her most radiant Saints.

Anyway, Saint Francis was a character whose ideals were impractical and exaggerated for his time. That is what the Popes who dealt with him, Cardinal Hugolino, his *Protector*, and even characters as circumspect as Saint Anthony of Padua (a spiritual son and contemporary of Saint Francis) and Saint Bonaventure himself —soon to succeed Francis as General of the Franciscan Order— thought of him.

The ensuing *Mitigations* of the Rule which, out of obedience he was obliged to accept, were always based on the same issue: Given the impossibility of a Gospel taken *to the letter*, it was necessary to find formulas to make it *more reasonable* and more *capable of being accepted* by some followers who, after all, felt themselves to be merely human beings and not heroes or titans.

It is often said, with some plausibility, that *History is the Master of life*. That is why it remains a sad fact that the recurrence of situations is almost never used by men to draw useful lessons — something that happens more frequently than is desirable. Well, we have here a reality that, by an astonishing wonder, has gone unnoticed by scholars: the similarity between the situation faced by Saint Francis and the doctrine advocated by current Modernism, which basically intends *to render the Gospel more reasonable and better adapted to the modern mind, so that it can be accepted by modern man.*

Or at least that is how it seems on the part of Modernism; however, the differences between the two situations are too deep to pass by unnoticed.

The fear, or refusal of practical acceptance of the Gospel by those in the Middle Ages is purely *external*, while the rejection of Revelation on the part of Modernism is entirely *internal*. This means that in the era of Saint Francis the truth of the Gospel was never doubted (even in all its literalness), although, in any case, it did cast doubts on the capability of men —or at least the vast majority of them— to carry it out; while the rejection accomplished by Modernism reflects the desire to *streamline* the Gospel, or *reduce* it to the measurement and interpretation of the categories of today's human thought.

At least that is how it appears from a first approach to Modernism. And, truly speaking, this is how that doctrine presents itself; and that is what even those who believe themselves to be most informed about that doctrine think about it. However, this interpretation is not at all the whole truth; in fact, it even contains no truth.

The Middle Ages was the bearer of an unconditional and absolute Faith in the Revealed Word of God. The heresies —which have existed throughout all ages— attacked few concrete truths of the Faith, and they were easily and promptly condemned and aborted by the Magisterium of the Church. It may be said about Modernism, however, that *it attacks all the truths of the Faith at once.* Saint Pius X firmly asserted that the Modernist heresy was, in fact, *the compendium of all heresies.*

And yet, this is not the whole truth. It would be difficult, and absurd, to imagine Modernism elaborating a list of dogmas and truths of the Faith to deny them one by one, or even all of them as a whole. Such a thing would imply a naïve simplification of the problem. What modernism really does is *attack the very root and foundation of the Faith.*[1] In other words, Modernism means the total and absolute denial of the entire supernatural world. The sequential relationship *God made Man*, accomplished in the Incarnation of the Word and proclaimed by the Faith, has been turned upside down by Modernism into the opposite one of *Man made God.*

It is not a matter of making a Christianity more and better adapted to the mentality of modern man so that it can be accepted by him, nor a matter of a more complete application of the modern techniques of investigation to get a better understanding of Revealed Scripture. Such slogans and similar ones are proclaimed by Modernism with the intention of deceiving the gullible (who, after all, are the species most abundant in the world). The purpose of the *New Age* Religion is the deification of man and the overcoming of all myths and beliefs of the past that referred to a transcendent Godhead. God is now, in fact, only an Idea developed by Man himself, which has evolved with him, and which now, once man has reached his maturity on this Earth, it is time to be kept in the attic with the rest of the junk.

The danger —which is immense— of this approach to the Faith of Christians is twofold:

---

[1] These are the exact words of the Holy Father: *Moreover they [Modernists] lay the ax not to the branches and shoots, but to the very root, that is, to the Faith and its deepest fibers. And once having struck at this root of immortality, they proceed to disseminate the virus through the whole tree, and to such an extent that there is no part of the Catholic Faith which they leave untouched, none that they do not strive to corrupt* (Saint Pius X, *Encyclical Pascendi*, n.3).

On the one hand, Modernism is an expert Master in the domain of language. It never presents itself to the community of believers with the authentic trappings of its doctrine. The employment of double–meaning language, of ambiguity, of words traditionally used in Christianity —which now are given, however, a different significance— etc., are techniques perfectly mastered by it.

On the other hand, Modernism has infiltrated today's Church and has a *full force there today* because it counts on the most earnest cooperation of much of the Hierarchy, even in its highest ranks. It is not strange, therefore, that much of the Worship which takes place at the present time as well as an infinite number of Catholics who still consider themselves such have become, in reality, both the former and the latter, unknowingly Modernist.

The phenomenon is so serious and so poignantly real that it deserves further and more careful consideration.

The Opposition between what the Gospel teaches and human weakness has been a constant feature in the History of Christian Spirituality. In this regard, people have taken either of two different attitudes.

On the one hand, there are those who have openly rejected the Gospel. On the other hand, there is an attitude which envisages, in turn, two different perspectives. In the first perspective are they who have tried to *interpret* the Gospel, minimizing its demands — although not abandoning them or stopping belief in them— to make them compatible with a more unchallenging human existence. The second perspective refers to those who have tried to adapt these demands to their own human subjectivity, accepting them only through the prism of human reason and to the extent that they are agreeable to it.

Let us try to delve deeper into these two schools of thought. The first stream of ideas —which *softens* the Gospel but without abandoning fidelity to the Revealed Word— has always existed within Christianity, walking always in parallel with the birth and the decline of Religious Orders and Congregations. The struggle between the *Strict Observance* and the *Mitigated Observance* reached full force in the Middle Ages. And as for the early Renaissance, we all are too familiar with the struggle that characters like Saint Teresa of Avila and Saint John of the Cross —supporters of reforming the Carmelite Order (The Discalced Carmelites)— had to maintain against the solid resistance of The Calced.

The second trend, or that which seeks to adjust Revelation to the measure of human subjectivity, and which squarely matches the Modernist Theology, is actually a falsehood.

Of course, Modernism, which is the principal sponsor and practitioner of this doctrine, presents it as the *authentic* interpretation of the Gospel. Christians who existed for the past twenty centuries somehow lived without knowing it, until the *New Pentecost* arrived with the Second Vatican Council to uncover this truth to all Christendom. Pope John Paul II, especially throughout his Encyclicals, imagined a very long *bridge* between the *Pentecost* of the first Apostles and the *New Pentecost* of the *New Era*, thanks to which Christianity would reach full maturity precisely at the beginning of the third millennium.

But the acceptance of such a premise would require the previous clarification of some important questions that must be taken into account. For it so happens that Modernism is a true artisan in the technique of Lying; a lesson that it has learned well from its Father, the Devil —since he is the Father of Lies and of all liars, according to Jesus Christ Himself. Modernism uses lies as befits every good liar, wrapped in the finest raiment of truth— a tithe that, after all, lies have to pay. For example, the art of the language of double meaning; of ambiguity; of the possible double and even triple interpretation; of the current orthodox terminology, which is also used by Modernism but in a totally different sense... all are skills perfectly dominated by Modernism.

Modernism is fully immersed in the immanentist doctrine of modern Existentialism, Personalism, and, above all, Historicism. Revelation has to be interpreted by man, although to the measure of his own reason and only in terms that can be accepted by the categories of human thought within each historic moment. Thus, what is true, legitimate, or false in a given historical moment or place *may not be such in another time or according to other categories of thought*. Therefore, man is not measured or configured by God's Revelation, but rather the opposite, for it is this Revelation which has to be determined by man. Now, it is no longer the Word of God that judges man, but man is the judge of the Word of God and the one who decides about It.

Apparently, this doctrine of Modernism would lead to a more *authentic* religion which would be more *consistent* with human nature —we see here, once again, the presumption of lowering Revelation to man's level instead of putting man at the prominence and in accordance with the demands of Revelation; in reality, such aim is nothing more than a façade (the Lie needs to disguise Itself). What Modernism seeks is to replace the worship of God with the worship of man; in other words, the disappearance of all vestige of supernatural or transcendent Religion.

Let us repeat it once more: the Gospel is perennially up–to–date. This means that Jesus Christ had foreseen and condemned this situation clearly and strongly; for instance, in the following passage from the Gospel of Saint Mark:

> *But He answering said to them:*
> *—Well did Isaiah prophesy of you hypocrites, as it is written:*
>
> > *'This people honours me with their lips,*
> > *But their heart is far from me.*
> > *And in vain do they worship me,*
> > *Teaching doctrines and precepts of men.'*
>
> *For leaving the commandment of God, you hold to the tradition of men.*
> *And He said to them:*
> *—Well do you make void the commandment of God, that you may keep your own tradition! For Moses said: 'Honour your father and your mother. And he that shall curse father or mother, dying let him die.' But you say: 'If a man shall say to his father or mother, Corban (which is a gift) whatsoever is from me shall profit you.' And further you allow him not to do anything for his father or mother, making void the Word of God by your own tradition, which you have given forth. And many other such like things you do"* (Mk 7: 6–13).

Except for disbelief and heresies, Christianity has never doubted the truth of the Gospel. That said, one has to make room for human weakness, which has always resisted taking seriously the practice of the Gospel. Jesus Christ already said that the path that leads to Life is hard and narrow, and few walk along it; whereas the path that leads to perdition is broad and spacious, and, unlike the former, there are many who enter by it (Mt 7: 13–14).

This explains the resistance to the *Rule* proposed by Saint Francis, as well as the fact that, although the true disciples of Jesus Christ, throughout the History of Christianity, have numbered many more than those whom the Church has proclaimed as such in her *Book of Saints*, the truth is that the authentic Saints —those recognized as titans in their Love for Jesus Christ and in their practice of the Gospel— have always been scarce... at least until the age that began with Pope John XXIII.

All this is rightly so, given the state of human nature and how sublime the Road of the Gospel is, on the one hand; and the exigencies attached to the character of the Hero (a synonym of Saint), on the other. The truth of the matter is that the Hero, like the Saint, would no longer be seen as such the very instant that there were an abundance of them; and they would consequently lose their rarity status. The human race only admires what is unusual and extraordinary, which is easily explained when one considers that what is common and vulgar does not attract anyone's attention.

But the admiration for the Saints, which is but a consequence of acknowledging their character as heroes and models, has, however, a very singular quality. First, it only occurs *post mortem* and over time (the so–called *Santo Subito* is, in reality, a completely dubious innovation); the reason being, perhaps, that with the passage of time the Saints have already acquired the status of *Legend*; and legends, as is well known, although they give rise to enthusiasm and feelings of respect for the numinous, pose no danger to anyone; that is, the possibility no longer exists that someone may feel belittled by them when he contrasts them with the mediocrity of his own life.

Secondly, the Saint is never recognized as such during his earthly existence. Quite the contrary: when all is said and done, he is a character who is bent on imitating seriously the life of Jesus Christ, which fully immerses him in the warning contained in the Second Letter of Saint Paul to Timothy: *Those who want to live godly in Christ Jesus shall suffer persecution* (2 Tim 3:12). And in this, as in so many other things, one cannot change the facts.

Apparently the reason for this is that his contemporaries may see in the Saint a constant accusation against themselves. It turns out that the Gospel is a reality that *is there, that can be both taken seriously and also carried out.* The Saint's behavior becomes annoying, therefore, when each party has already decided, in view of his own tranquility, that Christianity is merely a matter of devotion or, in any case, typical of those mysterious *Titans* who are said to have lived long ago and in the Dark Times of Humanity. And nobody likes to see his life made difficult.

Saint Francis was ignored even by his own spiritual children, including the most illustrious; even more so by the Hierarchy of the Church, whose main function has often been, apparently, to slow down heroic impulses: the more faithfully those impulses tried to adjust themselves to the Gospel, the more they were held back. As incredible as it may seem, to mention just one modern case, even Pope John XXIII accepted negative reports against Padre Pio of Pietrelcina which were furnished by detracting slanderers who had violated the secret of confession by hiding microphones in the confessional.

However, the rejection of the Gospel advocated by Modernism, as we have said in previous chapters, is of a different nature. It is no longer a matter of being afraid of the Gospel, but of a *lack of faith in its veracity, as a consequence of the general rejection of the supernatural.* Of course, as we have pointed out before, Modernism does not admit it. It is a matter, it says, of living a more sincere and realistic Christianity.

In the post–Council era, Progressive Theology insisted —despite all evidence to the contrary— that there was no contradiction between the post–Vatican II Magisterium and the previous one which had always been proclaimed by the Church in accordance with Tradition up to that moment in History.

But, when the evidence became too blatant, then that Theology was forced to change tactics. Once it was admitted that, in effect, there are such contradictions, It resorted to the theory of different interpretations, which depends on the circumstances to be considered in each historical moment. Thus, for example, some texts of the Magisterium which condemned errors and which were rightly issued at a particular time in history, as circumstances required it, may now have ceased to be effective because those circumstances have changed at the present moment in which we live.

The problem arises when one poses the question: who is the one to determine or assess that there has been a change of circumstances? Of course, according to Modernism, that one is not the Magisterium, for it is no longer reliable since —in the opinion of Progressive Theology— it is subject to change depending on the circumstances; therefore, it cannot confirm itself. Consequently, theologians are the ones called on to perform this task, for they must listen to and configure the *sensus fidei* of the Christian People, developing, in doing so, some patterns which ultimately —finally something!— can be collected and unified by the Magisterium. But then, what can happen, or what kind of certainty can be expected, when the feet have replaced the head? A text may be eloquent enough to illustrate this theme:

The Document [*Donum Veritatis* from the Congregation for the Doctrine of the Faith, 1990] *states, perhaps for the first time with such clarity, that the decisions of the Magisterium cannot be the last word about the issue they are concerned with, although they are substantially rooted in the problem at hand; they are, above all, an expression of pastoral prudence and like a provisional disposition. Their essential nucleus remains valid, but their aspects, upon which the circumstances of the historical moment have exerted their influence, may be in need of further modifications. One can think, in this regard, of the declarations of the Popes of the previous century about religious liberty, as well as of anti–Modernist decisions in the beginning of this century, especially of the decisions of the Pontifical Biblical Commission at that time.*[2]

The consequences can be deduced easily. As for the *theologians*, for example, it suffices to recall that during the Second Vatican Council they were directed entirely and precisely by the German theologians, whose orthodoxy was rather dubious, to say the least. And one should not forget that the Bishops (the Council Fathers) did not take a step without consulting them. As for the *sensus fidei*, or the sense of the Faith of the Christian People, it should not be confused with the manipulated thinking of so many people; let us just mention here also the decisive influence that the Press has had on the Faithful regarding that event. Summarizing, and in short: there is no more certainty of Faith.

Then...?

Then, the true Catholic who is, therefore, faithful to the Church and to the authentic Hierarchy, will continue trusting in the promises of Jesus Christ regarding the perennial nature of the Church. And, above all, he will continue praying and putting his hope in God. The Apostle already said it: *As the Scripture says: 'No one who believes in Him will be put to shame'* (Rom 10:11).

---

[2]Cardinal Ratzinger, in the *Presentation* of the mentioned Instruction, *L'Osservatore Romano*, Spanish edition, July 1, 1990, p. 12 (text quoted by Álvaro Calderón in his book *La Lámpara Bajo el Celemín*, Río Conquista, Buenos Aires, Argentina 2009, p. 94).

DON QUIXOTE AND THE "PROMOTION" OF THE PRIESTHOOD

It is not our intention in this chapter to outline an in–depth exposition of the so–called *priestly identity crisis*, about which so much was said during the first years after the Second Vatican Council and which is more alive nowadays than then.

Nevertheless, some clarifications must be made. The priestly identity crisis indeed became more acute in the aftermath of Vatican Council II, but its beginnings showed up before the Council, and several attempts had already been made at solving it. Efforts to confront the problem were intensified throughout several decades after the Council, but without satisfactory results; worse yet, those efforts contributed more than anything else to deepening the crisis.

As for the reasons that contributed to this worsening, it seems that there is an explanation: those efforts probably took the wrong direction; in fact, *it happened to be the polar opposite to the one which should have been trodden.*

The same happened to Don Quixote. Whereas all his contemporaries probably agreed on the necessity of righting all wrongs, somebody made the mistake of trying to achieve that goal by attempting to restore the Order of Knight Errantry. To say it more clearly: although the intentions may have been good, the methods used were far from being the most expedient ones. Likewise, the idea of adapting the Priesthood to the demands of the modern world (those demands, put forward as an urgent and pressing necessity, became an undisputed dogma for the conciliar and post–Conciliar Theology) was attempted through erroneous ways that in the end became pernicious. Nevertheless, this episode was but one more gust among those which blew —and are still blowing— along with the winds of reform at that time. It looked as if the Wind of the Spirit, in the *New Pentecost* of the Church according to the phraseology of Pope John Paul II, would actually be turned into the spirit of wind.

To be totally precise, there is one statement to be made which could seem astonishing: Christian Priesthood does not need to be *promoted*: it was sufficiently instituted by Jesus Christ as participation in his own Priesthood and having its same characteristics (Jn 17:18; 20:21). The Priesthood, therefore, has been *constituted* for men, once and for all and forever, according to the order of Melchisedech (Heb 5: 1 ff). To speak about the possible need for a future Council in order to confront this problem, as was done during the first post–Conciliar years (although almost no one alludes to it nowadays), would not make any sense. The alleged *promotion* of the Priesthood —should words have any meaning at all— would imply the need to elevate its *status*, which would lead to strange conclusions. One would necessarily have to admit, for instance, one of these outlandish possibilities: either the Priesthood has not already been given its proper place by Jesus Christ; or the Church can discover in the Priesthood a new identity or characteristic which has gone unnoticed for more than twenty centuries; or, and this is even more absurd, the Church can *elevate* it to a higher dignity and position than it has already been given.

Even more: If the Catholic Priesthood, given its present crisis situation, must be promoted, such promotion can only be attempted in a manner contrary to what is commonly thought and practiced, as we have said before. In other words, to dignify the Priesthood *does not mean to consider its elevation in rank, dignity, or significance according to world standards* (Jn 5: 41–44; 7:18; 8:50), *but rather to insist upon the way which leads to humility, suffering, persecution, and loathing on the part of the world.* It cannot be otherwise if we accept that the Priest is *another Christ* and that his mission is but a continuation of the mission and work of the Master (Mt 20:28; Mk 10:45; Lk 22: 26–27; Phil 2: 7–8). Consequently, the most effective way, in fact the only one, of promoting the Priesthood is to place it into its proper condition of permanent *kenosis.*

There were many post–Conciliar theologians who asserted as indisputable truth the identity crisis in the Priesthood. The idea that the Priest ought to appear no different from other men — his dress, his social condition, questioning the need for celibacy —became widespread. Moreover, it is not a question of denying the existence of the crisis, but it is true that its causes could have been explored more deeply. Evidence seems to indicate that it was artificially induced; finding support, above all, in the secularist environment that was looming upon the ecclesiastical ambience. It does not seem appropriate either to accept the attitude which puts all its effort toward suppressing all signs of differentiation of the Priest regarding the surrounding world; rather it is an idea contrary to the doctrine of the New Testament.

In reference to the artificial causes of the crisis —and the ensuing falsehood at the root of the problem— all one has to do is remember what has been said above about the identification of the Priest with Jesus Christ, Whose mission the Priest continues. If it is admitted that the identity crisis affects one of the two members of this partnership, one must also acknowledge that the other part is also affected by the crisis; which could result in a total disregard of the purpose of the Incarnation as well as of the mission of the Word Made Flesh and His coming into the world. The character of *co–redemptor* cannot be considered as alien to the office of the Priest, for he continues and *consummates* the mission of Jesus Christ —the Virgin Mary also being co–Redemptrix, and more properly so. There is no participation in the Priesthood of Jesus Christ without co–redemption (Heb 9:22) if one admits that Redemption is the chief reason for the Incarnation and the anointing of Jesus Christ as High and Only Priest. Hence, the tremendous importance of the passage of Colossians 1:24, and of other texts. (2 Cor 1: 5.7; Phil 3:10; 1 Pet 4:13; etc.)

We should add that the Holy Scripture passages about the Priests' distancing (estrangement) from the world are very clear; and that Tradition is just as forceful and far from hesitation.

In Hebrews 5:1 we must take both expressions *ex hominibus assumptus* and *pro hominibus constituitur* at face value; that is, each in its most profound meaning. There is no reason not to proceed in this way, since both are parallel and interdependent.

If you admit that the Priest has been *taken from* among men, you must also admit that he is somehow different from them. Once again we find ourselves before another of the numerous antithesis of Christian existence which, in this case, leads us to a double phenomenon that we may consider centrifugal and centripetal at the same time. The former, which would be determined by an *outward* movement expressed by *ex hominibus assumptus*, confirms the idea that the Priest has been separated from men *for the very purpose* of making him different from other people —by the attributing to or bestowing upon him of something that others do not possess— but he is still one of them. The efficient cause of this displacement or separation comes from Above (Heb 5:4) and is just what makes this situation possible and, at the same time, legitimate. At the same time, this distancing would make no sense without a simultaneous *centripetal* movement, expressed by *pro hominibus constituitur*. This is the same as saying that the Priest is someone who has been separated from men so that he can be sent back to them. This separation, which necessarily implies attributing to the chosen one an unmistakably distinctive character in regards to his brothers, not only does not estrange him from them but, in fact, it does just the opposite, for it makes him more intimate and close to his brethren. The first movement of separation is necessary to distinguish the Priest as a man of God and witness to Jesus Christ; otherwise, he would have *nothing* to give or communicate to his brothers. It is important to emphasize the fact that this distancing or separation from other men does not diminish the human condition of the Priest; on the contrary, it elevates and highlights it. It is similar to what happens to Jesus Christ in the Hypostatic Union: His Divinity does not diminish the fullness or realism of His Humanity —true *God* and true *Man.* And it may be appropriate to mention, in passing, that the antithesis separation–return is a paradigm of Christian existence (Jn 14: 3.28; 16:28).

It is beyond doubt that the expression *ex hominibus assumptus* implies an authentic *separation* from the world: *If the world hates you, know ye that it hath hated me before you. If you had been of the world, the world would love its own: but because you are not of the world, but I have chosen you out of the world, therefore the world hates you.*[1] *I have given them your word, and the world has hated them because they are not of the world, as I also am not of the world.*[2] That is why it makes no sense for the Priest, the closest

---

[1] Jn 15: 18–19.

[2] Jn 17:14.

disciple of Christ whose role it is to be *another Christ,* to insist on appearing as being identified with the world. They usually talk about *incarnationism* as a means of being accepted by the world, so that it would be possible for them to fulfill the mission entrusted to them. However, it is not licit to forget that the Incarnation does not involve identification with the world: *Just as I am not of the world... He came unto his own, but his own people did not receive him.*

Here again the *estrangement–approximation* antithesis, which is so specifically Christian, appears; without it the Incarnation would be void of content and intelligibility —and the same could be said about the mission of the Priest. That is why the *separation* and differentiation from the world is so essential to the Christian Priesthood. But we must not confuse this with a mere *distinction*, which indicates rather a difference of degree but not of quality. When this is not taken into account, when more emphasis is put toward identification with the world, then, and only then, is when the identity crisis appears. If the Priest is no different from other men, then what is he and what does he have to say to them? For that is precisely the tragedy of Protestantism: a man of the community, chosen from the community and appointed by it, *is not capable of giving to the community anything that it does not already have or does not know.* Nothing can come from the community that is not of the community, since from the wanting of something you cannot get even another wanting. The community in itself is *incapable* of giving someone the supernatural means that lead to Heaven for the simple reason that it does not have them. Ignorance, doubt, and hesitation about one's own identity is the tragedy in which the Priest has immersed himself when he tries not to feel different from the world. If a drop of water in the middle of the ocean does not try to be anything but part of the same water —really becoming one with it— how can someone even ask if that drop is different from the rest of the water? But the Priest, even though he is among men (Jn 17: 11.15), has been at the same time chosen from among men. It is true that the Word came to those who were His own, but *His own did not receive Him,*[3] as we have just seen. What men could not understand when they rejected Him is that they were fulfilling God's plan. The paradox or antithesis —revelation–concealment, wisdom–foolishness, greatness–smallness— became a reality.

Although Cervantes himself probably did not perceive it, there was no doubt that the [authentic] insanity of Don Quixote is the demonstration of the [even more authentic] insanity of those around him. At least Don Quixote was committed to righting all wrongs, while the men of his time (just like those of today) lived content with them and did not show any intention of righting them.

Forgetting what is fundamental is what leads Christians to make the mistake of not realizing that the Christian existence is a great paradox. The Incarnation, the greatest project of Divine Omnipotence and Wisdom, is, at the same time, the greatest wonder of emptying and humbling possible for those who have been driven by Love. The mystery in itself, which, given its double aspect, would have been unthinkable for mankind, is at the same time a display of the infinite magnificence of Divine Glory. As for the Priest in particular, who can do nothing but follow in the footsteps of the Archetype, he cannot achieve *promotion* except by humbling himself. In the present state of the Economy of Salvation, what is greatest cannot manifest itself except in what is smallest, just as the greatest sanity does not manifest itself in this Plan except through the greatest insanity —as can be seen abundantly in the texts of

---

[3] Jn 1:11.

Saint Paul and throughout the New Testament. If the Priest is
to be a testimony before men, he must necessarily appear distinct
from them; a differentiation which cannot come about by *rising to a
higher level* but rather just the opposite; if his testimony refers and
really points to Christ, the Priest has no other way except the one
that is already drawn and marked, which is the one Christ followed
from the *emptying* of Himself in the Incarnation until His death on
the Cross: *and where I am going you already know the way.*[4]

The Priesthood may be the institution most chastised by the
storm that lashed against the Church during Vatican Council II and
in its aftermath —and which is still beating against her today. Truly
speaking, the *identity crisis*, as we have said above, is a contrived
laboratory product since, in fact, the doctrine has been clear for the
Church, without any hesitation or doubt, for twenty long centuries.
At the same time, we must recognize that the recent Magisterium
has made no significant effort to clarify this issue.

In this regard, if any clarification is required, the text of Heb 5:1
is fundamental. It asserts that the Priest has been *taken from among
men*, while, at the same time, he has been *ordained for men*; which
could seem to be a paradox.

To tell the truth, the opposition between these two terms —being
in the world and not belonging to the world; which, on the other
hand, is a proper characteristic of any Christian— is particularly
prominent in the Priest, according to Heb 5:1, which includes both
positions. Evidently, unless the Priest *is in* the world, he cannot be
a living testimony of Jesus Christ; likewise, it is equally clear that
such a Priest is in no condition to bear that witness if he has not
been *taken from* the world.

---

[4]Jn 14:4.

The problem becomes even more serious when the necessity of being in the world is confused with the (supposed) need of *belonging* to the world: *I do not ask you to take them out of the world but to protect them from the Evil One.*[5] It is true that the Priest must be in the world; otherwise he would not be able to get close to his brothers and share their existence or even to become all things to all men (1 Cor 9:22). However, at the same time, he must appear to his brothers as somebody different from them, because of the need that weighs upon him to give testimony of Him Who, having become one of us (Jn 1: 11.14; Phil 2:7), remained, however, the *Absolute Other.* We must not forget that the Incarnation is the supreme manifestation (revelation) of God, and, at the same time, an absolute *kenosis* (hiding) of His Divinity. It should be clear that it is not enough for the Priest to appear as different from the world; he must also manifest himself as not belonging to it. Saint Peter, in his exhortation to all Christians, speaks of the obligation they have of appearing before men as *strangers and pilgrims* in the world (1 Pet 2:11; cf. Heb 11: 9.13); which obligation pertains especially to Priests.

All of this leads to living a new manifestation of that tense opposition we are talking about in this chapter.

On the one hand, the Priest must be *in the world* as the living testimony of his Master —a charge which must be very clear (especially to him). This is a fundamental truth which mysteriously goes unnoticed: the explicit reality of *being in the world* never becomes consciously factual to many priests. Here we are referring to an everyday expression that is practiced by very few: the necessity of having one's feet on the ground. Too many priests do not know the reality in which they live; moreover, they are not aware that

---

[5]Jn 17:15.

this problem affects them, hence the futility of their preaching. It is impossible to be conscious of the surrounding reality if you are not equally open to the other element that causes tension. In other words, the priest must be attentive to the world in which he lives without ceasing to be receptive to the reality from the World above —or, one might say, without ceasing to possess a deep interior life.

On the other hand, the Priest is forced to live in constant *absence* of his Master which may be described as an experience of Faith and which forces him to live in a continuous state of tension: *I am no longer in the world, but they are in the world.*[6] This effort is now much more painful and incisive since the Minister of Jesus Christ must live in a post–Christian society (including enormous masses of Catholics) that has renounced its Faith. In spite of this reality —or precisely because of it— the enthusiasm of his Faith must be patent before men, even to a level of resistance which does not exclude the shedding of his blood (Heb 12:4); or to a degree of intensity similar to the *insanity* of Abraham's faith (Rom 4: 19–20) although even more so, since the type or figure cannot be superior to the reality signified.

All of this would be impossible *if the Priest appears as just one more in the world and as belonging to it.* The Master was careful to point out that *no one lights a lamp to put it under the measure, but upon the lamp–stand, so as to give light to all in the house.*[7] Saint Paul, who had already spoken of hoping against all hope (Rom 4:18), could have equally spoken, in regards to Faith, of a force that inspires belief in what is *invisible*, in spite of what is *visible* (in the sense of Heb 11:19). We must keep in mind, as the text says, that Faith is the *proof of the things you do not see*, which is the

---

[6] Jn 17:11.

[7] Mt 5:15.

same as saying that the proof is indeed proof *in spite of what we do see*; which is what happens, for example, with the Mystery of the Catholic Church (for not everything in Her is holy). In this way, Faith can become the anti–evidence of what is evident (or the evidence of the anti–evident): or the proof that the Wisdom of God reaches much further than the wisdom of man, and also that God's insanity is wiser than human sanity.

In a post–Christian world as ours, the attitude of a Priest can be no other than as accepting God's point of view, so frequently contrary to the world's, and *in spite of all that could seem evident*. According to Saint John, Faith is precisely what overcomes the world (1 Jn 5: 4–5). This victory, especially for a Priest, given the situation of the world today, cannot become real without the sacrifice of his own life, whether we understand this in a metaphorical or in a very real sense. Truth be told, the offering of his own life bears no resemblance to a metaphor for a Priest; at least in the sense that his immolation, in one way or another, will always require a suffering that must find its consummation with his death. For the Minister of Jesus Christ cannot adopt any other position in the presence of the world than appearing before it as crucified (Gal 6:14); which becomes at least problematic if it is interpreted in a figurative sense rather than a literal one. The text from Galatians 6:17, *stigmata Jesu in super corpore meo porto,* has always seemed obscure to the commentators. It is evident that it can only refer to the fact that the signs of the sufferings of Christ —the most convincing testimony of all— are perceptible in the Apostle. This confirms that *his testimony of Christ is a true testimony.* The necessity of sharing in the death of Jesus Christ, induced at the moment of baptism, is an experience that must become reality during the life of any Christian, though it will not be consummated until the moment of his physical death. In the Priest, however, *it is already a reality* from the moment of his consecration by the Sacrament of Holy Orders: since the testimony he must give to the death of his Master is not destined to manifest itself in a constant process of slow maturing, but it must be an evidence that necessarily shows itself as such, that is, *already here and now.*

Whatever sense is given to Galatians 6:17, what clearly is derived from the text is that the living testimony of Jesus Christ, given by the Priest, must be as strong and as clear as the one the Apostle refers to. The textual expression *in super corpore meo*, added to the *stigmata* (whatever these stigmata mean), both point to a perceptibility that tends to acquire the level of evidence. Also, since the context shows that Saint Paul refers here to himself as an Apostle and not as a simple Christian, we must conclude that the appearance of the Minister of Jesus Christ must be distinctive enough as to *show himself* as somebody different from others. This is why the desire to appear before the world as having erased all differences between him and other men is contrary to the doctrine of the New Testament and any correct Theology of the Priesthood.

Of course what we have said here does not refer mainly to the merely external aspect of the Priest or the way he dresses. Affirming this would minimize and misinterpret the sense of what has been established so far. What has happened here is really a conceptual displacement that has caused a serious problem of profound importance; namely, the fundamental issue has been replaced by a superficial approach in order to substitute the form of the supernatural content with a purely natural one. This is an important subject and deserves further analysis which, although brief, provides a more in–depth consideration.

Few people could ever have thought about the possible connection —undoubtedly very odd— between the figure of the Priest and the Theater; and yet this is the reality: the Priest is the most important and most recognized actor in the World (or, rather, in the Universe) and, consequently, he is the most applauded and the most censured (the latter much more frequently) on the great stage of the Planet. It is no wonder that this be so, for his *role* is the most important and delicate, as well as the most decisive and determinant, in man's destiny that the Theater has ever known —the Theater of the World, in this case.

As an explanation of what we have just said, let us add that, according to Saint Paul, *God has set forth us the apostles last of all, as men doomed to death: for we are made a spectacle unto the world, to angels, and to men.*[8] No actor from all who have existed in the history of humanity could ever have dreamt of being contemplated by such a varied and multitudinous public.

Thus, the Priest is the lead actor in a performance that, having transcended drama, has entered the realm of tragedy: *novissimos ostendit tamquam morti destinatos.* Calderón, in his Sacramental Mystery Play *The Great Theater of the World* assigns only to God the role of spectator, while the solemn warning *Act well, for God is God!* is repeated regularly throughout the Play; reserving the condition of actors to humans —each in his own role. In this passage, however, the Priest is assigned the role of the main (and even only) actor. This undoubtedly produces within him a situation of extreme tension, similar to the actor who finds himself alone on stage, confronting both the responsibility of his performance and the contemplation of an expectant public. Additionally, the Priest's situation is, if possible, all the more tragic because he has not cho-

---

[8] 1 Cor 4:9.

sen it; God does not consult beforehand with those concerned to carry out His *free* election (Mt 3: 13–14; Jn 15:16; Heb 5:4). The spectators here are the collectivity of all men, good and bad (the world and men, as the text literally differentiates them), to which one must add all those who make up the supernatural realm (the angels).

Never has such performance been represented, neither so crowded (with Heaven and Earth in common contemplation), nor giving rise to such great suspense. The Greeks distinguished between the People —represented by the Chorus— and the tragic heroes; although the Chorus did partake in the action (a tradition which Calderón would continue in his plays). In contrast, the Scriptural texts of the *First Letter to the Corinthians* and the *Letter to the Hebrews* point to this very important fact: the Apostle is singled out as the only actor —clearly separated from all other rational beings (men and angels) to whom the position of mere spectator is assigned.

Under these conditions, it is difficult to claim that the Priest should not differentiate himself from the rest of men. In the Drama to be represented in the Great Theater of the World (which, in this case, encompasses even Heaven as spectator), just as it occurs in the human Theater, actors are never spectators. The so–called *Interactive Theater* is a hybrid product that has never prospered — though it has, in fact, been put into practice, just as attempts have been made to make the Priest perform tasks of the layman, and the layperson Priestly tasks. The results have always been the same in both cases: it is impossible to avoid the perception of witnessing a denaturalized product.

On the other hand, it is not a question of deciding what the Priest must or must not be, for the content and signification of the Sacrament of Holy Orders have already been determined solely and exclusively by God. The Priest is what he is, without his being able to structure himself as something different according to purely human parameters. Man would never have been able to configure, on his own, what pertains to the strictly supernatural order, such as the Christian Priesthood. He could not have ever fathomed that the function of his ministry —his role as *alter Christus*— would be accomplished based on a contraposition of wills: the election by God and the compliant answer of a human will freely accepting a destiny, knowing that that destiny will end in tragedy: *God has set forth us the apostles last of all, as men doomed to death...*

If the role to be played by the Minister of Jesus Christ, in accordance with the will of Him Who has summoned him, develops itself within a tragic drama with an expected and consequent end, to speculate about the *promotion* of the Priesthood makes no sense —at least in the manner in which one usually understands this term. Hence, one can safely say that the Church will do nothing to foster that *promotion*, neither in a next Council nor in any other Council. Nor can it be expected that the Church will display any intention whatsoever to promote a condition which has already been set in its proper place by God Himself. The drama–tragedy, along with its outcome which is proportional to the grandiosity and logic of the play, has already been written and revised by the Divine Author. Thus, the actor, in this case and as always, cannot intend to do anything except to perform his part well. The current crisis of the Priesthood within the Church has served to make it patently manifest that the post–Conciliar Priest finds himself with the possibility of reaching the loftiest point of his vocation and destiny, namely that, at the culminating moment in which the drama has reached its climax, he finds himself compelled to make his talents as an actor shine forth before an expectant public which is contemplating with eagerness, observing with curiosity, and awaiting with anxiety a successful outcome. It makes no sense to try to *promote* that which is destined to *descend* to its final destiny of immolation and death. Saint Paul explains it to the Faithful in Corinth: *We are fools for Christ's sake, but you are wise in Christ; we are weak, but you are strong; you are honorable, but we are despised. Even unto this present hour we both hunger, and thirst, and are naked, and are buffeted, and have no certain dwelling place; and labor, working with our own hands: being reviled, we bless; being persecuted, we suffer it: being defamed, we entreat: we are made as the filth of the world, and are the offscouring of all things unto this day.*[9] Just as it happened with the Cross of Christ, those who work to destroy the Priesthood are fulfilling, without intending it, the saving plans of God, Who has wanted to align some men with His own Passion in a particularly intimate way. For these men, this is about the fulfillment of a co–redemptive destiny which escapes human understanding and which counts, in this particular case, on the role and mission of the Priest as *alter Christus.* In the face of the most difficult moment which the Church has suffered throughout Her history, this is the opportune time for the grain of wheat to fall to the ground and die; never before has there been such a need to carry this out nor such a fitting occasion to see it through.

Progressive Theology and *Liberation Theology* have destroyed the possibility of the Priest giving testimony, and thus they have ruined the performance by depriving the Priest of his condition as sole actor of Quality Theater only to reduce him to the role of one spectator among many. There is no longer anyone whom the actor's representation could address and move, nor is there anybody for the spectator to contemplate and gaze at. By turning the Priest into

---

[9] 1 Cor 4: 10 ff.

a *leader* and a *guerrilla fighter* —the so–called defenders of mere political liberties and utopian social justice— they have obliterated his essential role of immolation and victimization which God has traced for him. There is not any possible salvation for the world without this divinely assigned role because *sine sanguinis effusione non fit remissio.*[10] The Priest is not any longer the man who shares the Passion of Christ and gives testimony of it to his brethren — as a grain of wheat that dies to yield fruit—, but rather becomes only one more man among many: a fierce avenger of social injustice, worried only about worldly affairs.

Now the *stage* has been left empty, and the Great Theater of the World can be no more. God has been deprived of the grandiose spectacle organized by Him, whose script He Himself had written. He no longer has anything or anyone to look at that may bring forth His mercy and placate His anger because of man's conduct. Consequently, it is to be feared that, driven by the example of what He now contemplates, God Himself might decide to become a Righteous, Out–for–justice Avenger —although, in His case, rightly so.

---

[10]Heb 9:22.

"DISPUTATIONES" ABOUT DIVINE–HUMAN LOVE

The starting point for this *quodlibet*[1] about the divine–human love relationship is the need that man has to listen to the divine voice, or to the voice of the Spirit,[2] as the element indispensable for rendering such a relationship possible. If man has been called to maintain a love relationship with God, since such relationship cannot exist without dialogue, we need to conclude that man *needs* to listen to God's voice.[3]

The Book of the *Song of Songs* already expresses the yearning and excitement of the Bride because she thinks that she has heard —at long last!— the voice of the Bridegroom.

> *The voice of my beloved...!*
> *He spoke and said to me...*[4]

---

[1]As already known, the Latin word *disputatio* means, rather than discussion, first and foremost a dissertation regarding a topic which one wants to go into more deeply.

[2]This article is a commentary of the text contained in the author's book *Siete Cartas para Siete Obispos*, Vol. I., Shoreless Lake Press, New Jersey, 2009, pp. 100 ff.

[3]We are not referring here to the creature's need to listen to the Creator inasmuch as it depends on Him absolutely and needs Him as a necessary means to reach its salvation once the creature has been elevated to the supernatural order. The course this discussion will take runs at a different, more elevated level —although finally both perspectives converge— for the objective now is to delve into the study of the divine–human love relationship.

[4]Sg 2: 8.10.

A superficial reading of the Sacred Book would consider such excited words from the Bride as mere exclamations of joy. And so they are, indeed; although, in truth, they answer to a far deeper feeling. The Bride expresses her longing and her restlessness because she wants to hear, as soon as possible, the voice of the Bridegroom. Given that her feelings spring now from the unfathomable and mysterious ocean of love, which in this case is also as intense as it is both eager and ardent, they transcend for the moment any type of description.

Anyone who has been truly in love and, to that extent, has also been in anguish and impatient to hear the beloved's voice, will be able to understand something of this. Although, in this case, something of no small importance must be taken into account; namely, the infinite distance mediating between merely human love —as pure and authentic as it may be— and divine–human love. For the latter, once it has been attained, is impossible to be satisfactorily, not even half decently, explained, as the mystics attest.

He also is wrong who tries to see in these exclamations a *superabundant* feeling of joy on the part of the bride. We are no longer dealing here with the intensity and degree of joy in the bride's spirit. The exclamations are rather an immense shout of longing and eagerness surging from the bride's heart, which is not possible to express beyond what the limitations of human language permit. The Bridegroom is no longer simply someone whose presence gladdens the bride to the extent of filling her with joy; *rather He is, truly, the very life of the bride.* The distance between this love exclamation from the bride and that which surges from a merely human love is the same distance that there is between Heaven and Earth: the distance between what cannot reach beyond human love, on the one hand, and the unfathomable depths of the divine–human intimacy, on the other. One can ardently *desire* the presence of the beloved person because of the joy of being at that person's side; or one can eagerly *need* that presence because nobody can live without what constitutes his own life (Gal 2:20).

In these post–modern times, although the process began its gestation during past centuries, the meaning of Christian existence has suffered a profound depreciation. The truth is that Christianity, rather than being a code of conduct or a doctrine about how to behave, *is a doctrine of life*. Jesus Christ did not come to improve the life of men (Lk 12:14; Mt 6:33) *but so that men may have life* (Jn 10:10; 20:31). Of course, He did not mean natural life, but one infinitely more elevated, belonging to a different order. There are many who continue to reduce the Evangelical Message, or the Message of Salvation, to the Social Doctrine of the Church. And there are also too many who are more interested in the Declaration of Human Rights than in the content of the Gospels. In truth, everything began when the question of *Who God is and what He means for man* started to be replaced by that of *who man is and what man means to himself*. It is usually stated that it was the Renaissance Man (whose prototype, according to many, was Petrarch) who was thought, for the first time, to have reached the conclusion that he was the center of the Universe; others say that the first glimpses of this realization can already be found in the philosophers from Classical Antiquity, who considered that *man is the measure of all things*. Be that as it may, the truth is that, since man was made by Love and for Love, the attitude of self–contemplation and, consequently, the attitude of remaining within himself because he considered himself self–sufficient has always been contrary to man's nature. Narcissism became a poor bargain for the human being; and the displacement of Theology in favor of Anthropology became in the end catastrophic. Man's persistence in knowing himself while departing from himself and remaining within himself, ended up in nihilism.

The reality is very different. Everything seems to indicate that man can reach certain knowledge of his nature only by looking outside himself or by looking at himself from the outside, or from *perspective*. If man wants to come to know what he really *is*, to discover the mystery of his *origin*, to know the *end* at which he is destined to arrive and even the best *path* to take to get there, then it is necessary that man, far from remaining within himself, look *beyond himself*. This means that the knowledge of the meaning of man's existence, together with the mystery of his origin and end could only be reached *outside himself*. Consequently, this is the only way through which Anthropology acquires its true sense, namely, indirectly, or as the contemplation of a ray of sunshine in a *refracted* mode, which is tantamount to saying reflected through a mirror. The best and most complete definition of man ever given in History is none other than that of Pilate, when he displayed a mangled Jesus Christ before the crowds and pronounced the words *Ecce Homo*. And so it is indeed, for only by contemplating Jesus Christ can man know what he really *is*; better yet, and above all, *how he should be*, or that which he is destined to be.[5]

Thus, the only road left for Anthropology to become constituted as a true science must go through love. Now, love is ultimately God, and what has been placed in the heart of man is nothing other than a participation (quite real) in such love. Hence it follows that Anthropology needs Theology; otherwise, it can do nothing but go round itself as a spinning sphere rotating ceaselessly... until the impulse stops and it remains motionless. In remote times, there were many who thought that the motto stating that Philosophy was *ancilla theologiae* supposed an intolerable subordination of Philosophy as a Science. That is exactly the reason why the majority of people will feel compelled to reject what has been affirmed here about Anthropology. Nevertheless, the reality of the world in which the human race lives —whether people admit it or not—, patently shows that there are many things whose nature may only be fully developed and their perfection consummated when they assume the attitude and role of *ancillae*. A so–called knowledge of man, for instance, that is not complemented by the knowledge of man's ultimate end (which would also imply ignorance about man's origin) would be incomplete and meaningless. Hence, one could develop a possible mathematical equation whose formulation would be more or less as follows: *Anthropology minus Theology equals nothing*.

To become convinced about the reality of such things, one has but to look at the results obtained by Anthropology so far, bent to the point of paroxysm on dispensing entirely with any supernatural sense: to say that the results are null without further comment would be tantamount to not be telling the truth; the sad reality is that they have been catastrophic. One result, for instance, is the great frequency with which man has been induced to consider himself as a beast —and not only in regard to his person, but also and especially with regard to his conduct towards others: Has the twentieth century not been for humanity the century of the great genocides?

---

[5]This has nothing to do with the tenets of Personalism which claim that the mission of Jesus Christ is seemingly to reveal to man *what he is* or who he is.

In conclusion: without having recourse to love, it is impossible to define man, to know what he is, or who he is, or where he comes from, or where is he going; at best, man would simply exist as a being lost in the Universe who, besides, as it could not be any other way, after thousands (millions?) of years of not knowing even himself, *is still fettered by his inability to know those surrounding him.* It is impossible to acquire a thorough knowledge of the human being if one focuses exclusively on the study of his nature, as if man had no *origin* and no *destiny*; for then, man would appear to be an insignificant being lost, after all, on an also insignificant planet, navigating through the infinity of a Universe of unknown dimensions. In the case of the human being, knowledge of his nature would require, as an essential condition, wisdom regarding the ends to which that nature is destined. Once more it is clear that it is impossible to know what things are, even to a merely sufficient degree of depth, unless we contemplate them in their reference to their Creator.

Unfortunately, the fundamental realities of Christian existence are frequently valued as secondary; at best, they are considered as belonging to the realm of mystical experience or proper to more perfect stages of Christian life ordinarily reserved for the chosen or the elected ones (the so–called *consecrated souls*). Nevertheless, the fact that Jesus Christ represents for Christians the possibility of making theirs *the very life of their Master* is something as transcendental as defining itself either as a complete success or perhaps as the total failure of a human existence. All of this, besides, bearing the imprint of eternity: *As the Father who sent me lives, and as I live because of the Father, so he who eats me, he also shall live because of me.*[6] One frequently forgets that man has been created *to love and to be loved* and that love does not know measurements. We are aware, of course, that the expression *to love and to be loved* is redundant. Loving necessarily supposes bilateralism and reciprocity, for there are always an *I* and a *thou.* Nevertheless, tautologies and repetitions are frequently useful in the art of human language. However,

---

[6] Jn 6:57.

it is a fact that all these realities are considered as something like
a plus or a windfall, reserved as a additional benefit for those who
wish to carry out specific tasks.

The *bilateral and reciprocal reality*, especially regarding divine–human love, is
clearly confirmed by texts such as those of John 15: 4–5; 15:9; 6:57; 1 Jn 3:24 or
Revelation 3:20.

However, the characteristic of *reciprocal possession*, though it is a clear feature
of divine–human love —*My love is mine and I am his*[7]—, is more diluted in
purely human love (understanding this as authentic love) even when elevated by
grace. In Genesis 2:24, the expression that manifests the singularity of each one
of *the two* is emphasized more, giving it an aspect of preeminence, than the text
that says that both will be *one flesh*; and the text clearly does not refer to the
supernatural order. On the other hand, though the act by which the conjugal
union is consummated best expresses the love between the spouses, in no way
does the desire to exchange and give to each other their own lives clearly appear
there. The Pauline text in which *neque mulier sine viro, neque vir sine muliere
in Domino*[8] must be understood in the sense of *ownership* rather than *possession*:
and we know that the concepts of ownership and possession are entirely different
in juridical order. And the sense of the concept of possession is even harder to
recognize in Ephesians 5:28, which says that, for the Apostle, *qui suam uxorem
diligit, seipsum diligit;* and he continues with the express declaration that (v. 29)
nemo enim unquam carnem suam odio habuit.

The idea of the interchange and *mutual surrender* in totality (ownership and
possession) of the life of each one to the other is practically nonexistent in purely
human love, even when it is elevated by grace. Here the distance increases between
simple human love and divine–human love and, consequently, also the degree of
participation of each one of them in Love. The texts that speak of this in the New
Testament must be understood in a real sense; and likewise in some texts from the
Old Testament, though in the latter, we must acknowledge a sense of perfection
and consummation that gives them a certain projection into the future, awaiting
the arrival of the Redeemer, when at last they would become a complete reality.

The problem we are considering here refers to maintaining the *singularity* and
the corresponding lives of each one of the persons that love each other. If each one

---

[7]Sg 2:16; 6:3; 7:11; cf. Gal 2:20; and the texts cited above.

[8]1 Cor 11:11.

gives his life to *the other*, truly and in all his being, how can the peculiarity and integrity of the person of each one of the lovers remain intact?

First, we should immediately dispel any suspicion of confusion in the sense of Pantheism. The singularity and particularity of each of the persons that love each other is an indispensable requirement for Love, since love is a *relationship* that can exist only between persons, completely distinct as such persons.

We may ask if the result of the interchange of lives, when the lovers seem to be joined by their mutual surrender, is compatible with the continuity of the singularity of the person of each one of them. Or, in other words, whether the fact that those who love each other become *only one thing* is reconcilable with the fact that each one remains *one and the same.*

In the Mystery of the Trinity, the doctrine has dispelled the problem as far as it is possible to do so. In the Divine Essence, each of the Persons that love each other and mutually surrender themselves to each other maintain their own singularity as a Person, even though their union and intermingling is so perfect that they are really identified in the unity and the oneness of only one Nature (numerically unique), which is unthinkable in a creature. The human nature cannot be *fused* forming a unity (numerically unique) with another nature, and even less so if that nature is divine.

To pose the problem correctly, we must insist that any shadow of Pantheism is incompatible with the concept of love. That is why certain expressions like *becoming one with God* or *losing oneself in God* should probably be avoided. There is no intention here of disseminating doubts about the integrity of venerable doctrines which are the fruit of the thoughts of illustrious Saints and magnificent Doctors who have been justly venerated for centuries by the Church and by all Christians without the least doubt. But it wouldn't be honest to conceal that certain expressions, as well as certain ways of considering the doctrine of contemplative prayer, could lead some people to perceive in their teaching faint indications of pantheism and even of *quietism*; doubtlessly they are groundless indications, but apparent indications nevertheless.

Regarding contemplative prayer, Saint Teresa's example of the water drawn laboriously from the well, compared to the torrential rain that falls from the sky and which has an effect without any effort on man's part —presented to illustrate the difference between simple meditation and contemplation (activity in one case, compared to pure passiveness in the other)— is open to some questioning. If we understand that contemplative prayer is an advanced stage of prayer life, or a phase in which we must recognize a high degree of intimacy in the love relationship between God and man, and given the bilateral and reciprocal character peculiar to such a relationship, it is difficult to think of an attitude of *pure passiveness* on the part of the creature. A love relationship is never passive for those who love; and even less if such a relationship has reached a high degree of intimacy and intensity. Of course the statement that *all is grace* is never truer than when applied to all that happens in contemplative prayer. But this is not sufficient to *eliminate human activity*, which is absolutely necessary as an element of a response that is real and supposedly essential in the love relationship. On the other hand, this claim would conceal a fundamental and inherent aspect of grace: which is without any doubt a gratuitous gift from God, but a gift that warrants the condition that the human act be truly human, that is, with personal and individual merit. Here we leave aside an explanation for the mystery, without forgetting to recognize the fact that because you cannot explain it does not mean it does not exist. Moreover, the Saint herself does not seem to agree entirely with this part of her doctrine: a careful reading of her *Autobiography* shows the obvious truth that the book is a passionate narration of her love relationship with Jesus Christ, an intimate and extraordinary reciprocity of dialogues and *affections on the part of one and the other*. And her *Interior Castle* is a description of the *difficult and arduous* itinerary that the soul must travel, sustained and vitalized always by grace, through the diverse *dwellings* that lead to the very center and definitive meeting point of union with God.

As for the mystical phenomenon of *transverberation*, as a singular grace given by God to the Saint, it seems more difficult to deny an attitude of pure passiveness. The occurrence seems to offer some similarities to the stigmata of Saint Francis of Assisi and other Saints. However, such graces from God, if we think about it, suppose an intense and extraordinary moment and an act of love: divine–human love, which consequently implies a greater excess and a more intense overabundance of love, on God's part as well as on that of the creature (love is never something of *only one*), to such a degree as to surpass any purely human love. Once we acknowledge this, it is practically impossible not to recognize in such occurrences, and precisely in these with more justification, a reciprocal and bilateral action on the part of the two that love each other.

It is convenient to establish certain principles to best approach this problem. First, we must begin with the certainty that the person, as such, is capable of giving up everything... except the capacity of giving everything up. If this were not so, it is clear that, when he realizes the supposed *surrender*, he would not be a person anymore; therefore, any possible existence of a love relationship would disappear. Does this mean that the person must reserve *something* in the love relationship that, on the other hand, is entirely real and authentic? Of course not exactly. In any case, and to avoid digression, we must keep in mind that we are talking here of the profound mystery of a concept, that is love, which in the end is identified with God (1 Jn 4:15).

To understand this to the extent accessible to human nature, we must again use Revelation. In the end, human love is a participation in Divine Love, and its character of *analogical similarity* to the Trinitarian Mystery is real, without the knowledge of which love would have remained forever the most inexplicable and profound mystery. Many centuries already have passed by Humanity in its effort to penetrate this Mystery, and it has resulted only in mere hints and stuttering truths isolated from an ocean of errors (Plato) before the Incarnation of the Word..., or of insufficient doctrines, though surer and closer to reality (Saint Augustine, Saint Thomas), after this event.

With the help of Revelation we know that the generation of the Word takes place *in the always actual and present instant of eternity*, without any *before* or *after* imaginable in it. The Psalm expressly affirms it: *Filius meus es tu, ego hodie genui te*;[9] where *hodie* is the word that expresses exactly the actual and present instant of eternity. The generation of the Son, with the loving surrender of the Father to his Word, is absolutely actual, without any possibility of conceiving in it a before or an after. It didn't have any beginning, as it will have no end. The Father surrenders himself in *totality* to the Son without ceasing to be the Person of the Father. Reciprocally, the same occurs with the Son in his Response to the Father. On the other hand, according to the words of Jesus Christ himself, *all the Father has is mine*;[10] a text that has three possible interpretations: (a) All the Father possesses in Himself has been given to Me by Him and pertains to Me; (b) All that is really Mine I have given to the Father; (c) After having given everything to the Father, nevertheless everything is still Mine. It is possible that none of the three interpretations exclude the other; and at the same time it is clear that, once the mutual surrender is realized, everything *remains belonging to* both.

If we apply the knowledge that derives from the *analogical* similarity to human love, and more properly to divine–human love, we will discover that the act of perfect love, precisely for being perfect and for supposing a total surrender, does not take place in a determined moment in such a way that afterwards something happens like an *it is done*, but, very much on the contrary, such an act is still being actual and in the present. The person who loves perfectly surrenders in totality and

---

[9]Ps 2:5; cf. Acts 13:33; Heb 1:5; 5:5.

[10]Jn 16:15.

continues surrendering in an act that is in some way *atemporal*, which means that love transcends the limits of time and any conditioning factor. The person who loves surrenders and continues surrendering, *and that is precisely why he never stops being a person*. Strictly, he would stop loving the same moment in which he stopped surrendering. The person surrenders everything and maintains at the same time, nevertheless, his capacity to surrender: without which *he would stop being a person* and the love relationship would disappear, as if by enchantment.

If what is said here is correct, we can deduce from it some interesting consequences.

In the first place, that the perfection of the love act requires the characteristic of eternity. According to this, true love would be, in every case and in any circumstances, destined to be *everlasting*, at least as a peculiar character that would demand its consummation.

If we start from the premise that *Perfect Joy* can only be the fruit of *Perfect Love* (and we know of nothing else that can produce it), and since Joy cannot really be perfect and complete if it lacks the condition of eternalness, the perennial quality of Love as well as Joy is confirmed even more. This leads to the conclusion that limiting the consideration of *Beatitudo* or the final end of man to the *satiating contemplation of Truth* seems to be insufficient, since Love, the source of all Joy and any *Beatitudo*, supposes *possession* as well as *vision* (and also it is perennial by nature). Because of this, if we admitted that the *Beatitudo* is also the fruit of Love, we would have to recognize in it the characteristic of reciprocity and exclude from it, because of this, pure passiveness. This seems to be confirmed by what the Apostle says: *Once perfection comes, the imperfect things will pass away*.[11] And he continues: *Now we see only reflections in a mirror, mere riddles, but then we shall be seeing face to face. Now I can know only imperfectly; but then I shall know just as fully as I am myself known*.[12] According to this, all seems to indicate that the Apostle is not only not adverse to reciprocity, but also seems to relegate pure passiveness to a secondary place: he says we will see *face to face*, adding right afterwards, *I will know as I am known*.

Another conclusion, not less important, would be that the capacity to love is inherent to the concept of person, which offers a greater and better foundation to the reality of the similarity between man and God.

---

[11] 1 Cor 13:10.

[12] 1 Cor 13:12.

Lastly, should this doctrine be accepted, one would have to admit the possibility that we may not be able to consider Boecius' definition of person, later adopted by the Scholastics, as complete; at least in the sense that it does not contemplate one of the fundamental elements of the concept of person which is the inherent possession of the capacity to love, which, in the end, is the most appropriate characteristic, as we have just noted, to explaining the similarity between man and God.

The passionate longings produced in the bride when she hears the voice of her Beloved are described in the *Song* in a very special way, as is fitting for a reality which also is very uncommon:

> *I sleep, but my heart is awake.*
> *I hear my love knocking.*[13]

This takes place, as we can see, during the day as well as at night, in waking and even during sleep; because love never ceases.[14] This interjection of the *Song* offers double evidence that confirms what we have been saying. First, because it is an allusion to a mystery, the mystery of love, that surpasses all a human being could imagine.[15] And secondly, because it is one more evidence of the anguish experienced by human language, which cannot help feeling distressed when it sees its own insufficiency.

---

[13] Sg 5:2.

[14] As we have already seen above, the character of love is, rather than *atemporal, eternal.*

[15] Love is, for the human being, at the same time and in conjunction, a secret mystery —the greatest of all Mysteries— and the most brilliant and magnificent reality. Always inaccessible and hidden, but also constantly manifest in works to which man owes firstly his existence —he was created by Love—, and secondly the Joy of his eternal destiny —he was created to Love—: *Sacramentum regis bonum est abscondere, opera autem Dei revelare et confiteri honorificum est* (Tob 12:7).

Insufficiency, insofar as its exhaustiveness yet not inasmuch as its (relative) effectiveness. The reality of Love is ineffable, although not impossible to ascertain and much less incapable of manifesting itself. The problem lies in that love identifies with God Himself. Hence, the more it is comprehended, the greater is the perception of a place and an ultimate goal... that is not final.

What is admirable of human language is its capability of not allowing itself to be intimidated because of its insufficiency. While it laments for that which it is unable to express, human language rejoices in the attempt to reveal with words, after its own fashion, something of what it perceives about that Infinite Beauty that draws the creature to Love. Hence, among the juggling and pirouettes it is forced to make, attempting to both disguise and transcend its very powerlessness while singing to Beauty and Love, human language views itself as being transformed into something resembling a bouquet of unusual flowers of astonishing charm and sublime splendor. Such an anguishing yet joyful attempt to surpass the insurmountable is known by many as *Poetry*. As an example of what has already been said, one can mention here the insuppressible emotion of the bride in face of the possibility of hearing again, from the bridegroom's own mouth, the bewildering confession *I love you* (the most beautiful and sublime expression Heaven and Earth could have conceived); which is not surprising if we consider that the one pronouncing it now is He Who thinks about the bride:

Arising as the dawn,
Fair as the moon,
Resplendent as the sun,
Formidable, as an army with banners.[16]

What is so strange, then, that the bride should feel *intimidated* (the anguish and torments of love also exist) in face of the possibility of knowing herself to be dying of excitement, should she hear again those *divine words* from the Bridegroom?:

If you should see me again,
Down in the glen where the singing blackbirds fly,
Do not say you love me then
For, were you ever to repeat that sweet sigh,
On hearing it, I may die.[17]

Still, the expressions of love between lovers also give way to *folly.* That is how others usually look at them, but it is not so for the lovers; after all, it is difficult for love to find ways of expressing

---

[16]Sg 6: 4.10. In the divine–human love relationship, the human being tends to place more emphasis on the love he feels for God rather than on the love God professes toward him; as a consequence, the marks of reciprocity and bilateralism become somewhat diluted. Strangely enough, it is easier for the creature to be conscious of his own love for God than to be aware of the ineffable reality that *God is in love with him.*

[17]Alfonso Gálvez, *op. cit.* n. 57. In the Spanish original:

Si de nuevo me vieres,
allá en el valle, donde canta el mirlo,
no digas que me quieres,
no muera yo al oírlo
si acaso tú volvieras a decirlo.

itself that will always satisfy; such is the poverty of language and the immense richness of the content. Hence, the absurdities and apparent contradictions which may appear incomprehensible to outsiders arise:

> *How I longed that you should hear me precisely,*
> *Sweet master, my spouse, my dearest friend, so true.*
> *And hearing from my lips the words 'I love you,'*
> *You would whisper those same words right back to me.*[18]

Indeed, the words that constitute the statement *I love* you form an entity that seems to possess the depth of the divine. Be that as it may, the attribution is not exaggerated. After all, this sentence contains most passionately and straightforwardly the expression of the love that an *I* feels for a *you,* in wait of being requited and of hearing exactly the same from such *you* who, in turn, is an *I.*

Moreover, the amorous language —language as an expression of love— is precisely what most intimately advances man towards God, Who is Love. As for the rest, the Bridegroom is for the bride *her life* (Col 3:4).[19] As for the Bridegroom Himself, unable in turn to express in human language what he feels for the bride and what she means to Him, calls her *formidable as an army with banners.* As it can be readily perceived, behold once more the unwonted language of lovers... It is necessary to recognize that the complex frame of tropes,

---

[18]In the Spanish original:

> *¡Cuánto anhelaba yo que tú me oyeras,*
> *mi tierno amigo, esposo y dulce amo,*
> *y al oír de mis labios "yo te amo",*
> *lo mismo que te digo, me dijeras...!*

[19]Cf. Phil 1:21; Rom 14: 7–8; Jn 6:57; 1 Jn 4:9; etc.

metaphors, allegories, epithets —all the luxuriant abundance of figurative language— is one of the most disconcerting, strange, and
mysteriously beautiful realities partaking of the bewitching world of
Poetry. It is fascinating the length to which Love and Beauty may
go, compelled as they are to not surrender themselves except partially to the creature, as they try to break in a thousand ways the
gags that would silence them. And although such an effort yields
fruit only to a small degree, not because of such limitation do both
refrain from trying once and again, their eyes always fixed on the
happy ending of an enterprise which, they know well, will only end...
the very moment of the final arrival of the lovers to the Homeland.

In any case, even when acknowledging the *folly* of amorous language and its
surprising and unexpected expressions, it seems more logical that the lovers are inclined to prefer the soft, caressing, delicate, trope–filled language where frequently
appear terms such as nemorous abodes, shady groves, backwoods, valleys, and
woodlands... in an attempt to express as best as possible, even stammer, the intensity of their mutual love.

> *Come, my dearest love, come to my side at last,*
> *My Spouse, my perfect one, my dove so serene,*
> *For already the night runs, hurrying fast,*
> *And behind the hill the sun can now be seen.*[20]

The language of human love is the same that divine or divine–human love uses.
After all, all manners of human love, when such love is genuine, are but diverse
levels of participation in Infinite Love. One should remember that divine–human
love is at a more elevated level than purely human love, not only by way of degree,

---

[20] Alfonso Gálvez, *op. cit.* n. 94. In the Spanish original:

> *Ven por fin a mi lado, bienamada,*
> *mi esposa, mi perfecta, mi paloma,*
> *pues ya la noche corre apresurada*
> *y el sol tras el otero ya se asoma.*

but also qualitatively. The problem lies —if it were indeed a problem— in its inexpressibility.

If mere human love becomes unintelligible —and in any case always difficult to comprehend in depth— to someone who has never experienced love, what is one to say about love whose nature is at a completely different, more elevated level? If the love of a human being for another is ineffable, how is one to explain the love of God emanating through the Person in Whom resides plenitude of both divinity and humanity? If Essential love was *ungraspable* to man in the reality of His Infinitude and the essentiality of His Being as Spirit, what may happen if such Infinite Love decides to *enclose* Himself in a human nature and become thus perceptible and *seizable* for the creature? That is the question: to love a man *to the highest degree man can be loved* and to love God *to the limit a human nature is able to that is now already capable of perceiving and interacting with Him tangibly* (1 Jn 1: 1–4). All of these having been performed with supernatural, rather than superhuman, strength. Man could never have fathomed such a notion. And yet, we are talking now about *loving both The Man and The God, both at the same time, to the fullness of the capacity of human nature elevated by grace besides...* such a thing has always exceeded —and will always exceed— all possibilities of the understanding, fantasy, excitement, and joy of the human heart. In this way, the Infinitude of Love Himself (still ungraspable to the creature) now appears condensed, contained, expressed, offered, and given through a Man (now, at last, within the reach of the creature).

Now, what does the expression *I love you* exactly mean? The only possible answer to that question is... that nobody knows. In spite of millions of human beings having pronounced it throughout centuries, nobody has ever known to this day how to offer an explanation that is entirely satisfactory. Nor does it seem very probable that anybody will do it in the future. Yet —and this is what is truly surprising— nobody doubts their meaning when pronouncing these words. Whoever does it feels sure about what the heart experiences, although he will never be able to offer a precise explanation of the content of his feelings.

What are, really, the feelings of the heart of whoever pronounces these words? Of course, everybody knows the easy and ready answer coming to mind: love, evidently. What this sentence expresses is the feeling of love towards the person to whom it is addressed. This is in truth, however, tantamount to remaining without any answer, for... what exactly is and of what does love consist?

Created love, granted generously to the creature as a participation of Infinite Love,[21] is in any case a *mysterium fascinosum*. For the sake of simplification, it could be qualified as a feeling of attraction on the part of the creature towards someone in whom he perceives the good and the beautiful, although it would perhaps be better to qualify it as *a set of feelings*. This is evidently insufficient, for love, as an ontological reality, is very far from being reduced to mere feelings.

In view of which one should ask, What kind of feelings? At this moment, one would feel something similar to what someone feels after finding himself all of a sudden in an unknown place in complete darkness: he does not know where he is, or why is he there, or what the surroundings are, or in which direction he should start moving. Yet such a person would understand the need to begin to walk towards some place until tripping on something, in a vigorous attempt to leave such a situation regardless.

And perhaps this is what may best be achieved here, namely, begin to take steps without, however, any predetermined course; perhaps going in circles, hoping to find something and to approach as closely as possible the kernel of the mystery.

The expression *I love you*, directed towards the beloved, answers in truth to a set of feelings: surprise, amazement, admiration, joy, tenderness, and some others —yet more, and above everything, attraction towards the beloved. In any case, since the conglomeration

---

[21]We are not claiming to talk about Infinite Love, which is God. The ideas presented here refer to created love and are but a simple approximation to the issue without aspiring to delve theologically into the mystery.

of feelings love carries is more intricate and profound than what is possible to express here, any attempt at a complete explanation would be a task doomed to failure.

The statement *I love you* entails the confession of *unconditional surrender to the beloved.* Whoever pronounces it is recognizing a desire to *belong* to the beloved, which cannot take place except through *self–giving* or donation. An initial approximation to this theme would reveal that the surrender to the beloved is subsequent to the desire of belonging to him.

Love offers itself to the consideration of the created being as a succession of feelings, among which is *submission* to the beloved. An illustrative episode in this regard is contained in the narrative of the events of the Last Supper. When Jesus is about to wash the feet of his disciples, Saint Peter refuses to accept such humiliation from his Master in regards to him. However, the examination of this peculiar characteristic of love would lead us to the posing and study of new problems, thus prolonging a task that does not belong here.

Index of Quotations
from the
New Testament

368

Books of the Bible

Acts, Acts of the Apostles
Amos, Amos
Bar, Baruch
1 Chron, 1 Chronicles
2 Chron, 2 Chronicles
Col, Colossians
1 Cor, 1 Corinthians
2 Cor, 2 Corinthians
Dan, Daniel
Deut, Deuteronomy
Eccles, Ecclesiastes
Eph, Ephesians
Esther, Esther
Ex, Exodus
Ezek, Ezekiel
Ezra, Ezra
Gal, Galatians
Gen, Genesis
Hab, Habakkuk
Hag, Haggai
Heb, Hebrews
Hos, Hosea
Is, Isaiah
Jas, James
Jer, Jeremiah

Jn, John
1 Jn, 1 John
2 Jn, 2 John
3 Jn, 3 John
Job, Job
Joel, Joel
Jon, Jonah
Josh, Joshua
Jud, Judith
Jude, Jude
Judg, Judges
1 Kings, 1 Kings
2 Kings, 2 Kings
Lam, Lamentations
Lev, Leviticus
Lk, Luke
1 Mac, 1 Maccabees
2 Mac, 2 Maccabees
Mal, Malachi
Mic, Micah
Mk, Mark
Mt, Matthew
Nahum, Nahum
Neh, Nehemiah
Num, Numbers
Obad, Obadiah

1 Pet, 1 Peter
2 Pet, 2 Peter
Phil, Philippians
Philem, Philemon
Prov, Proverbs
Ps, Psalms
Rev, Revelation
Rom, Romans
Ruth, Ruth
1 Sam, 1 Samuel
2 Sam, 2 Samuel
Sg, Song of Songs
Sir, Sirach
1 Thess, 1 Thessalonians
2 Thess, 2 Thessalonians
1 Tim, 1 Timothy
2 Tim, 2 Timothy
Tit, Titus
Tob, Tobit
Wis, Wisdom
Zech, Zechariah
Zep, Zephaniah

Contents

ECCLESIASTICAL WINTER